AN ENGLISH
MISCELLANY

WILLIAM SOUTAR MACKIE
(*Photograph: Terence McNally, September 1976*)

AN ENGLISH MISCELLANY

MISCELLANY

Presented to
W. S. MACKIE

Edited by
BRIAN S. LEE

Cape Town
OXFORD UNIVERSITY PRESS
London   New York
1977

Oxford University Press

OXFORD   LONDON   GLASGOW   NEW YORK

TORONTO   MELBOURNE   WELLINGTON   CAPE TOWN

IBADAN   NAIROBI   DAR ES SALAAM   LUSAKA   ADDIS ABABA

KUALA LUMPUR   SINGAPORE   JAKARTA   HONG KONG   TOKYO

DELHI   BOMBAY   CALCUTTA   MADRAS   KARACHI

ISBN 0 19 570101 1

*The editor gratefully acknowledges the financial assistance
of the Human Sciences Research Council and of the Frank
Connock University Trust towards the publication of this
work. Opinions expressed are those of the authors concerned,
and should not be attributed to the members of either the
Council or the Trust*

Set in 10 on 12 pt Times
Printed by Citadel Press, Polaris Road, Lansdowne, Cape
Published by Oxford University Press, Oxford House,
11 Buitencingle Street, Cape Town, South Africa

CONTRIBUTORS

NORMAN F. BLAKE: Professor of English Language, University of Sheffield.

ROBERT W. BURCHFIELD: Fellow and Tutor, St Peter's College, Oxford; Editor, Oxford English Dictionary Supplement, new edition.

DOROTHY L. CAVERS: formerly Professor of English Language, University of Cape Town.

RONALD P. DRAPER: Professor of English, Aberdeen University.

BRIAN K. GREEN: formerly Junior Lecturer in English, University of Cape Town.

GEORGE K. HUNTER: Professor of English and Comparative Literary Studies, University of Warwick.

MARK KINKEAD-WEEKES: Professor of English and Pro-Vice Chancellor, University of Kent at Canterbury.

BRIAN S. LEE: Lecturer in English, University of Cape Town.

BARBARA A. MACKENZIE: Emeritus Professor of English, University of the Orange Free State.

A. COOPER PARTRIDGE: Emeritus Professor of English, University of the Witwatersrand.

MARY C. PENRITH: Junior Lecturer in English, University of Cape Town.

MICHAEL C. SEYMOUR: editor, 'Mandeville's Travels'; co-ordinating editor, Trevisa, 'On the Properties of Things'.

A. JAMES SMITH: Professor of English, Southampton University.

CONTENTS

W. S. Mackie, seated, with H. M. Margoliouth on his left, and members of the first post-war English Honours class at Southampton, mid-1921, shortly before he left for South Africa to become the first De Beers Professor of English Language at the University of Cape Town.

(Photo by courtesy of the English Department, University of Southampton.)

WILLIAM SOUTAR MACKIE

William Soutar Mackie attained his 'undeserved nonagenariety', as he was pleased to call it, on 31 October 1975. A Festschrift to honour such a scholar and such a teacher as he, is not merely deserved but overdue.

He spent his early years in the manse at Drumoak, a village where his father was minister, not far from Aberdeen. He took his first degree, in English and History, at the University of Aberdeen in 1906, went on to read English under A. S. Napier and Sir Walter Raleigh at Christ Church College, Oxford, graduating with first class honours in 1908, and then proceeded to the Oxford History School in 1909. From 1910–20 he lectured in English at Southampton University College, acting as external examiner for Aberdeen University from 1914–18. In 1920 he was acting head of his department, and the following year was appointed to the newly created De Beers chair of English Language at the University of Cape Town, a post he occupied till his retirement in 1951. Not that his teaching stopped then, or his writing; till recently he was language adviser for several volumes of the *Standard Encyclopaedia of Southern Africa*; it is doubtful whether, on retirement, he found much more leisure for his favourite pastime, chess.

Among scholars he is best remembered for his edition and translation of Part II of the Exeter Book (E.E.T.S. 194, 1933); among former pupils for the humanity, humour, logic and lucidity of his expositions. The present collection of essays, a belated academic accolade, represents both the esteem in which he is held and something of the wide range of his literary and linguistic interests.

All four universities with which he has been associated are represented: Aberdeen by Professor Draper, writing appropriately on Hardy who received his first honorary degree, in 1905, from Aberdeen University while Mackie was a student there; Oxford by Mr Burchfield, who edits the revised *O.E.D.* Supplement to which Professor Mackie has contributed, as he did to the first Supplement; Southampton by Professor Smith, whose close reading of Dante and Milton demonstrates a technique of literary analysis which Professor Mackie introduced early on to the English department at Cape Town; and Cape Town by, among others, Professor Cavers, a former student of Professor Mackie's and his successor's successor in the

9

chair he occupied, whose essay on the medieval dialects of Surrey illustrates his philological interests. Fittingly for the translator of the Exeter Book, the collection begins with a translation from Old English by Professor Mackenzie, a member of Professor Mackie's first M.A. class in South Africa. Other contributors suggest, without exhausting, the variety of his interests and publications.

We offer these studies, comprising a selective survey of a thousand years of English language and literature, as manred to a fine scholar and respected teacher, ealdorwisa. We wish him, and others, much pleasure and profit from them.

B. S. L.

THE HAPPY LAND
Translated from *The Phoenix*

Barbara A. Mackenzie

I have heard of a wondrous country,
        to the east men say it lies,
But few have seen its glory,
        of the dwellers beneath the skies.
Far remote from evil-doers,
        it abides through God's own power,
And the fields are fair with beauty,
        with the fragrance of each flower.
For peerless is that island,
        and divinely was it wrought,
And there, as through gates of heaven,
        is the sound of singing caught.
There the pleasant fields and woodlands
        are forever fresh and fair.
For neither rain nor snow comes,
        nor a nipping frosty air,
No blazing fires or hail-storms
        or the touch of hoar-white rime,
Neither cold nor parching sunshine,
        nor the storms of winter-time.
But ever unscathed and smiling
        the flower-decked meads abide.
No precipitous crag or mountain
        there uprears its rugged side,
There no shadowy dales or valleys,
        or grim caverns are on the hill,
No perilous heights frown downwards,
        as do these upon us still,
But wide to the open heavens
        the fair plains stretch far away.
And from ancient tales of wisdom
        that were writ long since, men say
That the glorious land out-measures
        by twelve cubits – thus they read ··

In height our tallest mountain,
              to the stars that lifts its head.
Serene lie the pleasant meadows,
              and the sunny groves agleam,
And ever upon the branches
              the undying fruits shall teem.
In summer and winter season
              on the heavy laden trees
No leaf shall droop or wither,
              nor will fire consume the leas,
Till the last great day of Judgement,
              and the time of death and birth.
So of old, when the raging water,
              like a sea-flood, swept the earth,
Still stood 'gainst the billows scathless
              and unharmed the pleasant land,
Inviolate and peaceful,
              by the might of God's own hand.
And so shall it ever flourish
              till the coming day of doom,
When fire shall smite down from heaven,
              and the dead arise from the tomb.
There comes not age or hardship,
              and unknown are griefs or woes,
Or cruel death or evil,
              or the heavy hand of foes.
Nor with sin nor strife nor weeping,
              nor the pinch of bitter need,
Nor sickness nor weary sleeping,
              nor the curse of an evil deed,
Nor with wintry storms nor grieving
              is the pleasant country marred.
Nor does frost with death-white fingers
              on the earth below strike hard.
And no dark clouds burst in showers
              through the dim-oppresséd air,
But the streams with stately flowing,
              like clear wells upspringing there
Still lave with their quiet waters
              all the pleasant pastures green.

Remote in the shady woodlands,
   in the depths of groves unseen,
Each month through the sun-flecked greensward
   there comes bubbling up a stream
As fresh and cool as the sea waves,
   and with gentle flood agleam
It winds through the ageless woodlands;
   'tis the work of God's own hand
That each month of the year the water
   shall refresh the gracious land.
The trees bend down thick-laden,
   with their foison ripe always,
And the flowers grow not sere or wither,
   nor the luscious fruit decays,
But ever the laden branches
   are adorned and heavy-fruited,
For the grove, as the Lord commanded,
   on the bright green turf cool-rooted
Shall stand ever fair and stately;
   and immortal fragrance there
Is borne over fields and meadows,
   through the pleasant summer air.
And eternal is this beauty,
   for no change shall it ever know
Till it be by Him down-smitten,
   Who wrought it long ago.

The Phoenix: ll. 1–84.

THE DATING OF OLD ENGLISH POETRY

Norman F. Blake

In a volume in which we honour Professor W. S. Mackie, whose edition of the Exeter Book is still admired, I have thought it appropriate to write about the dating of Old English poetry. Quite a familiar topic many years ago, it seems to have fallen into disrepute more recently, perhaps because the results are so uncertain. One effect has been confusion, for most general accounts of Old English literature tend to assume that the bulk of Old English poetry was early, i.e. composed in the eighth or early ninth century, whereas editors of individual poems are often prepared to accept a much later date for their poems. Dunning and Bliss, in their edition of *The Wanderer*, were of the opinion that a date as late as the tenth century would be acceptable for the composition of their poem.[1] It seems, therefore, that it is time to reconsider some of the problems involved. In this paper I would like to approach the issue by raising points not usually taken into account in this connexion. I hope to show that they do have some bearing on this matter and may even provide us with a more fruitful way of looking at the poetry from Anglo-Saxon England.

The known limits for the composition of Old English poetry stretch from the late seventh century when Cædmon wrote, to a time after 991 when the Battle of Maldon was fought – an event subsequently commemorated in verse. It is often assumed that this was the last poem to be written in the classical alliterative style, and this view is reasonable since most other Old English poems are preserved in codices written about 1000 and in no case is there any likelihood that the poems in them are preserved in their original form. All show signs of copying and so they can be assigned dates earlier than *c.* 975. A feature which complicates the dating of these poems is that only a few poems at the beginning and end of the known period of composition can be dated fairly closely. In between there

---

1. T. P. Dunning and A. J. Bliss, *The Wanderer* (London, 1969), p. 104: 'There is no foundation for Cross's assumption that *The Wanderer* is early; the supposition that it was written in the first half of the tenth century would solve many literary problems'.

is a period of about 250 years in which no poem can be dated with any accuracy, though Sisam did try on philological grounds to date the poems by Cynewulf to the ninth century.[2]

The later poems, which apart from *The Battle of Maldon* are to be found in the *Anglo-Saxon Chronicle*, have attracted attention because of their style. Usually these poems are dismissed as decadent, and many scholars think that the classical alliterative style has been so weakened in them that they represent its death-throes. Since the earliest of the *Chronicle* poems celebrates the Battle of Brunanburh (937), this has been a potent reason for putting the composition of most classical poems not later than the ninth century. The same argument has not been applied at the beginning of the period, though it is accepted that *Cædmon's Hymn* and *Bede's Death Song* are indifferent creations. It might be suggested that consequently most classical poems are much later than these two. However, in this period the existence of the fragment of *The Dream of the Rood* on the Ruthwell Cross has prevented any such ready judgement, even though the dating of this fragment is itself fraught with difficulties. But if a poem like *The Dream of the Rood* may have come into existence about the same time as, say, *Bede's Death Song*, it ought with equal logic to be accepted that some of the better Old English poems may have been composed at the same time as the poor *Chronicle* poems. Good and bad poems can be composed at the same time, as any period of English literature makes clear. Scholars have been too prone to present Old English poetry in a finely descending curve of excellence, though there is little concrete evidence to support such a view. Indeed, it seems improbable if one considers other periods of English literature (including the Middle English period) and if one remembers how varied the conditions and the dialects were throughout Anglo-Saxon England.

We should not forget that we know nothing about the Anglo-Saxons' attitude towards English alliterative style or metre. We cannot tell whether they regarded things in the same light as we do or what movements of style motivated their approach. We may think that the style of *The Battle of Maldon* is decadent and so base our dating on that view – but there is no evidence that they saw the poem in this way. Their understanding of metre is also something that

2. K. Sisam, 'Cynewulf and his Poetry', *Studies in the History of Old English Literature* (Oxford, 1953), 1–28.

eludes us. We can try to decide when they used hypermetric lines, for example, but we cannot tell whether people then approved of them or not. In the same way most attempts to date the poetry by metrical tests are inconclusive, precisely because we can argue only from our own understanding of the metre, not theirs. In any case, it has so far proved impossible for modern scholars to achieve a consensus of opinion on the problem of metre; we must disregard it as any guide to dating.[3]

One theory about Old English poetry which has won widespread acceptance is Dr Sisam's proposal that it was written in a literary *koine* which did not represent any one dialect but included elements from them all. This theory has probably won support because it raised Old English poems above the merely local and dialectal level to the national one.[4] The theory is, however, open to serious objections. It was never clear from Dr Sisam's work whether he meant that this 'poetic dialect' existed at a spoken or at a written level, for he made the suggestion without exploring its wider implications. It is improbable that there would have been a spoken poetic dialect throughout the country, for even though poets may have used archaic words and constructions, they would hardly have bothered with other dialect forms. There was no reason for them to do so. If a poem was composed orally, it would be composed in the dialect of the poet or of the recipient. It would be composed for the moment, and a poet would hardly have worried about including other dialect forms to safeguard his poem's future reception when such forms may have jeopardized its immediate acceptance. Both what we know about the composition of medieval poetry and the advances made in our understanding of the workings of language through modern linguistics would seem to preclude that possibility.

If, on the other hand, we are asked to accept that this 'poetic dialect' existed only at a written level, we must naturally enquire what difference there is between that language and the mixed languages which arise through the normal processes of scribal copying. As Dr Sisam himself showed, the poetic codices underwent

---

3. The insufficiency of the earlier attempts at dating based on language and metre was illustrated by A. Ricci, 'The Chronology of Anglo-Saxon Poetry', *R.E.S.* 5 (1929), 257–66; see also D. Whitelock, *The Audience of Beowulf* (Oxford, 1951), pp. 26–33.
4. *Studies in the History of Old English Literature*, pp. 138–9.

several stages of copying and many of the discrepancies in dialect forms could have arisen in this way.[5]

Some poems at all events are not written in this poetic dialect. All the early Northumbrian poems that survive are written in the Northumbrian dialect and not in a mixed one. There is no trace of a poetic dialect at that time. Even some late poems, like the so-called *Kentish Psalm*, show pronounced features of one dialect and this helps to distinguish them from the bulk of the classical poetry. At the same time we may remark that when the late West Saxon written dialect was developed, it was accepted throughout the country as a written language without being diluted by other dialect forms. A mixed dialect was not necessary to promote widespread acceptance and permanence.

In fact, the linguistic mixture in most Old English poems consists principally of Mercian and West Saxon forms, and in this they are not very different from most Alfredian prose texts. Mixed forms in the latter resulted from the breakdown in scribal systems precipitated by the Viking invasions and from Alfred's attempt to piece together the fragments. In promoting scholarship he gathered together men from a variety of backgrounds and with a variety of speech forms. It is hardly surprising that the texts of this period should exhibit more linguistic diversity than those from other periods of Old English. It would not be unreasonable to suppose that the mixture in the poetic texts arose because the poems were also either written or composed in the late ninth or early tenth century before regularity was again established in what we call late West Saxon. At all events there seems little justification for a literary *koine*.

Because it is customary to isolate poetry and prose in two separate compartments, the help which prose can offer us in the dating of the poetry is neglected. It is well known that the prose of Alfred and his helpers is laboured, ponderous and Latinate, whereas that of Wulfstan and Ælfric is lighter and more fluent precisely because it is so strongly influenced by the alliterative style of Old English poetry. Since the influence of the Latin cursus on Ælfric's prose rhythm is now discounted,[6] the primary influence can have come only from the poetry. The implications of this are worth pondering over for

---

5. *Studies in the History of Old English Literature*, pp. 97–108.
6. See particularly, S. Kuhn, 'Cursus in Old English: Rhetorical Ornament or Linguistic Phenomenon', *Speculum* 47 (1972), 188–206.

they seem to be in conflict with the generally accepted canons of dating. According to Asser, Alfred memorized vernacular poems when he was a boy, and even before he could read Alfred used to listen to Old English poems. His children were brought up on the native poetry.[7] According to the accepted dating of the poetry, by the ninth century there was already a long tradition of composing Old English poetry and many of the extant poems were in existence by that time. It is surprising, therefore, that we can trace no influence of that poetry on Alfred's prose. It seems incredible that a man who had the rhythms of Old English poetry in his head and who lived at a time immediately following a flowering of the native poetry could have avoided using poetic rhythms and techniques in his own writing.

On the other hand, if, as is widely believed, Old English poetry went into a decline in the tenth century, we may well wonder why such acute writers as Ælfric and Wulfstan should have revived such a decadent form as a stylistic guide to their writing. Ælfric's work in particular is very closely allied to the poetry and it is composed in such a way that it is printed as poetry by some and as prose by others.[8] Attempts to explain his reliance on the alliterative style by conjuring up an otherwise untestified popular poetry are desperate and implausible.[9] The most reasonable explanation is that in Ælfric's time the alliterative style was a recognized medium of religious instruction, which in its turn implies that the use of vernacular poetry for religious ends was a common feature in the tenth century. When we consider that the majority of the extant poems are didactic in nature and that they are preserved in tenth-century manuscripts, this view seems quite acceptable. But such a view implies that the poetry was a living force in the tenth century; it had not become a kind of antiquarian curiosity. If so, it is likely that the bulk of the extant poetry was not very old by the end of the tenth century.

The failure of Alfred and his contemporaries to be influenced

---

7. W. H. Stevenson, *Asser's Life of King Alfred*, rev. ed. by D. Whitelock (Oxford 1959), ch. 22–23, 75–76 (pp. 19–20, 57–62).

8. A good discussion of Ælfric's prose style is found in J. Pope, *Homilies of Ælfric: A Supplementary Collection* (E.E.T.S. 259–60, 1967–8), I. 105–36.

9. See N. F. Blake, 'Rhythmical Alliteration', *Modern Philology* 67 (1969–70), 118–24.

in their prose by the alliterative poetic style suggests that no tradition of using poetry for didactic purposes was current during their lifetime. This would mean either that the poetry of the time was largely secular or, more probably, that the currently accepted dating is wrong and that we should regard Asser's testimony as at best dubious. It would, however, be possible to assume that Alfred, as part of his educational programme, encouraged the use of poetry for religious purposes. Indeed, the poetry complements the prose in many ways: the latter being suitable for the clergy (as the sending of the *Cura Pastoralis* to the bishops indicates), and the former for a wider audience. It may be for this reason that the poetry includes such subjects as biblical stories, simple explanations of Christian symbolism, and saints' lives.

If Alfred had encouraged poetry of this type, it is easy to see why it failed to influence his own prose, because it would not have been established long enough, and why Asser at a later date may have assumed that Alfred had a great passion for poetry. While it must be admitted that, although the composition of Old English poetry of a religious type fits well into Alfred's educational programme, this in itself does not prove that it was composed then, nevertheless to accept that it came into existence at that time provides us with a good reason for the rise and development of the poetry. In the past we have tended to ignore the reasons which may have prompted the appearance of this poetry, which has consequently existed in a vacuum unrelated to the social or historical conditions.

A feature of Old English poetry is the absence of classical allusions and of references to classical mythology. It used to be thought that this was because of the Germanic heroic nature of the poetry, though such an explanation no longer seems valid. The deliberate avoidance of such references can be traced most clearly in *The Phoenix*, whose first 380 lines are a translation of the *Carmen de Ave Phoenice* attributed to Lactantius.[10] Where the Latin refers to such figures as Phaeton, Phoebus, Aurora, and Aeolus, the Old English poet either omitted them or substituted a biblical image or general Anglo-Saxon circumlocution. The result is a loss in vividness and particularity.

This method of working is striking, for English poets have usually

10. Both the Old English and the Latin poem are edited in N. F. Blake, *The Phoenix* (Manchester, 1964).

been only too ready to borrow from classical mythology. Such borrowings are common in Middle English and are found particularly frequently in Chaucer, who does not hesitate to introduce such figures as Zephirus, Aeolus and Aurora into his poetry. It is clear that the poet of *The Phoenix* consciously avoided these names, but it has never satisfactorily been explained why. Classical names could be fitted into the alliterative metre and when in other poems they had to be included because their bearers, like Holofernes, play a prominent role in the action they caused little difficulty to the poet.

The answer may be found in the breakdown of classical learning following the Danish invasions of the ninth century. Before then, England had been one of the leading countries in the use of Latin and the knowledge of Latin authors. Writers like Bede, Aldhelm and Alcuin could write fluently in Latin prose and verse. Recondite allusions are common in their poetry which is itself rather precious and involved. It is highly unlikely that, in a period of this kind of accomplishment, classical allusions would be deliberately avoided because the author was afraid they would be misunderstood. But in the late ninth century the disruption caused by the Vikings led to a drastic reduction in the knowledge of Latin and of classical writings. The age of Alfred is an age of vernacular writing precisely because there were so few people who were familiar with Latin. It would make sense for any translator or adaptor at such a time to avoid unimportant classical names and allusions since there would be little point in putting needless difficulties in the path of reader or listener. Such avoidance would after all be in the same spirit as the substitution of Weland for Fabricius by the Alfredian translator of Boethius. This type of avoidance indicates a period of composition when the didactic message was put before any elegance in style or breadth of reference; and in Anglo-Saxon England that period was particularly the late ninth and early tenth century. Indeed, the addition of the final 297 lines in *The Phoenix* to the Latin source shows how anxious the poet was to drive home the Christian message, and thus provides confirmation of a date about that time.

As we have already noted, the majority of Old English poems are preserved in four codices dating from the end of the tenth century. Since at least some of these codices have passed through several stages of copying it is likely that their contents were collected together not later than 975. Probably this date is too late and the collections may have been formed in the first half of the tenth century. Two of the codices contain prose as well as verse pieces. This reinforces the point made earlier, that little distinction was drawn between the two forms. It also indicates that the same impulse (the desire to provide educational material for the Christian religion) lay behind the writing of the verse as well as of the prose. It may even be possible to think that in some cases the same author wrote both prose and poetry.[11] The assembling of the material in these codices has not received much attention. This may be because it is often assumed that Old English poetry existed in large quantities, so that collectors would have no difficulty in choosing pieces they felt in sympathy with. It is not of course possible to tell how much poetry was composed in the Anglo-Saxon period or to what extent the extant poems form a representative sample. It does, however, seem unlikely that there was a constant stream of poetry being transferred from Anglian to West Saxon areas, though naturally the Mercians called in by Alfred may have brought some poetry with them. What we need to consider is whether the gathering of these poems into collections was inspired by the same motives which led to the poems' composition.

Presumably the collectors wanted to assemble volumes which would be useful for educational purposes, and perhaps even to publish material useful for teaching the faith, as is true with the works of Ælfric. If so, it seems probable that the desire to assemble the material was very closely linked to the impulse to create it and that the two are not far separated in time. This might also help to account for the identity of material in some of the codices. It demands too much reliance on coincidence to assume that the biblical poems in the Junius manuscript were all written at very different times and in widely separated places only to be joined together in one manuscript at some later date. To make this view at all credible we would have to assume that biblical poems in Old English were so common that the original collector of the Junius material had no difficulty in assembling versions of Genesis, Exodus and Daniel. But if this were so, we would need to know why none of the other codices contains a biblical poem. The coherence of this collection and its difference

11. K. Jost, 'Wulfstan und die angelsächsische Chronik', *Anglia* 47 (1923), 105–23, suggests that Wulfstan may have composed two of the rhythmic passages in the Chronicle.

from the other collections suggest that the composition of the poems did not precede their gathering together by very long. As part of the *Genesis* is probably to be dated to the late ninth century, the collection itself can hardly have come into existence before about 900. But if the view I have put forward here can be accepted, that would mean that all the poems in the Junius manuscript were composed about or a little before 900. Let us look at this possibility more closely.

The poem *Genesis* in the Junius manuscript is of particular interest, because it consists of two parts: in addition to the major part written originally in Old English (*Genesis A*) there is a section of just over six hundred lines which is an Old English poetic translation of an Old Saxon poem (*Genesis B*). Extant Old Saxon fragments show that the Old English translation is only a small part of the original poem. It is universally acknowledged that the literary quality of this translated section is far superior to that of *Genesis A*. The relationship of this section to the rest of the poem has not been satisfactorily explained, perhaps because all commentators have started with the assumption that *Genesis A* is earlier than *Genesis B*. Timmer tried to show that it was the scribe of the Junius manuscript who was the first to unite the two poems, though his arguments based on the collation of the gatherings are not convincing.[12] This whole matter wants further investigation. Furthermore, Timmer could provide only vague aesthetic reasons to suggest why the scribe might have included *Genesis B*. He also linked the translation of *Genesis B* with the time of Alfred because Alfred recruited assistants in his educational programme from various countries, including the land of the Continental Saxons. Indeed, the name of one of his Saxon helpers, John, is known to us, though it need not be assumed that he was the translator since he was probably one of several. To the best of my knowledge Timmer's dating for *Genesis B* is widely accepted.

The important question about the translation is why it was made. If the translator was a Saxon associated with Alfred's attempts to re-educate the English, the answer must be to provide suitable material for preaching and instruction which could be used by those involved in this educational work. It would be part of the provision of material in the vernacular of which the Alfredian prose trans-

12. B. J. Timmer, *The Later Genesis* (Oxford, 1948), pp. 10–15.

lations represent a different facet. Here, however, we meet with a difficulty. If *Genesis A* and the other poems in the Junius manuscript were in existence before *Genesis B*, it would seem a pointless exercise to translate the Old Saxon version simply to provide educational material, for there would be plenty of material already available. And, as we have just seen, unless we assume that the collection of the poems in the Junius manuscript followed quickly on their composition, we have to assume that there were many such biblical poems in existence of which the Junius ones are a chance collection.

The best way out of this difficulty is to accept that *Genesis B* is earlier than *Genesis A*. The situation may have been something like this. One of Alfred's Saxon assistants was asked to provide suitable teaching material to help in the process of instructing the Anglo-Saxons in the basic beliefs of Christianity. He met this request by translating a section of the Old Saxon poem *Genesis* he had available and so produced *Genesis B*. An English helper imitated what he had done in order to supplement the teaching material. It would be natural for this helper to complete the *Genesis* story and to follow the Vulgate much more closely than the original Saxon poet had done for he would need a prop in his task. It need not surprise us that the final result, *Genesis A*, is much more wooden and stereotyped than *Genesis B;* indeed it is what one would expect. We need not assume that the other poems in the manuscript were written by the author of *Genesis A*, for no doubt Alfred had many willing helpers. But it may be that they were written in the same vicinity as and under the stimulus of *Genesis B*. In this way we can provide a satisfactory explanation for the appearance of these biblical poems in the same manuscript. I appreciate that as the view I have put forward runs counter to accepted orthodoxy it may be greeted with surprise. But I would like to re-emphasize that the metrical and philological criteria for the dating of the poems are so insecurely based that little reliance can be placed in them. It is for this reason that I have approached the whole question of dating from a different angle.

A paper on the dating of Old English poetry cannot fail to give special attention to *Beowulf*, although it is impossible in the space available to consider all the problems involved. An early date for the poem, say about 700, was favoured until Professor Whitelock suggested that there was no reason to exclude a date later in the eighth century, though despite her plea, Wrenn in his edition still favoured a date before 750. Few scholars have advocated a date later

than the eighth century.[13] The major reasons for dating *Beowulf*
so early have been philological, its relation to other poems and the
historical background. The philological arguments, as we have seen,
are insecurely based, and if the other Old English poems can be
placed in the late ninth or early tenth century, in themselves they
provide no argument for putting *Beowulf* much earlier than that.
The historical arguments have been more emotional than cogent,
for the early Anglo-Saxon period which produced Bede and the
Sutton Hoo treasure has seemed a more fitting environment for a
poem of the stature of *Beowulf* than has the later period which is
one of educational and cultural rehabilitation. As Professor Whitelock showed in her *The Audience of Beowulf*, such arguments carry
little conviction. Unfortunately, as we cannot agree whether the
poem is secular or religious and why it was written, it is difficult to
look for an appropriate historical context. If we accept it as a
religious poem, a date in the Alfredian period is acceptable since
it would fit in with the other poems in the programme of religious
instruction. If we accept it as a secular poem, though with a strong
moral base, the court of Alfred or of one of his successors would
provide as suitable a home for the poem as would the court of most
early Northumbrian or Mercian kings; in some respects, it might
be suggested, a more suitable one. For if Alfred and his successors
encouraged the cultivation of poetry for educational purposes it is
easy to appreciate why Asser thought he had a great interest in and
love for poetry and to realize why an Old English poet might have
thought it worth while to compose a poem for his court – possibly
even in his honour. The identification of the West Saxon court with
poetry is, after all, a sufficient reason to explain why such events as
the Battle of Brunanburh and the coronation of Edgar were recorded
in poems in the *Anglo-Saxon Chronicle*. *Beowulf* need be no different
in this except it was not about local events.

   We have, after all, assumed too readily that secular poetry was
very common in early Anglo-Saxon England, though there is almost
no evidence to support this assumption. That there was a form
of alliterative poetry among the Continental Germans does not mean

---

13. D. Whitelock, *The Audience of Beowulf*, pp. 1–33; C. L. Wrenn, *Beowulf*
    (London, 1953), p. 36, rev. ed. by W. F. Bolton (1973), p. 31. The reasons
    advanced by Schücking for a later date were not the right ones (see *The
    Audience of Beowulf*, pp. 24–6).

that there was a flowering of court poetry in England in the eighth
and ninth centuries. The absence of any reference to such poetry may
be significant. If we assume that there was little or no court poetry,
then England would be like the Continent, for there is little secular
poetry in Old Saxon, but unlike Scandinavia, for the Old Icelandic
scalds produced an immense quantity of court poetry. It is, however,
possible that the example of secular poetry among the Scandinavians
encouraged the development of a court poetry in England in the late
ninth century, even if we accept that stories about the appearance of
Icelandic scalds at the English court like the one found in *Gunn-
laugs Saga Ormstungu* are apocryphal.

   In her evaluation of the evidence Professor Whitelock could find
no firm grounds for putting *Beowulf* as early as *c*. 700. The only
terminus ad quem she could devise was the Viking invasions, for she
felt that after they began no Englishman would want to listen to
praise of the Danes.[14] This type of argument fails to respect the
figural nature of medieval poetry and implies the Anglo-Saxon could
not distinguish between a symbol and the reality. In any case,
although some monkish chroniclers, particularly at the commencement of the Viking raids, referred to the Danes in opprobrious
terms, by and large the *Anglo-Saxon Chronicle* is more moderate
in its attitude. We should also remember that after they had settled
in the North of England, the Danes were soon absorbed into the
West Saxon sphere of influence and adopted the Christian religion.
They must surely have been accepted by the English. On the other
hand, it is likely that the Danish invasions created an interest in Scandinavia – an interest which receives abundant testimony in *Beowulf*.
If the poem is late we could assume that such motifs as that of Gren-
del's mere which is closely paralleled by *Grettis Saga* were learned
from English Scandinavians rather than that they were part of the
Germanic folk memory and had been known to the Anglo-Saxons
even before they themselves had come to England. Various other
features of this type might support a late date. Some of the possible
sources of the poem, such as the *Liber Monstrorum*, can be better

14. 'Yet, I doubt whether he [i.e. the *Beowulf* poet] would have spoken in these
    terms during the Viking Age, or whether his audience would have given him a
    patient hearing if he had. It is not how men like to hear the people described
    who are burning their homes, pillaging their churches, ravaging their cattle
    and crops, killing their countrymen or carrying them off into slavery.'
    (*The Audience of Beowulf*, pp. 24–5.)

accommodated if the composition of the poem is brought forward
to the late ninth century. Similarly, the antiquarianism evidenced in
such descriptions as those of Scyld Scefing's burial and Offa accords
better with a later date. I would, therefore, suggest that a respectable
case for a late ninth century or early tenth century date can be put
forward; the matter is still quite open.

   Another aspect of *Beowulf* that is relevant here is that it is the only
Old English poem for which there is reliable evidence that it was used
as a source by another Old English poet as well as by a homilist.
For I am prepared to accept that *Beowulf* was the source of *Andreas*
rather than the other way around. That the description of the haunt-
ed mere in *Beowulf* was the source of the similar passage in the tenth-
century seventeenth Blickling homily is less certain, but seems probable.[15] If *Beowulf* is an early poem we have to consider how it could
have been used by the poet of *Andreas* and the Blickling homilist,
for the nature of some borrowings is such that they can be explained
only on the basis of borrowing from a written text. The further
away in time the source is from its beneficiaries, the more difficult
it becomes to explain the influence. To meet this difficulty, it would be
necessary to assume that there were many copies of *Beowulf*. Not
only does that seem inherently unlikely, but also it creates the additional difficulty of why more authors did not draw from this same
source. It is more natural to assume that *Beowulf*, *Andreas* and the
seventeenth Blickling homily are close in time, since the immediate
popularity of the one could account for its use by the others and a
speedy falling into relative obscurity would account for its failure to
influence more authors.

   In this connexion it may also be worth remarking that the unity
of attitude and outlook in Old English poetry is well known and that
it is also reflected in much Old English prose for which a tenth-
century date is beyond doubt. If we accept an early date for Old
English poetry, we have to assume that over a period of three to four
hundred years Old English literature remained uniform. This would
be surprising in view of the many political developments and of the
cultural and intellectual changes which can be traced in the Latin

---

15. A. G. Brodeur, 'A Study of Diction and Style in Three Anglo-Saxon Narra-
    tive Poems', *Nordica et Anglica*, ed. A. H. Orrick (The Hague, 1968), pp.
    97–114; and C. L. Wrenn, *Beowulf*, p. 210 (rev. ed. by W. F. Bolton
    (1973), p. 150).

literature of the period. With the accepted dating of Old English poetry, we are asked to believe that Old English literature remained static over a long period whereas Anglo-Latin literature showed many developments. This view is improbable and becomes unnecessary if we accept a later date for the bulk of Old English poetry.

It has not been my intention to suggest in this brief paper that all Old English poetry was written in the late ninth or early tenth century. This would clearly be impossible in view of the existence of the early Northumbrian poetry. I would merely like to suggest that some neglected aspects of Old English poetry indicate that a respectable case can be made for the theory that the poems in the four poetic codices were composed in the Alfredian period rather than earlier. While some of the poems, like *The Dream of the Rood*, may have existed earlier in whole or in part, it seems improbable that this would be true of many poems in the codices. Indeed, one would expect Alfred's Mercian helpers to have brought some vernacular poetry with them, but one cannot assume that they would have brought much for their number was small. How extensive poetry was in the pre-Viking age we cannot tell. Possibly a great deal may have been destroyed, though there is reason to think that the earlier age was very much a Latinate period in which the composition of Old English poetry was restricted. The destruction of learning by the Danes prompted the use of the vernacular – and in that respect we owe them perhaps a greater debt than we had previously realized. At all events it would seem that the whole question of the dating of Old English poetry needs a full-scale re-examination; perhaps what I have written may provide a stimulus.

SPES VIVA
Structure and Meaning in *The Seafarer*

Brian K. Green

In this essay I want to give an account of *The Seafarer* as a work of literature in its own right. Very often, in anthologies of Anglo-Saxon verse, *The Seafarer* accompanies *The Wanderer*, and the formal similarity of their titles induces the reader to think of them as an inseparable pair. But their literary kinship is a spurious one. For example, the just objection has recently been raised that a distortion of meaning results from forcing *The Wanderer* and *The Seafarer* into the same 'generic mould'.[1] The two poems are also unlike in their formal structures, since *The Seafarer* is less amenable to a dialogistic interpretation than *The Wanderer*. For one thing, *The Seafarer* lacks any internal textual cues such as *Swa cwæð*; for another, if a connected line of thought can be traced running through the poem, then, as Professor Whitelock has said, 'the reason for dismembering it vanishes'.[2] The two poems can also be separated on the basis of metre alone and, as to subject-matter, they are quite literally poems apart.[3] One critic has felt that the poems are close 'in tone and style', but another critic has convincingly argued that they actually diverge in respect of their poetic procedures.[4] Each poem, in fact, makes a

1. S. B. Greenfield, *The Interpretation of Old English Poems* (London and Boston, 1972), p. 18. See also, p. 134.
2. D. Whitelock, 'The Interpretation of *The Seafarer*', in *The Early Cultures of North-West Europe* (*H. M. Chadwick Memorial Studies*), ed. C. Fox and B. Dickins (Cambridge, 1950), p. 262. Indeed, a dialogistic interpretation needlessly disintegrates the poem in seeking to unify it. Thanks to Greenfield's defence of the poem as a monologue, in his '*Min, Sylf*, and "Dramatic Voices in *The Wanderer* and *The Seafarer*"',*J.E.G.P.* 68 (1969), 212-20, J. C. Pope has been forced to recant the dialogue theory he so skilfully proposed: see 'Second Thoughts on the Interpretation of *The Seafarer*', *A.S.E.* 3 (1974), 75-86.
3. T. P. Dunning and A. J. Bliss, eds, *The Wanderer* (London, 1969), pp. 77, 79.
4. The respective views of K. Sisam, *Studies in the History of Old English Literature* (Oxford, 1953), p. 291, and D. G. Calder, 'Setting and Mode in *The Seafarer* and *The Wanderer*', *Neuphilologische Mitteilungen* 72 (1971), 264-75. See my article 'The Twilight Kingdom: Structure and Meaning in *The Wanderer*', *Neophilologus* 60 (1976), 442-51.

different moral discovery. In the consolatory *Wanderer*, a man buries his lord and then seeks another in an attempt to regain his former happiness; in the admonitory *Seafarer*, a man leaves behind the joys of the world, knowing them for the false joys they are.[5] My own purpose in the ensuing pages is to demonstrate another distinctive feature of *The Seafarer*, viz., its peculiar metaphoric unity.

On a superficial view, the 124-line poem divides into 'two distinct segments' – the one to do with seafaring, the other purely homiletic – so that the poem 'begs for some kind of *rapprochement* revolving around this momentous "sea change" '; it seems to lack 'the unity, coherence, and emphasis demanded by our modern critical sensibilities'.[6] Even the possibility of the poem's unity has been categorically rejected: 'to me *The Seafarer*, in spite of all that has been said to the contrary, ends at 64a . . . the seafarer never returns after those lines. No allegorical or symbolic interpretation of the first 64 lines is in my opinion tenable, and no amount of sophistication can make it so'.[7] As I hope to show, in the detailed reading that follows, it is only when we are prepared to conceive of a metaphoric extension of the traditional title that we can begin to see the purpose and function of the logically incongruous components in the poem's structure.

I

The most obvious structural division of the poem is a tripartite one: seen in respective isolation, the first section (A1) describes a time of past tribulation; the second section (A2) a time of present conflict; and the third (B) the common homiletic theme *lif is læne*.[8] To these

5. See E. G. Stanley, 'Old English Poetic Diction and the Interpretation of *The Wanderer, The Seafarer* and *The Penitent's Prayer*', *Anglia* 73 (1956), 463.
6. S. B. Greenfield, *A Critical History of Old English Literature* (London, 1966), pp. 219-20.
7. A. A. Prins, 'The Wanderer (and the Seafarer)', *Neophilologus* 48 (1964), 247.
8. These are O. S. Anderson's designations ('*The Seafarer*: An Interpretation', *K.H.V.L. Årsberättelse* 1, 1937, 1-49), which I adopt here for convenience. He divides the poem as follows: A1 (1a-33a), A2 (33b-64a), and B (64b-124b). My section A2 includes 66a, while B runs from 66b to the end of the poem. According to Anderson, one of the main interpretative problems is to define the relationship between A1 and A2 (p. 12).

divisions and designations I would add the first four lines, and call
them A:

> MÆG ic be me sylfum   soðgied wrecan,
> siþas secgan,   hu ic geswincdagum
> earfoðhwile   oft þrowade,
> bitre breostceare   gebiden hæbbe[9]

These opening lines deserve careful attention, because it has not been
sufficiently appreciated in previous interpretations of the poem that
they do not expressly refer to the sea, and so cannot simply be assumed to share the ironic tone of section A1. The speaker says that
he has a 'truth-tale to tell', that he is going to present an actual
(soð) experience of his own, which we can expect him to portray
poetically (gied),[10] and the delayed fulfilment of the auxiliary verb
dramatizes the personal effort involved in the composition of a
poem expressing such momentous self-knowledge. The speaker says
that he wants to tell about his experiences (siþas) in a time of trial
(geswincdagum), of how, inwardly, he has gone through crisis after
crisis (earfoðhwile oft þrowade). These introductory interests are important because they direct and control the rest of the poem in
movement and in meaning.

Now, it is in order to interpret and to give greater reality to this
intense spiritual anguish (bitre breostceare) that the speaker summons
the sea images in the next part of the poem, A1 (5a-33a). In A1, the
speaker offers a description of his former spiritual condition in terms
of the sea, where the emphasis is on physical representation. He
makes seafaring the mirror-image of his past state of mind. The
images are all of the deprivation of physical ease and its psychological
effects. During 'dark winter nights', the speaker, alone and alert, had
repeatedly to be 'on watch in the prow of a storm-battered skiff',
i.e., his whole psychological being was tensed and taxed by mon-
strous insights and perceptions. There was constant anxiety: disasters
were a close menace; there was also excruciating despair, and warmth
of human fellowship was a remote comfort. In all of this, it was the
sheer immediacy of the experience that wore him out both mentally
and physically.

---

9. Extracts are taken from I. L. Gordon's text, *The Seafarer* (London, 1960),
   unless otherwise specified. I have unobtrusively corrected her lower-case *g* in
   the opening word.
10. See Stanley, pp. 450, 461.

Yet, the image of the speaker alone at sea, his state of mind ob-
jectified in the winter seascape, also opens up another dimension of
the same experience when it allows us to glimpse an alternative consciousness, that of the man 'þe him on foldan fægrost limpeð' (13).
This other dimension is not itself figurative. It is a very real part
of the speaker's painful delusion. But the figurative texture of lines
18a-26b vividly presents the impossibility of his reconciling the two
dimensions of the experience. Amid the squall's stinging flicks, the
speaker says,

> Þær ic ne gehyrde   butan hlimman sæ,
> iscaldne wæg.   Hwilum ylfete song
> dyde ic me to gomene,   ganetes hleoþor
> ond huilpan sweg   fore hleahtor wera,
> mæw singende   fore medodrince.
> Stormas þær stanclifu beotan,   þær him stearn oncwæð
> isigfeþera;   ful oft þæt earn bigeal,
> urigfeþra;   nænig hleomæga
> feasceaftig ferð   frefran meahte.   (18a-26b)

The language of the passage shows us that the poet's purpose is to
convey the dual subjectivity of the speaker's perceptions. The poet
achieves his purpose in two ways. First, Anglo-Saxon prosody enables him to bring together the two incompatible modes of consciousness; and second, this alliterative negotiation between the half-lines
is facilitated and confirmed by the analogy between birds and kins-
men. This basic analogy is set up in lines 19b-20a, and then remains
implicit in the rest of the passage. Thus, in a network of metrical
juxtaposition and implied predication, the poem weaves together
images of land and sea in order to articulate the superimposed experience, and so to enact the paradox in the speaker's affirmation of
worldly joy.

The poem depicts the speaker's suffering in a series of apparently
joyful analogies, and interprets his past unhappiness in terms of them.
The words *song, to gomene, hleoþor, sweg, hleahtor, medodrince,* and
possibly *oncwæð* (describing the reverberation of voices in a large
gathering of people) all have a festive register, so that the birds might
seem to supply his need for *winemægum* (16a). In effect, however, they
merely cast him back on his humanity and deeper into his spiritual af-
fliction. Like the speaker's, the true nature of the birds in the scheme
of Creation, their frailty and puniness, is graphically emphasized in

line 23, where the soft, flaky-feathered tern is pictured between
(*þær . . . þær*) the storm's boom and aggression on one side and the
towering, hard, granite cliffs on the other side. Of course, the 'singing' of the birds was illusory and, in the context, more discordant
and disturbing (like the *hleahtor* of a company of men) than har-
monious (as *hleoþor* would seem to suggest). The birds belong to the
land, and when they returned to shore the speaker had to resume an
isolation which had been intensified by their presence.

When, however, the speaker's former anxiety and the transparent
happiness of the 'land-dwellers' are counterpoised like this in the
same moment, the irony in the image forces itself upon us:

> For þon him gelyfeð lyt,   se þe ah lifes wyn
> gebiden in burgum,   bealosiþa hwon,
> wlonc ond wingal,   hu ic werig oft
> in brimlade   bidan sceolde.   (27a-30b)

The man who is intoxicated by the robustness and obstreperous
babble of human society can really have no inkling of an inner human
calm. And that point having been made in a vivid litotes, the land's
aspect changes with an ominous abruptness. It is now the land itself
that is bound by ice and flailed by *corna caldast* (33a), a cold cloud-
crop. Frost (*hrim*, 32a) and hail (*hægl*, 32b) reappear (cf. line 17,
both verbally and metrically). Even the figurative pattern of kinetic
antagonism is similar to the speaker's own suffering: *gebunden* (9b)
and *seofedun . . . ymb* (10b-11a), *bond* (32a) and *feol on* (32b). The
image of profusion, too, recalls the earlier oppressiveness in *geþrungen* (8b). For the first time in the poem, the land is seen as the
earth (32b), conjoined with the sea in a single image of the planet. The
land has ceased to represent a relieving psychological state, since it no
longer symbolizes human happiness.[11]

Within A1, then, the speaker gives a three-dimensional description
of his *bitre breostceare* by making an ironic criticism of the sea's
contrary. This thematic variation is intended to be not only dramatic,
contrastive, and ironic but, in a word, meiotic. Indeed, the poem's
technique so far is worth noting. First, it structures feelings of doom
and misery; then, it images a situation free from this state of mind;

11. The phrase *on foldan* (13a) refers not so much to the earth as to the civilized
    world. See Gordon, p. 34, n. 13, and Calder's valuable analysis of this whole
    passage (pp. 265-66).

and then it removes that exemption by exposing an inherent flaw in
the latter situation. In other words, the poem moves from a psycho-
logically harsh reality through an apparent physical ideal to a harsher
physical reality which itself implies an unbearable spiritual truth.
This, in crude short-hand, is the procedure of *The Seafarer*. It is a
rhythm of understatement which emphasizes three things in a precise
way: the speaker's rigorous consciousness of his spiritual paralysis,
his feeling of being alienated (*bidroren*, 16a) from his fellow-men, and
his delusion that the world gives security and fulfilment. But the total
effect of this section of the poem is essentially paradoxical, since it is
meant to startle us out of our simplistic preconceptions of happiness.
Arrogating to themselves dominion over the world, men are neglect-
ful of their inner vulnerability, and like to forget their physical
limitations.

All these contrasting perspectives notate an ambivalence towards
worldly happiness, and can most readily be seen in the bird-sequence
(19b-25a), in which images of land and sea interanimate one another.
These perspectives then co-operate to resolve partially the speaker's
ambivalence, by fusing the moral values of land and sea in the
concluding 'storm'-image of A1. In effect, then, since up to this point
the poem recounts a past experience, the sea throughout A1 actually
has been symbolizing all the tried happiness that life 'on land' could
offer. These are some of the deeper implications which the poem
explores in its first marine analogy.

II

Transcending the speaker's earlier disillusionment, lines 33b-38b
bring us back into the present, and give the position of the speaker in
his spiritual quest at the time of telling his 'tale'. The image is that of
a heart buffeted by a 'stormy' mind:

> Forþon cnyssað nu
> heortan geþohtas,   þæt ic hean streamas,
> sealtyþa gelac   sylf cunnige;
> monað modes lust   mæla gehwylce
> ferð to feran,   þæt ic feor heonan
> elþeodigra   eard gesece.[12]

12. *The Exeter Book*, ed. G. P. Krapp and E. V. K. Dobbie, The Anglo-Saxon
    Poetic Records, III (New York, 1936), 144.

Sustaining the metaphoric mode, the poem says that fancies 'toss' the speaker's heart now that he, relying on his own resources and initiative,[13] ventures into the 'tumultuous saltspray on the deep seas' (i.e., away from the coast); and that whenever he longs for the 'homeland of aliens', the worldly propensities of his mind accentuate his soul's desire to press on towards the true and happy 'land' of the devout Christian. This 'homeland of aliens' denotes the heavenly *patria* of Christian *peregrini* who, as God's people, are strangers or exiles in this world,[14] and we now become fully aware of the speaker's new spiritual orientation. We connect the speaker's trials with a man's efforts to achieve his social identity, to find salvation for his soul, and to discover a belief to which he can dedicate himself, once he has emerged from the delusion that happiness is to be derived from purely secular values.

At the same time, now that the speaker wants to reach this other 'land', he cannot escape having to venture through the same 'sea' of worldly 'happiness' in which he was before. By their immediacy, worldly attractions continue to embarrass his purpose and qualify his conviction. True, the speaker is no longer 'envious', casting 'wistful glances at the fortunate on earth'.[15] Nevertheless, the interlaced figuration in lines 40a-52b represents the host of worldly promptings that seek to impede the speaker's progress. Alfred's image defines further this notion of the passionately devout Christian's susceptibility to temptation, fear, and self-deception:

> Swiðe eaðe mæg on smyltre sæ ungelæred scipstiera
> genoh ryhte stieran, ac se gelæreda him ne getruwað
> on ðære hreon sæ & on ðæm miclan stormum. Hwæt is
> ðonne ðæt rice & se ealdordoom butan ðæs modes storm,
> se simle bið cnyssende ðæt scip ðære heortan mid

13. Cf. Pope, 'Second Thoughts . . . ', pp. 77-80. My two principal criticisms of Pope's new reading of the poem are: on the one hand, that it fails to appreciate the imaginative force of *cearselda fela* (5b) and, on the other hand, that it overlooks the fact that the poem contains no expression corresponding to *pro amore Dei*. In fairness, I should say that the second half of his reading is admirable.

14. I am conscious here of a debt, both explicit and implicit, to G. V. Smithers, without whose provocative and thorough articles, 'The Meaning of *The Seafarer* and *The Wanderer*', *Medium Ævum* 26 (1957), 137-53, and 28 (1959), 1-22, and 99-104, the present essay could hardly have been written.

15. S. B. Greenfield, 'Attitudes and Values in *The Seafarer*,' *S.P.* 51 (1954), 17.

ðara geðohta ystum, & bið drifen hider & ðider on
swiðe nearwe bygeas worda & weorca, swelce hit sie
ongemong miclum & monigum stancludum tobrocen?[16]

Creating some beautifully apt sea-imagery, the poem now describes
this susceptibility in terms of a man who has made up his mind to go
to sea and is about to set out (*modes fusne*, 50b). There is the natural
apprehension that comes to everyone, no matter the size, strength,
success, or service of his manly heart (39a-43b); such a person can
think only of the voyage and of his safety. And yet, as the pivotal
ambiguity in *longunge* (47a) makes clear – the line can be taken either
as a gnomic expression of a sailor's 'anxiety', or as an adversative
introductory comment on his eagerness, his 'longing', to stay ashore –
the earth seems to become especially attractive when one has to leave
it behind. The whole world is suddenly vibrant and lush with life and
beauty. As Professor Mackie has sensitively translated lines 48a-49b,

> The woods blossom forth, the cities become fair,
> the fields are beautiful, the world breaks into life[17]

it were as though, in going to sea, the sailor feels he is actually aban-
doning the very source of his own life. And indeed, everything that is
lovely serves only to remind the sailor of the perils of his journey. The
intensity of the feelings of the two seafarers, spiritual and literal, are
comparable, but their precise emotions are not. The man who seeks
the salvation of his soul knows that, in addition to the temptations of
the world, there is the fear of an ultimate death, i.e. damnation, and
there is the hope, latent and (to our modern minds, perhaps) paradoxical, of the blossoming orchards 'of the resurrection of man at the
Day of Judgement'.[18]

Lines 39a-57b, then, recapitulate the thematic rhythm of harsh
reality (*sæfore sorge*) mollified by apparent ideal (*wongas wlitigað*),
which is in turn ironically abrogated only to make the inescapable
reality (*wræclastas*) that much harsher. Like the opening line of the
poem, *sylf* (35b) affirms the speaker's essential being, and it enacts
his anxious compulsion to risk living virtuously in spite of the know-

16. *King Alfred's West-Saxon Version of Gregory's Pastoral Care*, Ch. 9 (Hatton MS.), ed. H. Sweet (E.E.T.S. 45, 1871), p. 59, ll. 1-7.
17. W. S. Mackie, *The Exeter Book, Part II: Poems IX-XXXII* (E.E.T.S. 194, 1933), p. 5.
18. N. F. Blake, ' "The Seafarer", Lines 48-49', *N. & Q.* 207, No. 5 (1962), 163.

ledge of his own moral guilt. What the word certifies is a freedom to
act, an action to be performed, and a potentiality to be realized. We
begin to see how crucially the energies of *MÆG* organize and animate
the whole poem.

It is at this point in the poem, in the final part of A2 (58a-66a),
that this meiotic pattern is most startlingly developed. The two escha-
tological ideas – the anticipation of heaven and the apprehension of
hell – become synthesized poetically:

> For þon nu min hyge hweorfeð   ofer hreþerlocan,
> min modsefa   mid mereflode
> ofer hwæles eþel   hweorfeð wide,
> eorþan sceatas,   cymeð eft to me;
> gifre ond grædig   gielleð anfloga,
> hweteð on wælweg   hreþer unwearnum
> ofer holma gelagu[19]

Here we return to the speaker's personal experience. Except for the
oblique reference to men in the MS. reading *wælweg* (which I have
retained), the poem now for the first time does not present the
speaker in terms of land-dwellers, for his life lies 'across the vast
sea', beyond the world of 'flesh'. Having said that, one may take this
secondary meaning of *wæl*, in conjunction with *anfloga*, as an iso-
morphous allusion to the conventional theme of the carrion bird
(cf. *wælgifre fugel, Judith* 207a).[20] In the lines quoted above, there is a
sudden notional switch from the speaker's emotions to a ravenous
bird that makes us see that the bird, immediate and impatient, perfectly objectifies those emotions and conveys the idea of an imminent
feast. The *anfloga*'s urgent desire is identified with the speaker's own.
We get a metaphoric utterance followed by a symbolic utterance,
intersecting at the point at which the metaphoric movement (*hweor-
feð*) is given an unexpected symbolic direction (*-weg*). The crucial
point is to see that the *anfloga* is not of the same imaginative order as

---

19. The punctuation is my own. See Greenfield, *The Interpretation of Old
   English Poems*, p. 44.
20. The idea most immediately suggested, in this context, by *wælweg* is 'water-
   way', as E. G. Stanley rightly points out in his rev. of Gordon's ed. (*M.Æ.*
   31, 1962, 58). Cf. W. F. Bolton, ed., *An Old English Anthology* (London,
   1963), p. 84. But see my exploratory paper, 'The Seafarer's Joy: The Interpretation of Lines 58a-64a', *U.C.T. Studies in English*, No. 5 (1974), pp.
   21-33, which was conceived before Pope's retraction came to hand.

the other birds in the poem. This 'bird' speaks to the speaker's heart as none of the birds in A1 do, and its cry penetrates his mind with its insistent exultation. Thus the attributes of the hungry bird – desire, impatience, delight, and anticipation – inform and discipline our own conception of the devout Christian, whose concentrated purpose is suggested by the element *an-*. In prayer, the speaker's thought leaves this world, has a kind of shamanistic foretaste of the heavenly life, and returns to inspire his willing soul to continue to seek God's 'fare'. The poem uses the emotional charge of the conventional image to convey the Christian's elation at the inward vision of the heavenly feast, a vision originating from the insight of his soul.

That is not all. The final wintry image in A1 carried powerful associations of death and of hell,[21] and there is now, to heighten the tension, an admonitory overtone in the *anfloga*-image which Gordon's comma, instead of the customary full-stop after *ofer holma gelagu* (64a), helps us to apprehend as part of an emotional continuum. The dependent clause which concludes A2

> for þon me hatran sind
> Dryhtnes dreamas   þonne þis deade lif
> læne on londe.   (64b-66a)

is not, in any meaningful sense, subordinate to the *anfloga*-clause so much as it is simultaneous with it. The pejorative connotation of *gifre ond grædig* (62a) is not inert either, since it initiates the interplay between *wæl* and *deade*. Indeed, the idea itself echoes Luke 17, 37, 'swa hwær swa se lichama byð þyder beoð earnes ge-gadered',[22] as if to say that the carrion birds have already begun to arrive. *Wælweg* may be a joyful experience, but it also has the resonance of the inescapable 'harsher reality' ironically understated as the model of the way to *elþeodigra eard*.

The closing lines of A2 are the poem's most explicit statement so far of the theme of worldly happiness. The *Nap nihtscua*-image made the point directly, that the earth and everything on it are dead. The

---

21. That the malignancy in the poem's winter images has a spiritual quality, V. Salmon helps us to see in 'Some Connotations of "Cold" in Old and Middle English', *M.L.N.* 74 (1959), 314-22.
22. 'The Gospel according to Saint Luke', in *The Gospel according to Saint Luke and according to Saint John*, ed. W. W. Skeat (1874 and 1878; rpt. 2 vols in 1, Darmstadt, 1970), p. 172, Hatton MS.

anfloga-image is less rationalistic. The joy that this earthly life offers
(*lifes wyn*, 27b) is transient and, compared with the joys of heaven –
it is metrically opposed to them – is as distasteful and as defiling as
death. But both life and death have to be faced and fully appreciated
if one is to realize at all one's sense of God. This whole passage, then,
is about a purification of purpose, as the powers of the mantic soul
are focused in the intense, spontaneous, and central action of committed prayer. It can only be in spite of part of himself that the true
believer aspires to heaven.

III

During the last part of the poem, B (66b-124b), the speaker's comments are less psychological and are more assured, reflective, and
gnomic. He now proceeds to show in what precisely it is that worldly
happiness is deficient. To do this, he employs again the meiotic
rhythm of a harsh reality setting off an apparent ideal which is subsequently revoked in order to reveal a harsher reality. The poem now
seemingly subverts death and decay by using heroic imagery to assert
immortality: a noble warrior can die happy because he knows that
his deeds of glory and honour will live on in men's praise, and that he
is assured of a place in the celestial *duguð* (72a-80a). *Lifgendra* (73a)
praise must pass away, but the hero's glory will live on (*lifge*, 78b).
The fact of the matter, however, is that the days of such heroism are
past, for no one any longer performs deeds of memorable nobility
(80b-85b). The poem now gives a penetrating critical account of this
decline in human achievement and, without denying the courageous
sacrifice involved in heroic attitudes, exposes the futility of this secular, aristocratic preference for 'eternal' fame among mortals:

> Dagas sind gewitene,
> ealle onmedlan   eorþan rices;
> nearon nu cyningas   ne caseras
> ne goldgiefan   swylce iu wæron,
> þonne hi mæst mid him   mærþa gefremedon
> ond on dryhtlicestum   dome lifdon.
> Gedroren is þeos duguð eal,   dreamas sind gewitene;
> wuniað þa wacran   ond þas woruld healdaþ,
> brucað þurh bisgo. Blæd is gehnæged,
> eorþan indryhto   ealdað ond searað,
> swa nu monna gehwylc   geond middangeard.   (80b-90b)

The syntactic equation of *Dagas* and earthly *dreamas* in metrically parallel lines casts all worldly happiness in a mould of feeble mortality. Moreover, in keeping with the universal frame of reference in B, all humanity and all the earth are seen together as parts of the same creation. And the passing of worldly splendour suggests not only the futility of earthly glory but also the vanity of all *eorðwelan* (67a). A noble life according to worldly standards is no longer possible for the simple reason that the noble spirit itself is dead; *eorðwelan* will not last for ever because the *eorðe* itself is about to die. The earth is in its old age, which is marked by the 'dwindling' of its 'life-force'. Its spirit broken by time, the earth has lost its own 'nobility'. The contrast with the 'perpetual vitality' (*ecan lifes blæd*, 79b) of the devout Christian is strong. In the metaphor, the earth takes on the infirm qualities of human *Yldo* (91a), namely, loss of vigour and enfeebled physical and mental activities. The disparity in the metaphor deepens our understanding of the idea, making explicit and effectively emphasizing the human properties of grief, joy, sensation, gesture, reason, and, above all, spirituality (92a-102b). There is further irony in the fact that a man has only one old age and cannot regain his former vigour on earth, while the earth itself undergoes seasonal rejuvenation. This discrepancy between the earth's real and apparent age is most vividly and succinctly imaged in the ambiguous *woruld onetteð* (49b). The superficial meaning, that the world is once again being charged with life, gives us the impression of eternal life. But the patristic notion of hexamerous time[23] is probably being alluded to in this image of spring. Charged with new life, the world is actually 'charging' to its end, and the Day of Judgement approaches with every season. And this is suggested particularly in the season of spring which, just as autumn suggests the deathly iciness of winter, suggests the parching heat of summer, when 'flos [foeni] decidit, et decor vultus eius deperiit' (James 1, 11).[24]

In the poem, we pass through winter (15a), spring (48a-49a), and summer (54a), and then we find ourselves in autumn, the time for

23. J. [E.] Cross, 'On the Allegory in *The Seafarer* – Illustrative Notes', *M.Æ.* 28 (1959), 105. But see, too, Cross's 'Aspects of Microcosm and Macrocosm in Old English Literature', in *Studies in Old English Literature in Honor of Arthur G. Brodeur*, ed. S. B. Greenfield (Eugene, Ore., 1963), pp. 1-22.

24. *Biblia Sacra iuxta Vulgatam Clementinam*, ed. A. Colunga and L. Turrado, Biblioteca de autores cristianos (Madrid: Editorial católica, 1946). Biblical quotations are from this ed.

dying. The shifting seasons recall the rhythm of understatement pointed out earlier. Spring and summer are a reprieve of winter, but a reprieve cancelled by the arrival of autumn, which is the warrant for another winter. Men are deluded by the superficial rhythms of the universe into believing that humanity will likewise continue to renew itself, and that death is somehow an abominable denial of an earthly, human prerogative. But to the man who fears mere oblivion, but who also looks forward to the apocalyptic *neowe eorðe*,[25] death does not come entirely 'unwelcome' (*unþinged*, 106b).

The image of sered human goodness thus reminds us that this half of the poem, in a style appropriate to its didactic purpose, organizes its Christian ideas through nodal (but not static) images of gold and heroic virtue. No amount of material wealth and martial prowess can absolve the human soul from its inherited sin and qualify it for heaven.[26] Then, through the metaphor of decay, the poem exploits the homiletic connotations of these images. In effect, it offers another reason for the deterioration of human *duguð* (86a). In the Sixth Age, noble conduct is undermined as moral evil increases among men, who become 'more degenerate', inwardly 'weaker' (*wacran*, 87a), as the earth provides the setting for the Antichrist's dominion.[27] By showing the moral poverty of the world itself, the poem bankrupts the idealistic hope that true happiness may be found either in worldly fame or in worldly wealth. The images of winter and of physical deterioration enact the traditional conception of Adam's punishment, owing to which 'omnis creatura ingemiscit, et parturit usque adhuc' (Romans 8, 22).

This idea of the earth's deficiencies is worked out finally in lines 103a-10b, where we get not so much a succession as a fusion of images. The foundation of the whole universe is described in a confident tone because the speaker has both accepted and assimilated Christian wisdom into his knowledge of human life. This confidence is grounded on a real personal experience, and this is reflected in the poet's individual interpretation of public knowledge. The MS. read-

25. Homily No. 28, *Early English Homilies from the Twelfth Century MS. Vesp. D. XIV*, ed. R. D-N. Warner (E.E.T.S. 152, 1917), p. 72, l. 11, cited by Smithers, p. 142.

26. M. D. Cherniss, 'The Meaning of *The Seafarer*, Lines 97-102', *M.P.* 66 (1968), 148, col. 2.

27. E.g. the Vercelli *Homiletic Fragment* 31a-34b and *Guthlac* 43a-92b.

ing *mod* (109a) is usually emended to *mon* on the assumption that the poet, if not the scribe, intended the gnomic comment 'Styran sceal mon strongum mode' (Gordon, p. 46). This assumption is not quite impregnable, despite the fact that the scribe of our poem would seem to have made an error in nearly every ten (editorial) lines he copied. Once one realizes that the poem deliberately distinguishes between two states of mind, between *þæt mod* (108a), which refers to *eaþmod* in the previous line, and *strongum mode* (109a), which refers back to 'Dol biþ se þe him his Dryhten ne ondrædeþ' (106a), the lines give good sense as they stand:

Meotod him þæt mod gestaþelað,   for þon he in his meahte gelyfeð.
Stieran mod sceal strongum mode,   ond þæt on staþelum healdan
(108a-9b)

'The Creator will secure that mind for him, because he trusts in His might; and that mind must steer the wilful mind, and still hold its own course'. The reverent and compliant mind, which is founded in faith, is encouraged by 'grace' (*ar*, 107b), i.e., by the assurance of the Creator's interest, and this faithful mind disciplines the wilful mind. The point of view here, or rather the centre of consciousness, incorporates humility, faith, and holiness (*wisum clæne*, 110b).

To illustrate this structure of pious feeling the poem dramatizes an extreme situation (111a-16b), just as it did earlier to describe the total futility of burying gold in graves. Again, as then (97a), the concessive *þeah þe*-clause emphasizes an important contrast. I follow the Holthausen-Mackie reading of line 112, *wiþ leofne [lufan] ond wið laþne bealo*,[28] and interpret this passage as follows. All men should be treated alike, one should become neither too attached to anyone nor too estranged from anyone, and regard friend and foe equally – though the one should kill the other. Even in such a grievous case, the Christian must not take sides, and God will give him the strength to restrain his worldly affections. Nor is this outlook an ideal of a passionless and therefore perfectly rational soul. Indeed, it is a decisive recognition that rationality by itself is insufficient to

---

28. Gordon, p. 47, n. 111-12; Mackie, p. 8. The idea conveyed by this line is not unlike Wulfstan's precept for the righteous king: 'þæt he be freondan and be fremdan fadige gelice on rihtlican dome' (*Die 'Institutes of Polity, Civil and Ecclesiastical'*, ed. K. Jost, Schweizer anglistische Arbeiten, Vol. 47, Bern, 1959, p. 54, II.30).

eradicate moral evil. Again, in terms of the poem's sea imagery, God is the destination of the repenting soul, and heaven is the native 'port' of the spiritual seafarer who, if his faith is fixed, will be able to give sound direction to (*mid gemete healdan*, 111b) every human relationship in which he is involved (*gewis werum*, 110a), i.e., to live a holy but active life. This moral notion of enduring *Wyrd* (115b) proposes not the sequestered adherence to a philosophical courage, but righteous engagement with life by a man whose courageous intention (*gehygd*, 116b) is to maintain a humble attitude of mind before God, who 'will help him to be impervious to the world around him'.[29] Contemplating worldly prosperity, the speaker thereby placed himself wholly in the power of Wyrd, and became 'storm-tossed'. But Wyrd is also the divine adjustment of the world to accommodate men's free choice of actions; it is 'the divine force that keeps human error from going too far and keeps the storm from sinking the ship'.[30] Thus, only if a man entrusts his will to Him can God make the optimum adjustments in the man's life:

> Swa eac þæt mennisce mod bið undereten 7 aweged of his stede þonne hit se wind strongra geswinca astyroð oððe se ren ungemetlices ymbhogan. Ac se þe wille habban þa ecan gesælða he sceal fleon þone frecnan wlite þises middaneardes 7 timbrian þæt hus his modes on þam fæstan stane eaðmetta, forþamðe Crist eardað on þære dene eadmodnesse[31]

IV

A final reduction of the topics in lines 66b-105b to a single theme would show that A1 and A2 are understatements of the overriding interest in the poem, namely, the inferior values on which men base their understanding of happiness. Both *cearselda fela* and *elþeodigra eard* have to do with some form of security and happiness. Each

29. A. Payne, *King Alfred & Boethius: An Analysis of the Old English Version of the 'Consolation of Philosophy'* (London, 1968), p. 94.

30. Payne, op. cit., p. 108.

31. *King Alfred's Old English Version of Boethius*, Ch. 12, ed. W. J. Sedgefield (Oxford, 1899), p. 27, ll. 2-7, contractions expanded. Indeed, the entire second book of the *Philosophiae Consolatio* provides an illuminating context of ideas for *The Seafarer*.

contributes in some degree to the meaning of *ham* (117a), which is the culminating image not only in the thematic structure of contrast between land and sea, but also in the total metaphoric strategy of the poem.[32] The complex of dwelling/building-images in the poem orders and binds the major theme through the agency of their common contextual connotations. Every phase of the experience which the poem creates is structured in terms of this single basic metaphor.

Taken in its immediate context (4a-5b), the ironic metaphor *cearseld* 'hall of anxiety' denotes a situation of distress.[33] The ensuing images (*atol . . . geweatc* and *cnossað*) clarify its meaning, and it comes to denote an appalling precariousness. The only 'security' the speaker was sure of was being firmly in the grip of unhappiness, a paralysing anxiety (*geþrungen* and *gebunden . . . clommum*). The whole poem holds together through this ambivalence between different kinds of insecurity and security. Used as an objective equivalent for anxiety, *cearselda fela* first stands in contrast to *burgum* (28a), but later, by extension in the transitional image of winter, takes in all dwellings on land. The halls of men are like ships at sea, their peace depends on joys which are always inconstant. In terms of the poem's metaphoric co-ordinates, then, *cear* = *wyn* (27b). Similarly, when the *byrig* in A2 (48a) please the eye in competition with the *elþeodigra eard*, which is invisible, we are meant to feel that such beauty is suspect because, as we have just seen in A1, the buildings themselves stand on the weak foundations of human nature. The first lines of B, 'Ic gelyfe no/ þæt him eorðwelan ece stondað' (66b-67b), thus bring to a climactic focus the metaphoric and thematic structures of A1 and A2. The apparently problematical relationship between A1 and A2 is thus explained by the fact that antithetical subjects, insecurity and security, derive their meaning from the same sphere of experience, seafaring, and their respective referents, *cearselda fela* and *elþeodigra eard*, are pressed into service in the same homiletic theme. In terms of the poem's total structure, if *cearselda fela* is the harsh reality then *elþeodigra eard* is the apparent ideal.

---

32. Calder, p. 269. But see N. D. Isaacs 'Image, Metaphor, Irony, Allusion, and Moral: The Shifting Perspective of *The Seafarer*', in his *Structural Principles in Old English Poetry* (Knoxville, 1968), pp. 33-4. Cf. C. L. Wrenn, *A Study of Old English Literature* (London, 1967), p. 144.

33. Gordon, p. 33, n. 5, and P. Gradon, *Form and Style in Early English Literature* (London, 1971), p. 161. Cf. Whitelock, p. 263.

Most critics easily connect 'the homeland of aliens' with *ham*
(117b), but overlook the clue to the speaker's tone given in the sub-
ordinating conjunctions *hwær* and *hu* (118b). This is no merely stoic
acceptance of cosmic doom, nor an attempt to rise above human
suffering. *Ham* is not conceived of as a direct escape from this world,
as *elþeodigra eard* was, but in living, human terms. *Ham* is revealed
to be the harsher, challenging reality because it implies a 'here',
where the heavenly life must begin in awful recognition of the Creator's might and righteousness, and in the practical appreciation of the
holiness of Christ's life by which our own lives will be judged. In
addition, *hu* has a twofold allusion: to the physical death of men,
which is a result of Adam's sin, and to the costly death of Christ
(*Halgan*, 122b), whose holiness made all Christians worthy (*usic
geweorþade*, 123a) to live in the presence of God. All Christians,
the poem says, should accordingly bear in mind[34] their Lord's
sacrifice; for, by accepting their lot as strangers in this dying world,
they have a regenerative *spem vivam* (1 Peter 1,3) in heaven (*hyht in
heofonum*, 122a), a hope that reinforces their responsibility for living.
The *hu*-clause thus notates the speaker's solemn recognition of the
inescapable harshness which this knowledge entails upon him. It
also certifies a new quality of inner strength, the courage to enjoy the
consecrated life which Christ inaugurated. It is this new vitality that
is the source of the *anfloga*-image we looked at earlier, and the whole
peregrinatio-analogy enacts the force of this spiritual creativity.[35]

Like its meaning, seeming at first plainly literal and obvious, the
imaginative unity of *The Seafarer* consists in its basically metaphoric mode, viz., the juxtaposition of figurative perspective and
homiletic ambiguity. In turn, the poem's meiotic rhythms grow from
a central paradox between appearance and reality which has its

34. *Geþencan* ' "to bear in mind" a fact (that should influence conduct or opinion)
stated in a clause', *An Anglo-Saxon Dictionary: Supplement*, ed. T. N. Toller
(Oxford, 1921), s.v., X. Blickling Homily No. 8, 'Sauwle Þearf,' offers an
instructive gloss: '& us is eac mycel nedþearf þæt we geþencean hu Drihten
us mid his þrowunga alesde from deofles onwalde . . . forðon þe he wolde us
from ecum witum generian, & us gelædon on þa ecean eadignesse', *The
Blickling Homilies of the Tenth Century*, ed. R. Morris (E.E.T.S. 73, 1880),
p. 97.
35. See F. N. M. Diekstra's penetrating commentary, '*The Seafarer* 58-66a: The
Flight of the Exiled Soul to Its Fatherland', *Neophilologus* 55 (1971), 433-46,
esp. 443.

germ in the poem's sea images. And the imaginative tension between these structures of thought and feeling is meant to exercise and strengthen the Christian reader's devotion. The Christian's happiness springs from the practice of hope, and the density of the poem's ironic understatements deepens and supplies that source.

MEDIEVAL AMERICA AND 'SIR JOHN MANDEVILLE'

Michael C. Seymour

Unlike Time, *Mandeville's Travels* does not claim to make survey of all the world, but there are very few countries within the world known to 14th-century Europe that do not get at least one brief mention. The most important exceptions perhaps are Iceland and the Norse settlements to the west. Iceland, known by vague report to Boethius, Orosius, and Bede as Thule, was well known to later medieval geographers. Thus, *De Proprietatibus Rerum* of Bartholomæus Anglicus, written probably in Saxony *c.* 1245, whose description of countries became a standard medieval gazetteer, gives this account, most likely derived from a near contemporary northern geography:[1]

> Iselandia est regio vltima in Europa, a septentrione vltra Noruegiam sita, perpetuo glacie in remotioribus eius finibus condemnata, protenditur autem super litus oceani maris versus septentrionem, vbi mare præ nimio frigore congelatur. Ab oriente habens Scythiam superiorem: ab austro Noruegiam: ab occidente oceanum Hybernicum: ab aquilone mare congelatum. Et est dicta Iselandia quasi terra glaciei, eo quod ibi dicuntur esse montes niuei in glaciei duritiem congelati. Ibi crystalli inueniuntur, in illa etiam regione sunt albi vrsi, maximi et ferocissimi, qui vnguibus glaciem rumpunt, et foramina multa, per quæ in mare se immergunt et sub glacie pisces capientes, eos extrahunt per foramina prædicta, et ad littus deferentes inde viuunt, terra est sterilis, quoad fruges, exceptis paucis locis, in quorum vallibus vix crescit auena, gramina tantummodo et arbores in locis vbi habitant homines, parturit et producit, et in illis partibus feras gignit et iumenta nutrit. Vnde de piscibus et venationibus et carnibus pro maiori parte populus terræ viuit, oues præ frigore ibi viuere non possunt, et ideo incolæ de ferarum et vrsorum pellibus, quos venatu capiunt, contra frigus se muniunt et corpora sua tegunt, alia vestimenta habere non

---

1. Cf. the anonymous *Historia Norwegiæ c.*1170, ed. G. Storm, *Monumenta Historica Norvegiæ* (Christiania, 1880), pp. 92–6, 211–13.

possunt nisi aliunde deferantur. Gens multum corpulenta, robusta et valde alba, piscationi dedit et venationi.[2]

Apart from the reference to the *albi vrsi*, polar bears which have strayed into this account and into the description of Norway from Greenland,[3] Bartholomæus knows nothing of Greenland and Norse America, and this ignorance is typical of the non-Norse-speaking world of the thirteenth and early fourteenth centuries in so far as the written records extend.

There is, however, the possibility that 'Mandeville', writing *c.* 1357, probably in the north-eastern French-speaking area, included one hearsay reference to these northern settlements:

> Et pur ceo mad il souenuz meinfoithe dune chose qe ieo oy conter, quant ieo fuy ieofnes, coment vn vaillant homme sen party iadys de noz parties pur aler cercher le monde; si passa Ynde et lez isles outre Ynde, ou il y a pluis de v^m isles, et tant ala par mer et par terre et tant enuirona le monde par mointes seysons qil trouva vne isle ou il oy parler son langage et toucher les boefs en disant tiels paroules come lem fait en soun pais, dont il se merueilla mult, qar il ne sauoit coment ceo poait estre. Mes ieo dy qil auoit tant irre par terre et par mer qil auoit enuironne tote la terre qil estoit reuenuz enuironant iusques a ses marches et, sil vousist auer passe auant, qil eust troue et son pais et sa conissance. Mes il retourna ariere par illeoqes ou il estoit venuz, si perdy assez de ses peines, si come il mesmes le disoit vne grande piece apres qil feust reuenuz. Qar il auient apres qil aloit en Norweye; sy ly prist tempeste en mer, et arriua en vne isle, et, quant it fuist en celle isle, il reconust qe ceo estoit lisle ou il auoit oy parler soun langage a mesner les boefs a la charue. Et ceo fuist bien possible chose.[4]

Since this little story, unlike the bulk of the book, has no known literary source, the commentators have generally passed it by, giving

2. Bartholomæus Anglicus, *De Proprietatibus Rerum* (Frankfurt, 1601), pp. 713–14. The reference to Wynlandia in some versions of the text (for example, in the English version, *On the Properties of Things*, ed. M. C. Seymour et al. (Oxford, 1975), II, 822–3) is to Finland. Cf. Higden, *Polychronicon*, I, 21, ed. C. Babington, Rolls Series (London, 1865), I, 322.

3. Polar bears could have drifted to Iceland from Greenland on ice floes. A few were taken thence to Norway, as in *Auðunar þáttr vestfirzka*.

4. G. F. Warner, *The Buke of Iohn Maundeuill* (Westminster, 1889), pp. 91–2.

most of their attention to the general statement of circumnavigation
which it embellishes, despite an early alerting to its significance by
Halliwell who claimed that 'this passage . . . proves, beyond a doubt,
that Maundevile had a distinct notion of the New World'.[5] In 1953
Letts wondered whether the story was an echo of the voyage of the
Vivaldi brothers who set out to circumnavigate Africa in 1291.[6] In
1954 Mrs Bennett stated that it was a deliberatively persuasive
fiction.[7] And the most recent comment is frankly sceptical, describing
it as 'a circumstantial story of a man who unwillingly sailed right
round the world in both directions, ending up each time at an island
off the Norwegian coast.'[8]

The critical approach of the last two of these comments is untena-
ble. Apart from the personal fictions which give his book coherence
and verisimilitude, 'Mandeville' is a serious writer, taking his stories
and descriptions from sources which he believed (generally rightly)
to be accurate. As an illustration of this general truth one may cite
the recent archaeological discovery that *planus* 'flat-faced' was used
to describe noseless lepers, which makes the *gentz qi ont la face tote
plate* reported by 'Mandeville' a real and not a fabulous people.[9]
And there may well be, therefore, some factual substance in his tale
of valiant voyaging.

Some elements in the tale may be usefully disentangled. First, the
date. 'Mandeville' wrote *c*.1357 and his youth might perhaps have
been between *c*.1300 and *c*.1320. Unless the reference *quant ieo fuy
ieofnes* is feigned (as, indeed, most of such personal references in the
book are, although here the context scarcely justifies the need) the
voyage of this circumnavigator was completed before 1320.

Secondly, the absence of written testimony of the voyage or at
least 'Mandeville's' awareness of it. Apart from this brief mention,
the voyage has apparently passed from human record unless, of
course, the story rests ultimately on the report of one of the trans-

5. J. O. Halliwell, *The Voiage and Travaile of Sir John Maundevile* (London, 1833, reprinted 1866 and 1883), p. 318.
6. M. Letts, *Mandeville's Travels*, Hakluyt Society CI (London, 1953), I, 130.
7. J. W. Bennett, *The Rediscovery of Sir John Mandeville*, M.L.A. Monograph Series xix (New York, 1954), pp. 232-6.
8. A. C. Cawley, '*Mandeville's Travels:* A Possible New Source', *Notes and Queries* n.s. 19 (1972), p. 47, citing Macrobius, *Commentarii in Somnium Scipionis* 2.5, ed. J. Willis (Leipzig, 1963), p. 114.
9. Warner, p. 100.

atlantic voyages related in the Norse sagas or annals. This is a real possibility. Both the first and the last recorded Norse voyages to North America were tempest-tossed; in 986 Bjarni Herjofsson on passage to Greenland from Iceland was blown onto the North American coast, and in 1347 a ship on passage from Markland to Greenland was blown into Iceland.[10] However, the oral traditions which lie behind such reports and other histories, like Adam of Bremen's account of these northern lands c.1057,[11] were so well developed that 'Mandeville' could easily have heard such a tale, as he claims, *quant ieo fuy ieofnes.*

Thirdly, the language of the voyager. He was *de noz parties*, that is (if one may side-step the question of the author's nationality) a man of north-western Europe. The casual mention of *Norweye* as the starting-point of his second voyage is particularly interesting. All Norse-speakers, whether of East Norse or West Norse, were mutually intelligible to each other throughout the medieval period.

Fourthly, the circumstance of its context. The *tempeste en mer* was a natural hazard of these northern waters and, in addition to the two examples already noted, the Norse records are full of mariners' being blown off course by foul weather.

Now, against this background, if one asks oneself what elements in this tale (as 'Mandeville' tells it, confessedly by ear) could perhaps be factual, one is led inescapably to one conclusion. The only long sea-voyage possible to a man of north-western Europe before 1320 which could link lands peopled by Europeans of one language, and which would be least likely to be recorded in written form in the more developed European countries but would be most naturally available in oral tradition, would be from Norway and Iceland to Greenland and Norse America.[12]

Conversely, if one assumes that 'Mandeville' or the earlier narrator

10. *Gottskálksannáll s.a.* 1347, ed. G. Storm, *Islandske Annaler indtil 1578* (Christiania, 1888), p. 353, and *Skálholtsannáll hinn forni s.a.* 1347, ibid., p. 213.
11. Adam of Bremen, *Gesta Hammaburgensis ecclesiae pontificum* iv. 37, 39, ed. H. B. Schmeidler (Hanover-Leipzig, 1917), pp. 274–6.
12. Language and date militate against a non-Norse voyage. The evidence for Irish transatlantic voyages, as in the *Navigatio Sancti Brendani*, ed. C. Selmer (Notre Dame, 1959), and for the Venetian claim, made in 1558 on behalf of the Zeni who allegedly sailed c.1380, is too flimsy for consideration. The earliest Portuguese claim is based on the occurrence of Antilia on the Zuane Pizzigano marine chart of 1424.

50   MICHAEL C. SEYMOUR

of this tale of 'circumnavigation' invented the story, one must then
explain the remarkable fact that the fiction contains so distinctly
woven a pattern of reality. Given the essentially truthful nature of
Mandeville's Travels and the known distortions inherent in oral
tradition, it is surely much less incredible, even much more likely,
that 'Mandeville' is here relating a genuine experience of his youth
which ultimately depends on a report of a genuine voyage to Norse
Greenland or Norse America.

These distant lands are first recorded in written form by Adam of
Bremen, whose descriptions are known to be based on information
reported to Svein Ulfsson, king of the Danes (*d*.1076), perhaps by the
Icelander Auðun.[13] An account of North America was thus available
in Europe about sixty years after Thorfinn Karlsefni established the
first known European settlement in America.[14] Thereafter, however,
all other written reports of Greenland and Norse America until the
latter half of the fourteenth century (that is, after the date of composition of *Mandeville's Travels*) are confined to Norse sources, of
which Ari Thorgilsson's *Íslendingabók*, *c*.1127, is the earliest,[15] and
the *Grænlendinga Saga* and *Eiríks Saga Rauða* (which, in their extant
form, belong to the first part of the thirteenth century) the most widely known. However, it needs to be stressed in passing that the coming into existence of written records did not (as some have claimed
or implied) involve the extinction of the oral tradition; in all societies
both traditions have happily co-existed to their mutual advantage.

This restriction of written record of Greenland and Norse America
to Iceland is no doubt due to the failure of the more remote colonies
to develop into settlements important enough for sustained European
interest. After 1200 the southward advance of ice and Eskimo put
Vestribyggd increasingly at risk;[16] late in the thirteenth century the

13. *Auðunar Þáttr Vestfirzka* in *Flateyjarbók*.
14. As recorded in *Eiríks Saga Rauða*, ed. M. Thórdarson, *Íslenzk Fornrit* iv
    (Reykjavik, 1935).
15. See M. Magnusson and H. Pálsson, *The Vinland Sagas. The Norse Discovery
    of America* (London, 1965), and G. Jones, *The Norse Atlantic Saga* (London,
    1964).
16. On the deterioration of the climate see W. Dansgaard, in *Nature* 255 (1 May
    1975), 24. Contemporary comments are given by Konungs skuggsjá *c*.1260, ed.
    F. Jónsson (Copenhagen, 1920), and *c*.1341 by Ívar Bárdarson, *Det gamle
    Grønlands Beskrivelse*, ed. F. Jónsson (Copenhagen, 1930). On the Eskimo
    advance see G. Jones, op. cit., and (for a different point of view) T. J. Olsen,
    Early Voyages and Northern Approaches (Ottawa, 1964), pp. 70–86.

grant to the Bergen merchants of the monopoly of trade with Greenland by the king of Norway, who had gained control of the Icelandic trade in 1261, likewise threatened Eystribyggd; and voyages to
Norse America were impossible without a viable base in Greenland.
Moreover, it is clear that the standard of shipbuilding in these farther
regions had declined to a very low point; the ocean-going *knerrir*,
built in southern Norway of pine to withstand the pounding seas,
were no longer available, and without them Greenland was virtually
isolated.[17]
However, where the written records falter, archaeology provides
some evidence. The discovery of the settlement at L'Anse aux
Meadows in Newfoundland and of chests at Herjolfsnes made of
Labrador larch attests a continuing interest in Greenland for the
American lands.[18] And one intrepid friar, commonly identified as
Nicholaus of Lynn, is known to have visited Greenland and Norse
America before 1360 and to have written an account of those lands
for Edward III in Latin, the *Inventio Fortunata*. This account is now
lost apart from a fragment in Middle English translation,[19] but it
was incorporated into a geography of Jacobus Cnoyen of Hertogen-
bosch (also now lost) and thence into a summary made by Mercator
at the request of Dr John Dee.[20] Nicholaus' observations of the
lands and people of Norse America, made about the time when
Vestribyggd had finally succumbed and when Eystribyggd had less
than one hundred years left to it, were the last to be made for
European record. Coincidentally they were made about the time
Mandeville's Travels was completed.

17. A. W. Brögger and H. Shetelig, *The Viking Ships* (Oslo, 1953), and O. Crum-
lin-Pedersen, 'The Viking Ships of Roskilde', in B. Greenhill, *Aspects of the
History of Wooden Shipbuilding* (Greenwich, 1970). There is no record of a
ship from Norway to Greenland after 1367, and the last ship from Greenland may have sailed in 1410. On the navigational problems involved see
E. R. G. Taylor, *The Haven-finding Art* (London, 1956).

18. T. Vilmundarson in *Lesbók Morgunblaðsins* (30 September and 14 October
1962), and P. Nørlund, *Viking Settlers in Greenland and their Descendants
during Five Hundred Years* (Cambridge, 1936). See also T. J. Olsen, op. cit.

19. See M. C. Seymour, *The Metrical Version of Mandeville's Travels* (E.E.T.S.
269, 1973), p. 126, note to line 2598.

20. British Library MS. Vitellius C vii ff. 264ᵛ-9ᵛ (damaged by fire), printed by
E. R. G. Taylor, 'A Letter Dated 1577 from Mercator to John Dee', *Imago
Mundi* xiii (1956), 56–68. Cf. R. A. Skelton, 'Mercator and English Geogra-
phy in the Sixteenth Century', *Duisberger Forschungen* vi (1962), 161–2.

Nicholaus of Lynn[21] may have left Bergen in the *knörr* of Paul
Knutson in 1354 which sailed at the command of King Magnus. His
arrival in Greenland and Norse America in 1360 and his writing of
those northern lands were reported to Magnus in 1364 by a party of
eight travellers, the majority of whom were probably settlers from
America. Jacobus Cnoyen, described by Mercator in 1577 as one
who *orbem peragravit ut Mandevillanus sed meliore iudicio visa anno-
tavit*, may have been one of them. From Cnoyen's account, supplemented by two other sources,[22] it is clear that the friar visited
Eystribyggd and the deserted Vestribyggd, saw active volcanic
islands, reached Markland, and travelled widely in Norse America,
first north of latitude 54° N and later (according to the Middle English fragment) south to New England and beyond. His account of
those lands, fragmentary as it now is, is the most detailed description
of Norse America now extant, including a report of a native village
where the menfolk were away hunting or fishing:

> Ende dit gheberchte duert in de breede 8 mijles. Ende in al dien
> circkel seide de minnebroer en was gheen habitatie den aen die
> oost [*lacuna*] daer dat smalle landt voic ereben aen quamen

21. A note added to MS. Vitellius C vii, f.267ᵛ, quotes Bale's reference to the
otherwise unknown Hugh of Ireland O.F.M. Nicholaus of Lynn was a
Carmelite and so describes himself in the *kalendarium* for the years 1387–1462
(now being edited by S. Eisner at the University of Arizona; see his
'Chaucer's Use of Nicholas of Lynn's Calendar', *Essays & Studies* 29 (1976),
1–22); cf. Mercator's *minnebroer*. But unlike the Carmelites, the Minorites
were renowned for their world-wide missions, and it would be natural for
anyone in the late middle ages and after to style an unnamed travelling friar
a *minnebroer*.

22. L. A. Vigneras, 'A Letter of John Day, 1497', *Hispanic American Historical
Review* 36 (1956), 503–9. Johann Ruysch, *Nova et universalior Orbis cogniti
tabula* (Romae, 1507 and 1508), a world map based on the Contarini map
which contains legends from the *Inventio Fortunata*. D. B. Quinn, *England and
the Discovery of America, 1481–1620* (London, 1974), pp. 107–9: the claim
there that the reference to *el libro llamado Inventio fortunata* by *Bartholome
de Las Casas, Historia de las Indias* in 1570, ed. J. Perez de Tudela, *Obras
Escogidas* (Madrid, 1957), I, 48, is not to the work ascribed to Nicholaus
of Lynn, depends on the fragmentary nature of Mercator's summary without reference to the Middle English translation.
    On the continuity of English interest in the North Atlantic routes be-
tween 1360 and the precursors of Cabot at Bristol, see B. Thorsteinsson,
Enska Öldin í Sögu Íslendinge (Reykjavik, 1970).

waren 23 Leiden, bouen vier voeten niet [*lacuna*] waer of de 16
vrouen waren.

Its air of compelling authenticity reminds one always of Óttarr and
Wulfstan who described northern Norway to King Alfred five centuries before.[23]

Since the friar clearly sailed over established trade routes before
beginning his exploration of Norse America, his voyage alone provides confirmation that these northern lands were known by repute
to Europe during the lifetime of 'Mandeville'. No doubt, if the
Inventio Fortunata had been available at the time of writing, 'Mandeville' would have journeyed to the New World himself. As it was
not, he had to rely on vague oral reports. And since in the late middle
ages the world was thought to contain only three continents, and
therefore the American littoral could only be (in that geography)
the farther shore of Asia, he very plausibly incorporated those reports into his statement of the rotundity of the world.[24]

---

23. T. J. Olsen, 'Inventio Fortunata', *Timarit Thjodræknisfelags Islendinga* xliv
(1963), and *Early Voyages* . . . , pp. 106–8, claims that the *Inventio Fortunata*
derives from Ivar Bardarson's account of Greenland *c.* 1341.

24 C. K. Zacher, *Curiosity and Pilgrimage. The Literature of Discovery in
Fourteenth-century England* (Baltimore and London, 1976), pp. 149-50,
187-8, believes that this statement has a moral purpose and was probably
influenced by the *Imago du Monde* of Gautier de Metz.

IN SUPPORT OF THE USE OF PLACE-NAMES AS AN AID TO THE STUDY OF MIDDLE ENGLISH DIALECTS

Dorothy L. Cavers

I Introduction

Though an advance has certainly been made since the days when the value of Pl-Ns as an aid to the study of ME dialects formed the subject of hot controversy,[1] even now not enough use is made of them, particularly in attempting to ascertain fairly exactly the provenance of an ME text. In default of adequate material such as literary works of known provenance and local documents written in English, Pl-N material from reliable sources may safely be used for this purpose as well as for general dialect study.

An advantage of the use of these forms in general dialect study is that they cover the whole period being investigated, and thus provide evidence of developments not adequately shown in texts.

It must be conceded that their evidence is limited almost entirely to the field of phonology, and that even there the record is not as complete as could be desired: some OE sounds whose various developments are crucial tests of dialect character occur only rarely in Pl-N elements, and such elements as do contain them may be altogether lacking in the names of a particular area. The information that they do provide, however, fully compensates for these lacunae.

The publications of the English Place-Name Society can assist the investigator, especially in identifying localities,[2] but since his aims are different, material for his dialect-study must be obtained from primary souces. Such materials falls into two groups. The first contains local records such as land charters, custumals, monastic registers and, in the later period, wills; among the more general docu-

---

1. The writer remembers well a clash between Professor H. G. Wyld and Dr C. T. Onions. The display of erudition was impressive, as was the ability on both sides to frame 'the retort courteous' to imply: 'You're talking nonsense'.

2. In this study much use has been made of J. E. B. Gover *et al., The Place-Names of Surrey*, E.P.N.S. 11 (Cambridge, 1934), which has considerably lightened the task of locating places named.

ments that comprise the second group are collections such as Inquisitions Post Mortem, Forest Pleas, Pipe Rolls. Local Place-Name sources should be used as the basis of an investigation. No conclusions can safely be drawn from types found in public collections only, as these are obviously less reliable, being apt to show at least occasional influence of the London dialect.[3]

Every effort should be made to locate all places whose names are used as evidence. The identification becomes doubly necessary in dealing with sounds whose developments vary in different parts of the area concerned.

II The Development of OE[y̆] in the Dialect of Surrey in Middle English

The results of investigations into the ME dialect of Surrey support the view that it was a border dialect.[4] As such it provides an excellent field for a study such as this. Judging by the testimony of the early forms of Pl-Ns and the linguistic character of available documents in English, there appear to have been four fairly clearly defined dialect areas within the county. In these, as will be shown below, South-Western and South-Eastern features occur in varying proportions, these dependent upon the dialect characters of adjacent counties.

a. Western Area: In the West of the county is the large area that extends from just E of Chertsey to about Chiddingfold in the S; it is characterized by several S-W features found also in the neighbouring counties of Berks and Hants.

b. North-Eastern Area: This extends from Kingston to Croydon and includes Southwark, Wandsworth, Lambeth, etc. The influence at work here is that of London (City).

3. Percy H. Reaney, 'On Certain Phonological Features of the Dialect of London in the Twelfth Century', *Englische Studien* 59 (1925), 321–45, has shown that the forms of Pl-Ns in the Pipe Rolls, for example, reflect the type of London City, with only slight local influence.

4. See e.g. H. C. Wyld, 'The Surrey Dialect in the Thirteenth Century', *English Studies* 3 (1921), 42–5; Mary S. Serjeantson, 'Distribution of Dialect Characters in Middle English', *English Studies* 4 (1922), 93ff., 191ff., 223ff.; and P. H. Reaney, 'The Dialect of London in the Thirteenth Century', *Englische Studien* 61 (1926–7), 9–23. The writer's own investigations confirm this view.

c. South- and Central-Eastern Area: Flanked to the E by Kent, the area extends from Croydon to the N border of Sussex.

d. Central Area: This large tract stretches from the extreme N, where it abuts on Middlesex, to the N border of Sussex. It is bounded on the E by Areas *b* and *c* and on the W by Area *a*.

It is generally accepted that the development of OE $\breve{y}$ in Surrey follows both the usual South-Western and South-Eastern patterns. The aim of this study is to investigate the development more closely (in the various areas) and while so doing to demonstrate the reliability of carefully chosen Pl-N material. The sources consulted are documents containing Pl-Ns (see Appendix A), local documents written in English, and literary texts (see Appendix B). Material from Pl-N sources of the second type has been used only when the overall evidence of the documents concerned tallies with that provided by sources of the first type.

The literary texts examined require further comment.

In his brief discussion of the provenance of *The Owl and the Nightingale*, E. G. Stanley states that 'there is nothing known to make it impossible that the original dialect was that of Guildford'.[5] Very few useful rhymes with OE $\breve{y}$ occur in the poem; thus for the study of this sound practically the only evidence available is spelling.[6]

The original version of *King Horn*, the dialect features of which are adduced from the rhymes occurring in the three extant MSS, appears to the writer to have been composed in N-E Surrey.[7] The line numbers are quoted from C. C+ indicates that the forms referred to are found in all three MSS.

All the usual ME spellings of OE $\breve{y}$ (*u* = [y], *e* and *i*[8]) are found

5. *The Owl and the Nightingale*, ed. E. G. Stanley (1960; Manchester, 1972), p. 18. This opinion, as he points out, is that of most recent commentators. My own investigations into the ME dialect of Surrey, which have given rise to this study, point clearly to Western Surrey for O & N and – rather more tentatively, owing to complete dependence upon rhymes for evidence – to North-Eastern Surrey for the original version of KH.
6. The spelling of OE $\breve{y}$ is generally identical in C and J.
7. The extant texts do not belong to this area. Most investigators believe that the original version was written in the South-East. Wissmann, with whom McKnight agrees, postulates Essex. See, however, Note 5 above. Wissmann's suggested reconstruction of the original (*Das Lied von King Horn:* see List of Sources) is a valuable aid to the study of the poem.
8. Since *i* and *y* are interchangeable spellings in ME, *i* is used to refer to both.

in ME Surrey documents and in Pl-N forms belonging to the period, but in proportions that differ widely according to area and date, as will be demonstrated below. For the sake of brevity, except where the numbers are small the lists of significant forms are not complete; the total number found is stated in brackets at the end of each list. Pl-N forms are grouped according to centuries.

The Western Area
As might be expected, the documents relating to this area have an overwhelming majority of *u*-spellings in Pl-N forms. In the 15th c, however, the proportion drops sharply as *i*-spellings increase in number (see below):

Cateshull, Chatishull (Godalming), 12th c VCHS iii/32(2); *Cuserugia* (Farnham), 12th c Dugd v/237; *Guldeford*, 1181–1204 MPR 46; 1186–96 ib. 39; *Riehullam, Riehulle* (Peper Harow), 12th c Dugd v/242; 1147 BMCR i/584; *Richardishulle* (Farnham), 12th c Dugd v/237   (8).

Ayshurst (Chiddingfold), 13th c VCHS iii/11; *Busheley* (Bisley), 1284 ib. iii/398; *Catteshull*, 1241 BkF ii/1377; 1212 ib. i/67(2); *Guldeford, Gudeford(e)* 1250 BSC 48; 1266 SDMC 646, fol. 96; 1228 FFS 16; 1277 ib. 51(2); 1256 CAD v/149; *Horishull*, 13th c VCHS iii/427; *la Hulle* (Artington), 1218–9 VCHS iii/6; *Putfold* (Frensham), 1285 BMCR i/590; *Sorbeshull* (Godley H.), 1225 HAS i/6(2) . . .   (60).

As(she)hurst, 1310 VCHS iii/65(2); *Busseleye*, 1317 FFS 87; *Catteshull(e)*, 1332 STR 19; 1324 FFS 94; *Clayputte*, 1327–47 MSL 434, fol. 69b; *Cuserugge*, 1310 Dugd v/238; *Denebrugge* (Chiddingfold), 1357 VCHS iii/10; *Guldeford(e)*, 1301 CAD i/325; 1303 BSC 46; 1350 ib. 29; 1332 STR 1; 1311 MPR 205, 206; *Guldenelond* (Chertsey), 14th c MSL 435, fol. 124b; *Horisull*, 1370 FFS 140; *la Hurst*, 14th c MSL 435, fol. 179; *Langgehurst* (Chertsey), ib. 434, fol. 77b; *M(o)us(h)ulle* (Witley), 1332 STR 18, 45; *Putfold(e)*, 1317 CAD iii/159; *Sittinghurst* (Haslemere), 14th c VCHS iii/10; *Southbrugge* (Chiddingfold), 1357 ib. iii/10; *Stonhulle* (Chertsey), 14th c MSL 434, fol. 77; *Stonhurst* (Chertsey), 14th c ib., fol. 240b; 1342 FFS 221; *Wyndmullehulle* (Chertsey), 14th c MSL 434, fol. 7 . . .   (90).

Cucmulle (Chertsey), 15th c CLB ii/242; *Guld(e)ford(e)*, 1402 FFS 165(2); 1484 SrW 2; 15th c CLB ii/169; *Horshull*, 1485

SrW 18(3); *la Huthe* (Egham), 1435 CAD iii/475; *Mowshull,*
1488 BMCR ii/814; *Praushull* (Frimley), 15th c CLB i/26;
Rammeshurst (Godley H.), 1446 CLB i/28; *Thorphull* (Egham),
15th c ib. i/55; *Thornehulle* (Frimley), 15th c ib. i/28; *Wyneshurst*
(Chertsey), 15th c ib. ii/187 . . .   (45).

Spellings with *i* become frequent in the thirteenth and fourteenth
centuries. By the fifteenth century the number has increased considerably:

>   *Chatishille*, 1131 BMCR i/151; *Riehell, Riehullam, Riehulle*
>   (OE *ryge*) (Peper Harow), 1189 Dugd v/237; 12th c ib. v/242;
>   1147 BMCR i/584   (4).
>   *Catteshill*, 1225 BkF ii/1363; *Gildeford, Gyld(e)ford(e)*, 1258
>   FFS 39(3); 1267 ib. 44; 13th c Dugd vi/1493(2); 1250 BSC 48;
>   *Horishill, Horyshill*, 1278–9 VCHS iii/428; 1238 FFS 22; 1260
>   ib. 40 . . .   (20).
>   *Bothedenesbrigge* (Chiddingfold), 1357 VCHS iii/10; *Gild(e)-*
>   *ford, Gyldeford*, 1320 FFS 90(4); 1370 ib. 140(3); *Hazelbridge*
>   (Chiddingfold), 1357 VCHS iii/10; *Litelcroft* (Egham), 1319
>   VCHS iii/422; *Patteshill* (Egham), 14th c VCHS iii/422; *Synder-*
>   *hill* (Chertsey), 1335 CAD i/300 . . .   (21).
>   *Bysley*, 1484 SrW 8; *Cat(te)shill*, 1428 FA v/127; *Cokhill*
>   (Godley H.), 1446 CLB i/128; *Crocfordbrigge* (Godley H.), 1446
>   ib. i/127; *Gildeford, Gyl(de)ford*, 1414 BMCR ii/542; 1402 FFS
>   165; *Gyldeshamele* (Egham), 1432 CLB i/55; *Horsill*, 1487 SrW
>   iv/63(2); *litilmede* (Frimley), 1432 CLB i/27; *millewhele* (God-
>   ley H.), 1446 ib. i/128(2); *Mymbrig(ge)* (Godley H.), 1446 ib.
>   i/127(2); *Southmill* (Godalming), 1409 VCHS iii/24; *Synderhill*,
>   1469 CAD i/298 . . .   (42).

A small number of *e*-spellings occur in the names of places in the
eastern part of this area, mainly 'Guildford' and places near Guildford and Godalming:

>   *Cateshella*, 1141 BMCR i/154; *Geldeford*, 1186–98 MPR 40;
>   *Geldesdone* (nr Guildford), 12th c VCHS iii/547; *Riehell*, 1189
>   Dugd v/237   (4).
>   *Cateshell*, 1219 BkF i/273; *Est Caterselle*, 1272–1307 BMCR
>   i/154; *Gelderford(e), Geudeford*, 1208 FFS 9; 1201 ib. 5(2); 1255
>   ib. 36(2); 1259 ib. 39; 1200–16 MPR xxxiii; 1221 ib. 79; 1212
>   BkF i/66; *Saresberi* (nr Hambledon), 1242–3 ib. ii/687   (12).

Cathell, 1350 MPR 250   (1).
Assherst, 1428 FA v/111; *Geldeford,* 1423 SDMC 3013, fol.
190; *Mechelshete* (Godley H.), 15th c CLB i/28   (3).

The thirteenth-century Chertsey Chartulary generally writes *u* for
OE $\breve{y}$:

buri, ii/363; *brugge,* v/987(2); *cuðe,* iv/844, 849; *gridbruche, grit-
bruche, griðbruche, grythbruche,* iv/848, 849, 850; Dugd i/431(3);
hulle, v/987; *huðe,* v/987(2); *kuðe,* iv/848, 856; *muchele(re),*
iv/844, 848; *mulle,* v/987(2); *munstre,* iv/844, 856 . . .   (37).

There are also a few *i*-spellings:

gelitlað, iv/844; *ilitlade,* iv/844; *kiðe,* iv/850; *micelre,* iv/850   (4).

Spellings with *e* are even fewer:

menechene, v/987; *wertuualen,* v/987   (2).

The proportions of *u*-, *i*-, *e*- spellings in ChCh agree quite well with
the proportions in the 13th c Pl-Ns near Chertsey found in local
documents:

	u	*i*	*e*
13th c Pl-Ns:	10	2	0
Ch Ch:	37	4	2

The Owl and the Nightingale agrees with the 13th c Pl-Ns of the
Western area of the county in having a very high proportion of *u*-
spellings for OE $\breve{y}$. The forms quoted occur in both MSS:

bugge(n), 1368; *cunde,* 87, 251, 276; *custe,* 9, 1398; *dude,* 1016,
1089; *duntes,* 1227; *dusi, dusy,* 1466; *fulste,* 889; *gult(e),* 874,
1410, 1523; *hud(e),* 164, 265, 1113; *hurne,* 14; *ifurn,* 1306;
lust(e), 213, 287, 1193; *lutle,* 631, 802, 1404 . . . ; *muchel(e),* 847,
1207, 1217 . . . ; *mulne,* 778; *murie,* 345; *mus,* 87; *pulte,* 1524;
rugge, 775; *sunne(n),* 858, 974, 1395; *sunfulle,* 891; *spus-bruche,*
1368; *s(w)uch,* 1415, 1433; *uuel(e), vuel(e),* 63, 247, 1051 . . . ;
wuste, 10 . . .   (118).

The rhyme *i-munde: funde,* 1515f appears to indicate a retracted
vowel arising from [$\ddot{y}$].[9]

---

9. There are a few rhymes with forms descended from OE $\breve{e}o$, but in a dialect
   area such as Surrey these cannot be relied upon as evidence of the quality
   of either vowel.

A few *i*-spellings are found, mainly before front consonants, including *n*:

> *litle*, C only, 1776;
> *þincþ*, 1787; *þinchest*, 578; *þinche(þ)*, 225; *þincþe*, *þynk*, 46;
> *triste*, J only, 1273; *wirche*, C only, 722.
> There is one rhyme of OE *ẏ* with OE *ï* in *ofligge: bugge*, 1505f
> (7 + 1).

O & N contains practically no *e*-forms. The word *herst*, 970, occurs in C only, and *sweche*, 1711, in J only. There is, however, one rhyme with OE *e: cunde: s(ch)ende*, 273f. (?2 + 1).

In the following comparative table the Pl-N forms totalled are those found in local documents relating to the area near to and west of Guildford:

	u	*i*	*e*
13th c Pl-Ns:	52	15	6
O & N:	118	7 + 1	?2 + 1

The proportion of *u*-forms is higher in O & N and may indicate that the poem was written some distance west of Guildford. The later documents belonging to the Western area often have *i* or *y* for OE *ẏ*. On the whole *u*-spellings are still rather more frequent. Only one *e*-spelling has been noted:

> Godalming Custumal (early 15th c): *myche*, 134; *mylle*, 130, *dydde*, 131; but also: *hulle*, 130; *muche*, 133(2), 134.
>
> Godley Metes and Bounds (1466): *brigge*, 127(2); *first*, 127; but also: *bussh'*, 128; *put(te)*, 127(2).
>
> Surrey Wills (late 15th c): *buried*, *buryed* (Worplesdon, Peper Harow, Guildford, Pirbright, Farnham), 4, 12, 31, 78, 94; *buryeng* (Chobham), 52; *ffurst* (Worplesdon), 4; but also *(f)first* (Peper Harow, Pirbright), 12, 78; and *beried* (Guildford), 61.

Summary

The evidence of both Pl-Ns and other material shows that in the Western area of Surrey, as in Berkshire and Hampshire, *u* is usual for OE *ẏ*. Spellings with *i* occur, increasing considerably in number in the 15th c. Much less frequent are *e*-spellings, which are found mainly in Pl-Ns belonging to the neighbourhood of Guildford and Godalming.

The North-Eastern Area
In the earlier centuries of the period the Pl-Ns of this part of the country have more *e*-spellings than *u*- and *i*-spellings taken together. In the later centuries the proportion of *e*-spellings drops:

Lamheda (Lambeth), 1190 FFS 5; *Mecham*, 1199 ib. 4(2); *Melneham* (Bermondsey), 1152 Dugd v/97; *Rederhitha, Retherhithe*, 12th c ib. v/87, 100, (6).
Beleannesbregge (Bermondsey), 1295 CAD v/172; *Lambeth(e), Lam(ih)eth*, 1261 MSAsh 1146, fol. 59; 1279 CAD iii/410; 1202 FFS 5; 1248 ib. 32; 1272 ib. 49; *Mech(eh)am*, 1201 ib. 5(2); 1218 ib. 9; 1232 ib. 18; *Retherheth(e), Retherhithe*, 1243 ib. 27; 1267 CAD iii/142; 1230 Dugd v/98; *Stodmerbreg* (nr Southwark), 13th c BMCR i/679; *Velepetten* (Cuddington), c1280 SDMC 1105, fol. 129 ... (48).
Bregge (Lambeth), 1330 FFS 99; *Lambeth, Lameht*, 1316 FA v/107; 1317 MPR 218; *Meleward* (Malden), 1325 SDMC 1057, fol. 157; *Northbery* (Croydon), 1385 BMCR i/545; *Potenhethe, Puttenheth(e)* (Putney), 1386 FFS 153; 1387 ib. 154; 1332 STR Appendix 1; *Retherheth(e)*, 1313 CAD v/175; 1315 ib. iv/231; 1340 ib. iii/256; 1315 FFS 82, 83 ... (37).
Hakebregge (nr Mitcham), 1429 CCR 46, 48; *Lamb(e)heth*, 1428 FA v/113; 1432 Dugd v/100; *Melneham*, 15th c BAnn 439, *Meytchame*, 1485 SrW 33; *Northlambheth*, 1404 CAD i/433(2), *Retherhithe*, 15th c BAnn 434; 1446 FFS 188 ... (19).

A fair number of *u*-spellings occur in this area, the proportion dropping considerably in the 15th c:

Claiputte (Wandsworth), 1180 BMCR ii/523; *Duneshull* (nr Merton), 1185 MPR 38(2) (3).
Bredinghurst (Camberwell), 1218–19 VCHS iv/31; *Bromhulle* (Cuddington), 13th c CAD i/316; *Lamehuth*, 1266 FFS 43; *Mulewardestrete* (Bermondsey), 13th c CAD v/173; *Mucham*, 13th c BMCR i/520; *Rutherheth, Rethurhuth*, 1268 ib. i/626; 1293 CAD iv/249; *Suwerk Brugge* (Southwark), 1266 FFS 21 ... (15).
Goodrichesbury (Wandsworth), 14th c VCHS iv/109; *Lamchuth(e)*, 1307 MSLaud 723; 1315 FFS 81; *Leuehurst* (Camberwell), 1353 ib. 124; *ate Mulle* (Merton), 1315 SDMC 1056, fol. 152; *Muleward* (Merton), 1345 ib. 1058, fol. 161; *Northlam(be)*-

huth, 1317 FFS 86; 1360 ib. 130(2); *Retherhuth(e)*, *Rutherhuth(e)*, 1313 CAD v/181; 1359 ib. ii/369(2); 14th c ib. iv/230(2) . . . (27).

Blachemeldesbusch (OE*bysc) (Cuddington), 1406 CAD i/326; *Bramblehulle*, *Bromhulle*, *Underbramblehulle* (Cuddington), 1406 ib. i/326; 1441 ib. i/325(2); *Diversbussh* (Richmond), 1401 Dugd vi/31(2); *Levehurst*, 1449 VCHS iv/33; *Sulstrete* (OE *syle*) (Peckham), 1472 CAD i/401; *Suzfarnhulle* (Cuddington), 15th c ib. i/316   (9).

Spellings with *i* become much more frequent in the fourteenth and fifteenth centuries:

Micheham, *Michelam*, 12th c Dugd vi/169; 12th c CAD iii/16 (2).

Hackbrigge, 1230–40 BMCR ii/698; *Lamhithe*, 1229 Dugd v/90; *Mich(eh)am*, 1201 FFS 5; 1242–3 BkF ii/687; *Retherhith*, *Retherhythe*, 1230 Dugd v/98; 1298 ib. v/98; 1284 FFS 57; *Seynt Johnesmylles* (Southwark), 1277 CAD vi/72 . . .   (17).

Lam(b)ehith, 1331 FFS 102; 1396 ib. 161; *le handbrigge* (Rotherhithe), 14th c CAD iv/244; *Littleworthe* (Surbiton), 1356 ib. i/373; *Micham*, 1382 ib. ii/318; 1308 BMCR i/514; 1332 STR 61; *Northlambhith*, 1361 FFS 131; *Retherhythe*, *Ritherhethe*, *Rutherhithe*, 1358 FFS 128; 14th c CAD iv/244; ib. iv/230 . . .   (25).

Briggefeld (nr Wandsworth), 1440 CAD vi/352; *Howelle Pytte* (Cuddington), 1451 ib. i/325; *Lam(b)(e)hith(e)*, 15th c BAnn 457; 1454 FFS 191; 1486 SrW 144; *Lambehythemershe*, 1427 FFS 178; *Mi(c)cham*, 1402 FA vi/389(2); *Pistilhill* (Malden), 1428 SDMC 4791; *Potenhith*, 1473 FFS 195; *Retherhith(e)*, 1416 Dugd v/100; 15th c BAnn 434, 467; *Stonhyll* (Richmond), 15th c SCMS fol. 286 . . .   (32).

In the forms developed from OE y̆ *King Horn* appears to agree quite well with the Pl-Ns of this area of Surrey.

There are several rhymes of OE y̆ with OE ĕ:
ferste, firste, furste: berste, 703f, 1297f; *fulle, felle: telle*, 1237f; *hudde: bedde*, 1281f C only; *hurede, herde: ferde*, 805f; *kesse, cusse: (W)est(er)nesse*, 1295f; *keste, kuste, custe: reste*, 1275f; *leste, luste: beste*, 505f; *leste, liste, luste: reste*, 917f, 431 L, H only; *merie: werie, serie*, 1489f; *rigge, rugge: legge*, 1136f;

s(c)hredde: bedde, 895f; *þenche, þinche: adrenche*, 111f C, H only.
Rhymes with *ĕ* of OE *ăn – i* are:
dunte: wente, 647f C, L only; *ken(ne), kyn: men(ne)*, 671f; *kenne, kinne, kunne: Sud(d)enne, sodenne*, 156f, 189f, 923f, 1061f C, H only.

A rhyme of OE *y̆* (lengthened before – *nd*) with OE *ēo* occurs only in L, but these lines are obviously original: *kende:fende*, 1479f.

Rhymes with OE *i* exist; but see Morsbach on the question of *ĕ: i* rhymes in ME:[10]

kesse, cusse: (y)wisse, 461f C, H only; *pelte, pulte, pylte: hilte, hylte*, 1529f; *swymme: brymme*, 203f C only; *þinke: drinke, drynke*, 1233f.

The occurrence of [y̆] in an ME text is generally impossible to establish from rhymes. What may be rhymes with OE *ŭ*, indicating retracted forms arising from [y̆], and therefore significant, are: *turne: murne, morne*, 1037f; *turne: (un)spurne*, 1153f C, L only; *cunde: bunde*, 451f C only, but these are not satisfactory evidence, since an unmutated form *turnian* also existed in OE, and Wissmann does not regard the *cunde: bunde* rhyme as original. The rhymes with *i* listed above, if reliable, point to earlier rounded forms.

Comparison of the proportions of forms in KH and in 13th c Pl-Ns in the extreme N-E:

	e	*u*	*i*
13th c Pl-Ns	10	5	3
KH	21	?	4

Fifteenth-century documents written in this area usually have *i* or *y*, but *e*- and *u*-forms also occur in SrW:

Surrey Wills (late 15th c): *bye* (Richmond), 82; *(f)first, ffyrst* (Malden, Southwark, Wandsworth, Kingston, Richmond), 25, 34, 40, 67, 74, 82; *fulfyllyde* (Richmond), 82; *kynn* (Southwark), 40; *kyrtell, lytel* (Richmond), 82;
but also: *berede, beret, beried, beryd, berynge* (Wandsworth, Southwark, Richmond), 34, Furnivall 29(3), 40, 82;
and: *buried, buryed* (Kingston, Malden, Southwark), 93, 26, 41; *churche(werk)* (Southwark), Furnivall 29(2); *ffurst* (Kingston), 93.

10. L. Morsbach, *Mittelenglische Grammatik* (Halle, 1896), §132, Anm. 1.

Sheen Documents have only *i*- and *y*-spellings:

SCMS: *lytle* (3), *myll*, *pytle*, fol. 286;
SLMS: *firste* (2), fol. 60, 60b.

Summary

The North-Eastern area, which abuts upon London, agrees with the City in having a clear majority of *e*-forms in the earlier centuries.[11] Spellings with *u* and *i* are also found, the latter increasing considerably in number in the later centuries. By the fifteenth century *i*-spellings are the most frequent in both Pl-Ns and documents written in English.

The South- and Central-Eastern Area

Except in the fifteenth century the evidence here depends on Pl-N material only.

The area borders on Kent along its whole length. It is thus not surprising that *e*-spellings are in the majority in all centuries under consideration:

> *Billesersse* (OE *hyrst*) (Lingfield), 1197 FFS 2; 1198 VCHS iv/307; *Cherchefelle* (E of Reigate), 12th c ib. iii/229; *Crechesfeld* (Tandridge), 1154–89 BMCR ii/622; *Sideluue melne* (E of Horley), 12th c ib. i/380; *Tanregge*, 12th c Dugd vi/604(2)   (7).

> *Casherste* (Caterham), 13th c BMCR i/153; *Croherst*, 1220 FFS 12; 1228 ib. 14, 16; 1278–9 VCHS iv/275; *atte Melne* (E of Caterham), 1278 FFS 52; *Pereslond* (OE *pyrige*) (nr Farley), *c*1250 SDMC 583, fol. 42; *Tanregg(e)*, 1262 FFS 41; 13th c SAC ix/120; 1242-3 BkF ii/684 . . .   (18).

> *Crauherst, Crouherst, Croweherst*, 1311 L & B 161 (2); 1386 FFS 153; 1394 ib. 159; *La feldbregg* (nr Tandridge), 1355 BSC 25; *Geldenewode* (nr Tandridge), 1311 L & B 138; *melle, mellefeld* (nr Limpsfield), 1311 ib. 159, 160(2), 161; *Musherst*, 1311 ib. 145, 146; *Reyecroft* (Limpsfield), 1311 ib. 157; *Tanregg(e)*, 1311 ib. 162; 1321 FFS 217; 1355 BSC 25 . . .   (37).

> *Crouherst*, 1435 FFS 182; *Crowherstmelle*, 1406 VCHS iv/278; *atte Melle* (Lingfield), 1400 FFS 163; *melstrete* (Oxted), 1421 SAC vi/146; *Pendell* (OE *hyll*) (Bletchingley), 15th c BMCR i/582; *Tanregge*, 1458 FFS 192 . . .   (14).

---

11. See Barbara A. Mackenzie, *Early London Dialect* (Oxford, 1928), §156.

The following are representative of *u*-spellings that have been noted:

Tenruge, 12th c CAD iii/16   (1).

Crauhurste, *Cro(we)hurst*, 1228 FFS 16; 1271 ib. 46; 1270
MPR 151; *Hursta* (Horne), 13th c BMCR i/381; *atte Muln*
(Walkingstead), 1271 FFS 47; *Tan(e)rugg(e)*, *Tenrugg(e)*,
Turugge, 1297 MPR 181; 1225 FFS 13; 1271 ib. 46; 1225 CAD
iii/27 . . .   (16).

Crowehurst, *Crouhurst*, *Crow(e)hurst*, 1301 SAC ix/123; 1303
BSC 46; 1317 FFS 86; 1371 ib. 141(2); *Giffreyshull'* (nr Limpsfield), 1311 L & B 157; *Halemulle* (Nutfield), 1359 BMCR i/560;
la Hulle (nr Limpsfield), 1311 L & B 138; *mellehull*, 1311 ib.
159; *Tanrug(g)e*, *Tenrugge*, 1303 BSC 46; 1324 CAD iv/49(2);
1316 FA v/107(2) . . .   (29).

Billeshurst (Lingfield), 1403 VCHS iv/307; *Crauhurst*, *Crou-
hurste*, 1428 FA v/114, 120; *Rugge* (Crowhurst), 1431 VCHS
iv/278; *Tanrugge*, 1404 FFS 167; 1437 ib. 183; 1407-8 SAC
ix/55; 1428 FA v/115, 120   (9).

Spellings with *i* are not frequent. The only twelfth-century one noted
occurs in the 1190 Pipe Roll, p. 154 – *Tenriggehundredo* – of doubtful
validity for this study.[12] The proportion of these spellings increases
considerably in the fifteenth century:

Tanrich, *Tenrig(g)e*, 1234 FFS 19; 1247 ib. 31; 1267 ib. 44;
1235 BkF ii/1362; 1271 MPR 151   (5).

la Bysshe (OE*bysc) (Horne), 1355 VCHS iv/293; *Tan(e)-
rigg(e)*, 1301 SAC ix/123; 1324 ib. ix/133, 134; 1327 FFS 97;
1361 ib. 131 . . .   (11).

Bysse, *la Bysshe*, 1407-8 BSC 53(3); *Frith* (Farley), 1458
SDMC 687, fol. 210; *Gyldenhyll* (Chelsham), 1499 VCHS iv/271;
Tanrig(g)(e), 1421 FFS 224; 1487 SrW iv/68; 1488-9 ib. iv/84 . . .
                                                                  (10).

In the late fifteenth-century Surrey Wills belonging to this area
seven *i*-forms, four *e*-forms and two *u*-forms have been noted:

byried (Limpsfield), 94; (*f*)*first* (Sanderstead and Warlingham),
18, 20, (Farley), 47; *fulfilled* (Warlingham), 18; *hirith*, *mychel-
nesse* (Farley), 47, 48;

12. As pointed out in Note 3. See *Pipe Rolls*, Record Commission (London.
1884 –).

beried, beryd, beryed (Farley, Limpsfield, Warlingham), 47, 82, 17, 18;

buryed, furste (Sanderstead), 20.

Summary

The evidence indicates that in this area, as in Kent, *e* is usual for OE *ȳ*.[13] The *u*-type is, however, quite well represented, and *i*-spellings also occur, increasing in proportion in the later centuries.

The Central Area

The Pl-Ns of this large area, which extends from Middlesex to Sussex, have, over the centuries, *u*-spellings in the main, a fair proportion of *e*-spellings (occurring in Pl-Ns from all parts of the area) and a good few *i*-spellings, which increase in proportion in the 15th c. Here, too, conclusions must be drawn almost entirely from Pl-N evidence.

The following are representative of *u*-spellings:

Aldebury, 1235 BMCR i/7; *Danhurst* (Bramley), 1234 FFS 20; *Emelebrugg'* (Elmbridge H.), 1241 BkF ii/1377; *Gom(m)eshulne* (OE *scylf*), 1291 FFS 61; 1298 BMCR i/305; *la hurst* (Epsom), 13th c MSLaud fol. 9b; *Knavenhurst* (nr Cranleigh), 13th c Dugd vi/833; *Minthurst* (Reigate), 1231–8 MPR 95; *Uhurst, Ywhurst*, 1297 FFS 67; 1291 MPR 75; 1295 BMCR i/268; *Wintereshull, Wyntereshull* (Bramley), 1250 FFS 33; 1257 ib. 37(2) . . .   (31).

Ald(e)bury, 1332 STR 28, 29; 1335 FFS 105; *bielesmulle* (Banstead), 1325 BH 322; *Coppedehulle* (Banstead), 1378 ib. 359; *Furshull(e)* (Cranleigh), 1304 BMCR i/295; 1338 BSC 28; *Gomeshulne*, 1363 CAD iii/16(3); 1396 FFS 160; *Holehurst* (Blackheath H.), 14th c VCHS iii/87; *Horshulle* (Banstead), 1325 BH 318, 319; *Knavenhurst*, 1304 BSC 40(2); *Newhurst, Uhurst*, 1321 BMCR i/268; 1333 FFS 104; *Pynehurst* (Leatherhead), 1315 CAD ii/243; *Shulf* (Banstead), 1368–9 BH 120; *Waybrugge*, 1398 FFS 162; 1372 CAD vi/178(2); *Wyldebrugge* (Walton-on-Thames), 1377 VCHS iii/472 . . .   (80).

13. It is worthy of mention that the 9th c Surrey Charter, which was probably written in this area, still has *y* for OE[*ȳ*]. However, it seems very likely that the change had already taken place, and that the vowel represented is really [*ĕ*]. Jane Weightman, 'Vowel-Levelling in Early Kentish; and the use of the symbol ę in OE Charters', *Englische Studien* 35 (1905), 337–49, uses the spelling *styde* (OE *stede*) as evidence of the change: pp. 342–3.

Aldebury, 1415, 1439 BMCR i/7(2); 1428 FA v/121; *Combehuthe* (Blackheath H.), 1428 FA v/122; *Derhurst* (nr Leigh), 1400 FFS 163; *Ewhurist*, 1486-7 SrW 52; *Gumshulue*, 1427 BMCR i/305; *Waybrugge*, 15th c CLB ii/277; *Wyntreshull*, 1412 FA vi/518 . . .   (19).

Forms with *e* are much less frequent over the centuries. Only one reliable 12th c entry has been found:

Waibreg, 1196 FFS 2   (1).

Ewerste, Yweherst, 1207 MPR 64; 1271 FFS 46; *Gomeshelle, Gumeselue, Gumeshelve*, 1245 CAD iii/419; 1232-3 BMCR i/305; 1235 BkF ii/1362; *Redinghers*, 1272-1307 BMCR i/205; *S(c)helwood* (Leigh), 1231-8 MPR 95; 1226 ib. 87; 1239-48 ib. 103; *La Slefherst* (Ewhurst), 1216-72 BMCR i/268 . . .   (24).

le Bery (Hersham), 1374 CAD iii/306; *Gomshelve, Gumshelue*, 1333 FFS 104; 1361 BMCR i/305; *le Herst* (Hersham), 1369 CAD iii/308; *Lampet* (Banstead), 1325 BH 334; *Redingherst, Ridinghers*, 1388 BSC 28; 1300 ib. 39; *Wyntersell'*, 1311 L & B 147 . . .   (14).

Ewerst, 1488 SrW 84; 1489 BMCR i/268; *Gumshelue, Gumshelve*, 1407 FFS 176; 1428 FA v/121; *Redyngherse*, 1494 BMCR i/205; *Shelwode*, 1468 MPR 301   (6).

Before the 15th c the *i*-spellings are also fewer:

Mikeleham (Mickleham), 1197 FFS 2; *Waibrige*, 1199 ib. 4   (2).

Aldebir, Aldebyr, 1260 FFS 41; 1242 BkF ii/684; *Emelebrig(g)*, 1212 ib. i/67; 1235 ib. ii/1363; *Gumeshylle*, 1216-72 CAD iii/444; *Hupmilne, Upmilne* (Molesey), 1215 MPR xlii; 1212 VCHS iii/455; *Micheleham, Mikeleham*, 1242-3 BkF ii/687; ib. ii/64 . . .   (20).

Emelebrigg, Emilbrigge, 1316 FA v/iii; 1359 FFS 221; *Gumshylue*, 1353 BMCR i/305; *Lampytt*, 1325 BH 134; *Mykelham*, 1316 BMCR i/514; *Rysbryg* (Wonersh), 1349 CAD ii/419; *Sedelewumille* (Banstead), 1378 BH 359; *Waybrigge*, 1372 CAD i/447 . . .   (15).

Coppedhille, 1489 BH 155; *Emelbrigge*, 1404 FFS 166; *furshill* (Cranleigh), 1485 SrW 9; *longrigge*, 1428 BSC 33; *Mikilham*, 1487 SrW 65; *atte Mille* (Ockham), 1412 FA vi/518; *Milton Strete* (Ashstead), 1486 SrW 32; *Sidlomyll*, 1489 BH 155; *Way-*

brigge, Waybryg, 1486 FFS 199; 15th c CLB i/34; *Wyntereshill,*
1428 FA v/123 . . .   (22).

Spellings with *i* are almost invariable in 15th c documents belonging
to this area:

> Banstead Petition (1413–19): *first,* 151.
> Surrey Wills (late 15th c, all relating to Leatherhead): *ffirst,*
> *fyrste,* 33, 95; *fulfyllyde,* 33; *girdyll, gyrdyll,* 95; *kyrtyll,* 95(2);
> *litell,* 95; *synnys,* 33;
> but also *beried,* 95.

Summary

The dialect of this part of the county treats OE $\breve{y}$ as might be expected in a central area. It agrees with the dialects of Middlesex[14] and
North Sussex in having more *u*- than *e*-spellings. The proportion
of *e*-spellings is larger than in the Western area, but smaller than in
both the Eastern areas. As in the rest of the county the proportion
of *i*-spellings increases considerably in the fifteenth century.

III General Summary and Conclusion

The use of reliable Pl-N material has made it possible to examine
closely the development of OE $\breve{y}$ in the four areas of the county.
The tables that follow are based upon the complete numbers of
significant Pl-Ns found:

(a) Western Area			(b) North-Eastern Area		
u	*i*	*e*	*u*	*i*	*e*
12th c	8	4	4	3	2	6
13th c	60	20	12	15	17	48
14th c	90	21	1	27	25	37
15th c	45	42	3	9	32	19

(c) South- & Central-Eastern Area			(d) Central Area		
u	*i*	*e*	*u*	*i*	*e*
12th c	1	?1	7	–	2	1
13th c	16	5	18	31	20	24
14th c	29	11	37	80	15	14
15th c	9	10	14	19	22	6

14. See B. A. Mackenzie, loc. cit.

The Pl-N figures above show that while the South-Western *u*-type may be regarded as being basic in the county, in each area the pattern of *u*- and *e*-forms is dependent upon the development in neighbouring areas. This is to be expected in a border area such as Surrey.

The *i*- spellings, most of which must have arisen from earlier ME [y̆], and which therefore strengthen the South-Western element, are of particular interest. The earlier examples generally occur before front consonants, but in all areas this spelling becomes more and more widespread over the centuries, until in the 15th c it is the most common in the county. The vowel [y̆] was here obviously undergoing the regular process of gradual unrounding; by the 15th c *u* and *i* may well both represent the unrounded vowel. It is significant that, taken as a whole, the 15th c ME documents examined show the same preponderance of *i*-spellings as do the Pl-Ns.

The other points that emerge in support of the use of Pl-N material are that the earlier ME documents consulted also show much the same pattern as the Pl-Ns, and that it has been demonstrated that the evidence afforded by the forms containing this vowel in O & N and KH agrees quite well with that of the Pl-Ns of the areas to which they have been tentatively ascribed.

APPENDIX

LIST OF SOURCES AND ABBREVIATIONS

The following list contains the names of sources of forms quoted in this study.
The full list of Group A sources consulted is considerably longer.

A. PLACE-NAME SOURCES (LOCAL COLLECTIONS AND GENERAL COLLECTIONS CONTAINING LOCAL DOCUMENTS)

BAnn   *Bermondsey Annals.* MS Harley 231 (mid 15th c). Vol. III of *Annales Monastici*, Rolls Series, ed. H. Richards Luard (London, 1864–9).

BH   *Banstead, History of,* ed. H. C. Lambert (Oxford, 1912).

BkF   *Book of Fees,* 2 vols., Public Record Office (London, 1920–3).

BMCR   *British Museum Charters and Rolls,* 2 vols., ed. H. J. Ellis and F. B. Bickley (London, 1900, 1912).

BSC   Surrey Charters in the Bodleian Library, 13th, 14th and 15th c MSS (Nos. 1–70).

CAD   *Ancient Deeds, Descriptive Catalogue of,* 6 vols., Public Record Office (London, 1890–1915).

CCR   *Carshalton Court Rolls* (temp. Edward III – Henry VII), Surrey Record Society, viii (London, 1916).

CLB   *Chertsey Leiger Book* (1432), Surrey Record Society, v and xxvii (London, 1915, 1928).

Dugd   *Monasticon Anglicanum,* Wm. Dugdale (London, 1846).

FA   *Feudal Aids, Inquisitions and Assessments Relating to* (1284–1431), 6 vols., Public Record Office (London, 1899–1920).

FFS   *Feet of Fines for Surrey* (Richard I – Henry VII), ed. F. B. Lewis, Surrey Archaeological Collections, extra Vol. I (Guildford, 1894).

HAS   *History and Antiquities of Surrey,* 3 vols., O. Manning and W. Bray (London, 1804).

L & B   'Lymnesfeld and Brodeham, Extents and Custumals of the Manors of' (1311), in *Battle Abbey Custumals,* ed. Scargill-Bird (Camden Society 41, 1887).

MPR   *Merton Priory Records* (12th to 16th c), ed. A. Heales (London, 1898).

MSAsh   MS Ashmolean 1146 (13th c) (Bodleian Library).

MSL   MSS Lansdowne 434 and 435 (1307–47 and 1307–44) (Bodleian Library).

MSLaud   MS Laud 723 (13th & 14th c) (Bodleian Library).

SAC   *Surrey Archaeological Collections,* Surrey Archaeological Society (London, 1858 –).

SCMS   Sheen Documents. See Group B, below.

SDMC   Surrey Documents in Merton College, Oxford, transcribed by W. H. Stevenson.

SrW   *Surrey Wills.* See Group B, below.

STR   *Surrey Taxation Returns,* Surrey Record Society xviii (London, 1922).

VCHS   *Victoria County History of Surrey,* Documents quoted in.

B. LITERARY TEXTS AND DOCUMENTS EITHER ENTIRELY OR PARTLY IN MIDDLE ENGLISH

BPet   'Banstead Petition' (1413–19), in *History of Banstead* (See Group A).

ChCh   *Chertsey Chartulary* (*c*1259–80), ed. Kemble, *Codex Diplomaticus Aevi Saxonici* (London, 1839–48).

GCust   *Godalming Custumal* (early 15th c translation from Latin), ed. P. Woods, *Surrey Archaelogical Collections* (see Group A).

GMB   'Godley Hundred, Metes and Bounds of' (1446), *Chertsey Leiger Book*, Vol. I, pp. 127–8 (see Group A).

KH   *King Horn* (Original text early 13th c), MSS C(*c*1260), L(*c*1310), H(*c*1314–20). Various editions, including J. Hall (Oxford, 1901); G. H. McKnight (E.E.T.S. 14, 1901, 1962); T. Wissmann, *Das Lied von King Horn* (Strassburg & London, 1881). E.E.T.S. line nos. quoted.

O & N   *The Owl and the Nightingale*, MSS C (early 13th c) and J (late 13th c). Various editions, including J. E. Wells (Boston, 1907, rev. ed. 1909); E. G. Stanley, (1960; Manchester, 1972) (based on MS C). References are to Wells's parallel text edition.

SCh   *Surrey Charter* (871–889), ed. H. Sweet (E.E.T.S. 83, 1855).

SCMS   Sheen Documents, MS Cotton Jul. Cii, fols. 286 ff. (15th c).

SLMS   Sheen Documents, MS Lansdowne 1201, fols. 59b – 61b (15th c).

SrW   *Surrey Wills* (15th c), Surrey Record Society, xvii (London, 1921); also F. J. Furnivall, *Fifty Earliest English Wills* (E.E.T.S. 78, 1882).

A POEM 'CLEPID THE SEVENE AGES'

Brian S. Lee

Analogues to Jaques' famous speech on the Seven Ages of Man include, according to H. H. Furness citing Halliwell in *The Variorum
As You Like It*, a poem 'clepid the sevene ages' in the Thornton MS.
of the fifteenth century in Lincoln Cathedral. The reference is a
tantalizing one, since there is no indication where Halliwell makes
the alleged statement, and the Thornton MS. contains no such poem.[1]

One runs the will-o'-the-wisp to earth in Cambridge University
MS. Ff. 2. 38 (subsequently called C), where a rubric on f. 20ᵛ reads
'here endiþ the *profitis* of erþeli anger and begynneþ þe mirro*ur*
of vices & of vertues which also ys clepid þe seuene ages'.[2] The poem,
written in double columns as verse but without breaks between the
eight-line stanzas, is incomplete after 186 lines, as ff. 22-7 are missing
from the manuscript. Halliwell listed the contents of this manuscript
in the preface to his edition of *The Thornton Romances*,[3] and in citing
item 18 of the list, Furness failed to notice that Halliwell had already completed his catalogue of the Thornton MS.

The poem thus detected is not unknown, though it hardly seems to
have received the attention its literary merit and interest as an exemplar of a common form of medieval schematization deserve. F. J.
Furnivall edited it in 1867 from MS. Lambeth 853 (subsequently
called L), where it runs to 82 stanzas, calling it *The Mirror of the
Periods of Man's Life, or Bids of the Virtues and Vices for the Soul of*

---

1. *The Variorum Shakespeare: As You Like It*, ed. H. H. Furness (Philadelphia, 1890), p. 124. For the contents of the Thornton MS., see R. M. Woolley, *Catalogue of the MSS of Lincoln Cathedral Chapter Library* (Oxford, 1927) entry 91 'The Thornton Romances'; also the Scholar Press facsimile, with introductions by D. S. Brewer and A. E. B. Owen (London, 1975): contents pp. xvii-xx.

2. I have consulted the MS. on microfilm, by courtesy of the Cambridge Uni-versity Library. The foliation refers to the original order in which the manu-script was rebound in 1972. The entry for this poem in Carleton Brown's *Register of Middle English Religious Verse* (Oxford, 1916), I, 180, contains some errors of transcription.

3. *The Thornton Romances*, ed. J. O. Halliwell (Camden Society, 1844), pp. xxv-xlv. *The Mirrour* is item 18 on pp. xxxviii-ix.

72

ffor þe loue of owre lorde ihesu
And for hym specyally ye pradye
þ þe gode in to euerlastyng loue
þat he hym silf þis on gode frydaye
þis yowys naylyd on þe rode a slowe
and graunt vs þo blisse þt euer shall ay
In heuene þro yere þt owre nebur Amen

here endiþ the passioun of crist auctor
And begynneþ þe mirror of vices &
of vertues whiche is clepid þe
seuene aȝeȝ

Holy mankinde doþ bygynne
    þus worche to dyȝ ȝe soo
    In name he ys conseyued wt synne
    þe chylde ys þo modued dede soo
    Or they be fully perfyȝd on thynne
    In yeft of dethe ben bothe twoo
    þore he come þe worlde wt inne
    wyth sorowe and pyne owt / stiff þo rood
    In wynt in ryȝt or y wakyd
    In my slepy y dremyd soo
    y fond a chylde modre nakyd
    wtse borne þe modre froo
    All alone all god hym makyd
    In wyȝernesse he þud rood
    & yt I wod in wommanes þt hed onfed
    An almyȝt frendis an almyȝt foo
    And the worlde to þe chylde how many folke
    haþte y brouȝt y yeuþose now fat þo
    thou pryutyȝt dye for hmwne y cold
    But y lenne mete and clothe to thd
    y wold the fynde tyll you be oold
    how write you quyte þo me
    Quod dystruye he ys dombe & solde
    And dye & he ende made styll wo
    And þe chylde y come poso þo worke wt inne
    ȝe clewe a wondurfull aduntuse
    haþ ys one of þe uyches of hyme

Man.[4] Versions are extant in eight manuscripts, but in only three of them is the poem reasonably complete.[5] E. C. York, in an unpublished dissertation, concludes that MS. Pepys 2125 (subsequently called P) preserves the most authoritative text, and provides a diplomatic edition, with variant readings, which are extensive, from the other manuscripts.[6]

The Mirror has little relevance to Jaques' speech. Even though 'clepid þe seuene ages', it deals in fact with eleven, which run from birth to the ages of seven, fourteen and twenty, and then in ten-year intervals to a hundred. The presiding Virtue is Conscience; Vices are numerous. Up to fifty Man indulges his free will and treats Conscience with cheerful scorn; from sixty onwards he is contrite but insecure to the end. The introductory rubric in P summarizes these distinctions: 'Here begynneþ materes of ʒouthe & of age And of vertues & of uices wyþ her kyndely condiciouns'.[7] Coxe in 1852 catalogued the poem as 'The life of man, corrected by Conscience, by Lydgate?, in eight-line stanzas'.[8] Coxe wrote before MacCracken

4. *Hymns to the Virgin & Christ*, ed. F. J. Furnivall (E. E. T. S. 24, 1867), pp. 58-78. Unless otherwise stated, references are to L in this edition. The poem belongs to the late fourteenth or early fifteenth century: *M.E.D.*'s date *c.* 1450 (e.g. s.v. 'gesoun' (b), s.v. 'hachet' (c)) is evidently too late.

5. Lambeth 853, pp. 120-50 (L): 656 lines.
Balliol 354, 194r-99r: lines 1-496. Ends at L's line 488: stanza 50 not in L.
Camb. Un. Ff. 2. 38, 20v-21v (C): lines 1-186.
Pepys 1584, 14r-28r: 664 lines. Stanza 50 not in L.
Pepys 2125, 60v-65r (P): 654 lines. Omits L's stanzas 24, 29, 30, 82; includes 1st six lines of 50 and 3 stanzas after L's 78.
B.L. Add. 36983, 298r-305r: 'complete' in 482 lines. Omissions and transpositions, apparently arbitrary, suggest the original of this version was transcribed from memory.
B.L. Add. 37492, 90v-92v: lines 1-142. Omits stanza 14; ends 'be he bolde wykeþ or lyʒt' (variant of L 150).
Huntington HM 135, 83r-86r: acephalous, with omissions and transpositions.
Of these I have inspected the Pepys and Additional manuscripts.

6. E. C. York, 'The Mirror of the Periods of Man's Life' (Pennsylvania, 1957): see *Dissertation Abstracts* 17 (1957), 1079.

7. Only C has a title stipulating seven ages. In Pepys 1584 it is 'The Merour of Mankynde', in B.L. Add. 36983 'Gubernacio Hominis', and in the list of contents prefixed to Richard Hill's commonplace book (MS. Balliol 354) 'The treatyse of ye ages of man'.

8. See *Songs, Carols and Other Miscellaneous Verses from Richard Hill's Balliol MS*, ed. R. Dyboski (E.E.T.S. e.s. 101, 1907), p. xlvii.

investigated the Lydgate canon,[9] and when any anonymous fifteenth-century poem might as soon be ascribed to Lydgate as not: *The Mirror* is metrically too various, and in language and imagery too startling, vivid and colloquial, to be by Lydgate.

A brief comparison of variants reveals that the early copyists treated their exemplars cavalierly. The basically four-beat line tends on the whole to be shorter in P than in L, which sometimes expands for clarity: e.g. L 79 'Course of kynde is for ȝouþe to be wilde' reads in P 'Cours of kynde wul ȝouþe be wilde'. There are exceptions: for L 367 'To þi mercy, lord, me vndirfonge' P, anticipating the metaphor of the ebbing tide in the next line, has 'And biddeþ me to go lond for shipmans þrong'.[10] C, as far as it goes, keeps fairly close to L, though with a tendency to abbreviate. C omits the following initial words in L: 52 Mi, 72 To, 81 Thus, 86 Þe, 92 And, 133 And, 169 Þanne, 180 For. L 173 'Do þou to euery man þat is due' is contracted to 'Do þou euery man dewe'. Rarely, C is closer to P than to L, describing the fallen Lucifer as 'al aungels page' where L 142 has, uniquely, 'moost looþeli page'. The Lambeth scribe is doubtless responsible for this 'improvement', since the common ancestor of L and C must have had the reading that was also in the exemplar of P. In 101 C mediates between L and P: L has 'Quod lust to conscience, "ȝouþe so muste" ' (rhyme words *coost*, *loost*, *post*), P 'What conscience q^d ȝouþe þ^u it wost', and C 'What conscience youþe so moste'.

P has some inferior readings, but corrects certain errors in L. L is obviously wrong at 617 to begin a speech belonging to Man 'Quod þe worlde, "Y wole hise dettis quyte"'; P omits 'Quod', while the somewhat later MS. Pepys 1584 expands to 'Quod man to þe worlde'. In 505 P has 'The' for L's 'Þre': the former is preferable, as all the Sins speak, and not only the three in the first of the two stanzas allotted to them. L 531 'Whanne sijknesse comeþ men to craue' is more forcefully rendered in P ' . . . somneþ men to graue'. L 558 'He siȝkeþ for synnes ben not vnbounde' obscures the meta-

---

9. *Lydgate's Minor Poems*, ed. H. N. MacCracken, Pt I *Religious Poems* (E.E.T.S. E.S. 107, 1910), pp. v-lviii.

10. This is garbled. Add. 36983 provides an intelligible reading:
        He biddeth go to þe lond from shipmans throng
        ffor þe tyde is ebbed, no more wil flowe (301^v).
It is a vivid and affecting picture of retirement in old age.

phor and is possibly unintelligible: P has 'his sak of synnes is nat vnwounde', a reading confirmed by the imagery in L 589–90, where confession is likened to shaking out a sackload of sin in front of the priest. In 416 P has the Devil speak where L only mentions him: Youth warns Age to make up his accounts 'Or þe deuel bringe þe countirtaile'; in this case P's reading 'Q^d þe deuel, I bryng þe countretaille' though possibly more dramatic seems to rob Youth of the necessary climax of his moral admonition.

The Mirror makes moral capital of a scheme originally neutral. The ancients had no religious motive in dividing the Ages of Man. Aristotle distinguished three ages in his treatise on Rhetoric: youth, prime and old age: ἡλίκιαι δέ εἰσι νεότης καὶ ἀκμὴ καὶ γῆρας. His purpose was to help orators adapt their matter to the interests of their listeners. He noted contrasting characteristics of youth and old age: καὶ δειλοὶ καὶ πάντα προφοβητικοί· ἐναντίως γὰρ διάκεινται τοῖς νέοις· κατεψυγμένοι γάρ εἰσιν, οἱ δὲ θερμοί [old men are nervous and anxious about everything, for their dispositions are opposite to those of the young: cold as against hot.] The age of prime shares the advantages of both extremes, and occupies the position of the golden mean between their excesses and their defects: ὅσα μὲν διῄρηνται ἡ νεότης καὶ τὸ γῆρας τῶν ὠφελίμων, ταῦτα ἄμφω ἔχουσιν, ὅσα δὲ ὑπερβάλλουσιν ἢ ἐλλείπουσιν, τούτων τὸ μέτριον καὶ τὸ ἁρμόττον. But he had some difficulty in deciding at what age the golden mean lay, as man is a composite being: ἀκμάζει δὲ τὸ μὲν σῶμα ἀπὸ τῶν τριάκοντα ἐτῶν μέχρι τῶν πέντε καὶ τριάκοντα, ἡ δὲ ψυχὴ περὶ τὰ ἑνὸς δεῖν πεντήκοντα [the body reaches its prime between thirty and thirty-five, the mind about forty-nine][11].

Horace evidently had Aristotle's views in mind when he advised the aspiring dramatist to assign parts suitable to the ages of his characters.[12] Horace describes four ages: the child is playful and his moods change rapidly, the youngster is feckless, prodigal, eager and a lover of vigorous sports, the man is ambitious and acquisitive, the ancient is querulous, timid and nostalgic about the past. Morality is not in question: to please his audience the dramatist should always suit the correct attributes to whichever of the four ages he is dealing with:

11. *Aristotelis Ars Rhetorica*, Bk II chs 12-14, ed. W. D. Ross (Oxford, 1959), pp. 100-4.
12. *Ars Poetica*, 153-78.

Ne forte seniles
Mandetur iuveni partes pueroque viriles;
Semper in adiunctis aevoque morabimur aptis (176-8).

If, in classical antiquity, the treatment of the Ages of Man was
pragmatic, in the Renaissance of the twelfth century the scheme was
subsumed into theology.[13] Theologians were developing a Bibli-
cally-orientated view of world history, and they correlated the historical dispensations with the periods of man's life. The schemes
they elaborated are conveniently summarized by Hugh of St Victor,
who divides the contents of Scripture, and therefore the history of the
world, into two 'status' (an old and a new dispensation), three
'tempora' (those of natural law, of the written law, and of grace),
and six ages. Of these the first five, from Adam to Noah, and then to
Abraham, to David, to the Babylonian captivity, and to the coming
of Christ, are in four successions, those of the patriarchs, the judges,
the kings and the priests. 'Aetates dicuntur sex,' Hugh explains,
'ad similitudinem aetates hominum. Fuit enim mundus et infans et
puer, &c.' [The Ages are six, like man's : for the world has also been
through its infancy and childhood, etc.][14]
Isidore lists these six Ages of Man as 'infantia, pueritia, adolescentia, juventus, gravitas, atque senectus', answering to the years
between birth and seven, fourteen, twenty-eight, fifty, seventy and
however much of life is left. He adds 'Senium autem pars est ultima
senectutis' [Extreme age is the last part of old age][15]. Honorius of
Autun has a similar list, except that he terminates *adolescentia* at
twenty-one, calls the fifth age *senectus* and the sixth *decrepita*, and
extends this last age 'ad centum annos vel usque ad mortem' [to
a hundred or right up to death].[16] The gloss on 'Agis sevyn' in the
Promptorium Parvulorum is based on Isidore, but adds '7' est in

13. See M.-D. Chenu, *Nature, Man and Society in the Twelfth Century*, selected,
    ed., and translated J. Taylor and L. K. Little (Chicago, 1968), ch. 5 'Theology
    and the New Awareness of History', especially pp. 181-3.
14. Hugh of St Victor, 'De materia sacrae Scripturae', *P.L.* 175, 24. For
    Hugh's discussion of the 'tria tempora' see *P.L.* 176, 32 (repeated, cols.
    312-3).
15. *Isidori Etymologiae*, ed. W. M. Lindsay (Oxford, 1911), II, Lib. XI, Caput II,
    'De Aetatibus Hominum'; also *P.L.* 82, 415-6.
16. Honorius of Autun, 'De Imagine Mundi' II, 75: *P.L.* 172, 156.

resurrectione finali' [the seventh age consists in the final resurrection].[17]

These lists lack moral or religious comment. Bonaventure, however, elaborates. He links the Ages of Man to those of the world by a sort of analogous necessity between the microcosm and the macrocosm, it being fitting that 'maioris mundi decursus correspondeat decursui vitae minoris mundi, scilicet hominis, propter quem factus est' [that the history of the macrocosm should match the lifespan of the microcosm, man, for whom it was created]. The periods of world history correspond to the six days of creation by apt analogies: for instance, the sixth age in which Christ was born in human form answers to the sixth day on which the first man was made. Similarly Bonaventure justifies the relationship between human and cosmic ages: the first age, consumed by the Flood, is fittingly called *infantia*, since infancy is obscured by total forgetfulness; and the sixth *senium*, 'quia, sicut illa est quae copulatur cum morete, habens tamen magnam lucem sapientiae, sic sexta aetas mundi terminatur cum die iudicii, et in ea viget sapientia per doctrinam Christi' [just as extreme old age couples with death but has a great light of wisdom, so the sixth age of the world ends at doomsday and in it flourishes wisdom because of the doctrine of Christ].[18] The seventh age is the eternal Sabbath of rest, as Augustine noted at the end of his *De Civitate Dei*.

It was the connection between the coming of death and the wisdom of repentance that later medieval treatments of the Ages of Man took over when they applied them to the moral exhortation of the individual. For the theologians, the implication of the correspondence was that the world, now in its sixth age, *senium*, was declining, doddering towards doomsday in a sort of cosmological decrepitude. For the moralist, old age was a warning to youth to prepare for the end:[19] 'þi reckenyng bi tyme bisili þou make' (*The Mirror*,

---

17. *Promptorium Parvulorum*, ed. A.L. Mayhew (E.E.T.S. e.s. 102, 1908), s.v. 'Agis'. *Adolescencia* goes up to a curious 29; otherwise the ages are named and delimited as by Isidore.

18. Saint Bonaventure, *Breviloquium: Prologue*, II, 2-3, ed. Jacques-Guy Bougerol (Paris, 1966), pp. 96-100.

19. For example, the Vernon lyric 'Þenk on ʒuster-day', 97-108, ed. Carleton Brown, *Religious Lyrics of the Fourteenth Century*, 2nd ed. revised by G. V. Smithers (Oxford, 1957), No. 101, suggests that God allows crooked and feeble old men to survive as warnings to young men.

415). This is the theme of many a *timor mortis* poem about the brevity
of youth:

> Wyle Y was ȝonge Y myght nat see
>   þe strayte waye to my last age . . .
> þer was neuer ladd þat leuyt so long
>   þat ne deyyt or dede schall be;
> þerfore, bycauce Y haue lyuyd wrang,
>   'Timor mortis conturbat me.'[20]

It is also the point missed, or ignored, by the Victorian scholar
Sidney Colvin in his romantic description of the flower-surrounded
figures depicted on the floor of Siena Cathedral, in a mosaic dated
1476:

> The seven ages of man are shown in single white figures set in
> squares or diamonds of black. These ages are not divided as usual:
> four divisions are given to the time before manhood, as if to draw
> out as much as possible that season when life is life indeed. There
> is no mewling and puking, nor any whining school-boy: *Infantia* is
> a naked child playing among flowers; *Pueritia* an Italian boy in
> short cloak and cap walking in the fields; the season of youth is
> spun out, always among flowers, through *Adolescentia* and *Juven-*
> *tus*; manhood is not a soldier full of strange oaths and bearded
> like the pard, but a studious citizen walking with open book;
> *Decrepitas* moves, over a land flowerless at last, on crutches to
> his open grave.[21]

What is unusual is not the division of the ages, or even Colvin's
omission of one of them, but the idyllic viewpoint, which smacks
more of the nineteenth than of the fifteenth century. The mosaic is
reproduced by Edgar Fripp, who also provides a more detailed description than Colvin's. He adds that *Juventus* has a falcon on his
fist; that *Virilitas* is 'a learned doctor in his robes, carrying a book of
the law'; that *Senectus* holds a rosary; and that the flowers represent the Garden of the World, while *Decrepitas* 'looks with bowed
head into his tomb, within the House of God: *the largest and central*

---

20. Ed. R. L. Greene, 'A Middle English "Timor Mortis" Poem', *M.L.R.* 28
    (1933), 234-8.
21. Sidney Colvin, 'The History of a Pavement', *Fortnightly Review* (July, 1875),
    53-4.

picture of the series, with a Cross behind it'. Fripp goes on to contrast what he calls Jaques' smart and cynical travesty of this happy
and dignified representation of Life.[22]
  Nevertheless the sobering and centralized conclusion of the series
shows *Decrepitas* approaching his tomb. The iconography of the
Ages almost inevitably has this sobering emphasis.[23] In the sumptuous but fragmentary De Lisle psalter of the fourteenth century, the
figures of Infantia, Juventus, Senectus and Decrepitas represent the
four ages at the corners of an illustration of a ten-spoked wheel de-
picting stages of life from the cradle to the grave.[24] The emphasis on
death is apparent in Wynkyn de Worde's woodcut illustrating the
chapter on the seven ages in John of Trevisa's translation of the *De
Proprietatibus Rerum.*[25] In a landscape containing a castle, a terrace
and a hill, with birds flying above, are drawn a naked infant, a child
playing with a hobby-horse and a windmill, a boy bending a bow, a
gallant wearing a tall-feathered hat and holding a falcon on his wrist,
and three soberly-dressed but scarcely differentiated figures; below
the seven a physician scrutinizes a vial beside the bed of a sick man;
the head and trunk of a corpse are visible behind the castle wall,
and a surgeon is apparently cutting the throat of an unhappy-looking

22. E. I. Fripp, *Shakespeare, Man and Artist* (Oxford, 1938), II, 533-4.
23. The iconography of the Ages has been extensively studied by Samuel C. Chew,
    in 'This Strange Eventful History', *Joseph Quincy Adams Memorial Studies,*
    ed. J. G. McManaway *et al.* (Washington, 1948), pp. 157-82, and in *The
    Pilgrimage of Life* (Yale, 1962), pp. 153-73.
24. MS. B.L. Arundel 83, f. 126ᵛ. On f. 122 a note dated 'mil ccc xxxix' mentions
    'Robert de lyle'. The fine half-page illustration is reproduced (p. 176) by
    J. Winter Jones, 'Observations on the Origins of the Division of Man's Life
    into Stages', *Archaeologia* 35 (1853), 167-89. Winter Jones also reprodu-
    ces and describes a fifteenth-century woodcut showing a 'rota vite' with re-
    presentations of the seven ages around it, pp. 186-8. Cf. J. G. Waller, 'The
    Wheel of Human Life, or the Seven Ages', *Gentleman's Magazine* (May,
    1853), 494-502; also Chew in *Adams Studies,* pp. 166-7. Four quatrains
    describing man at twenty, forty, sixty, and in his last age called 'decrepitus',
    occur as part of a poem about death in Richard Hill's commonplace book:
    ed. Ewald Flügel, 'Die lieder des Balliol MS. 354', *Anglia* 26 (1903), 223-4;
    and as 'Death and the Four Ages of Man', ed. R. Dyboski (E.E.T.S. E.S.
    101, 1907), p. 93.
25. Wynkyn de Worde, n.d. (1494?), sig. M2ʳ, preceding Bk 6, ch. 1. For the
    text see *On the Properties of Things,* ed. M. C. Seymour *et al.* (Oxford, 1975),
    pp. 291-3.

figure reclining on a stool. The chapter following concentrates on the medical or at least physical aspects of the ages, detailing especially the disabilities of old age. The author seems to have as much difficulty as the artist in distinguishing the last three ages, perhaps because Isidore, whom he acknowledges as his source, is somewhat confusing about the distinctions between *gravitas, senectus* and *senium*.

Comparison with the physical changes of human life made the theological divisions of history more readily intelligible, but the scheme proved less tractable when pressed into the service of moral exhortation. For the theologians, the analogy of the seven ages cut down the vast range of history to manageable proportions, but for the homilists it was more extensive than necessary. A life-span is not the appropriate object of moral exhortation, which requires a response from the individual addressed at the present stage of his life.

A case in point is the extended review of the seven ages in the Scots poem *Ratis Raving*, intended as a father's guide to practical morality for his son.[26] The review, which the author claims is 'vrytin in lytill space' (1099), although it takes up some 700 of the poem's roughly 1 800 lines, is provided to help the son

> To knaw the cours of thi ȝouthede,
> and of the mydys, and of thin eild,
> As þow has feld and mar sal feild (1101-3).

Any resemblance to Aristotle's three ages is accidental: the author's concern is with the development of reason and the virtue it should promote, which he calls 'bounté'. The first two ages, up to three and seven years, are devoted merely to nourishment and innocent play, and have no homiletic value; but in the third, from seven to fifteen, 'springis rutis of resone' (1152), and here the author warns against the frivolity of too much play, and the evil of dicing. The fourth age, fifteen to thirty, when man grows to the perfection of reason, is the time to develop 'bounté'. In the fifth age, thirty to fifty, man should reach 'the perfeccioune Of resone and discreccioune' (1414-5). But

---

26. *Ratis Raving and Other Early Scots Poems on Morals*, ed. R. Girvan (S.T.S. 11, 1939), pp. 31-51 (lines 1098-798). Girvan explains the title (p. xxi) as the advice (? 'raþing') of one Rate, which whoever added the epilogue assures us is not 'raving' but good moral sense. Also ed. J. R. Lumby, *Ratis Raving and Other Moral and Religious Pieces* (E.E.T.S. 43, 1870).

too often this age is given over to vice and tyranny: here the verse becomes a satire of contemporary oppression, with one Mortimer as an example, whose evil ways were confessed, if not in life then on his epitaph, in a version of Psalm 51, 3-9. The sixth age, fifty to seventy or eighty (the terminal alternative agrees with the proof text, Psalm 89 [90], 10), is too often covetous although the Psalter says 'That halynes in eild suld bee' (1648).[27] The last age, eighty and beyond, is a time of toothless senility, with Albert Magnus's reputed lapse into childishness as an example. The moral, wise rather than particularly spiritual, is that even if Hell and Heaven didn't exist, philosophers agree that it's better to be virtuous than vicious.

If the survey in *Ratis Raving* is unwieldy, the problem of achieving unity is neatly solved in the poignant lyric *The Hours of Man's Life*.[28] Here the survey is presented as the reminiscence of a hoary old man lamenting his misspent life, whom the poet overhears while (ominously) 'on(e) my playing' (1; 77). The narrative framework thus brings the substance of the old man's monologue into the present with dramatic immediacy, and its obvious though unstated relevance to the carefree mood of the reckless young poet gives it homiletic impact. Each stanza ends with the refrain 'This wor(l)d ys but a wannyté', insisting on the poem's single theme. Moreover, the ages are concentrated into the passage of a day, to make an admonitory point about the brevity of human life:

---

27. Psalm 54, 24: 'Viri sanguinum et dolosi non dimidiabunt dies suos': 'bloody and deceitful men shall not live out half their days' (55, 23: A.V.). Cf. Proverbs 16, 31: 'Corona dignitatis senectus, quae in viis iustitiae reperietur': 'Grey hair is a crown of glory, and it is won by a virtuous life' (N.E.B.). *The Mirror* has

> Quod Conscience, 'certis it were riȝt
> To be holi now or neuere moore' (343-4)

when Man at sixty grows old ('Myn iȝen daswen, myn heer is hoore' 338) and ashamed of his sinful past.

28. I use the title suggested in Carleton Brown and R. H. Robbins, *The Index of Middle English Verse* (Columbia, 1943), No. 349, and quote the edition by Carleton Brown, *Religious Lyrics of the Fifteenth Century* (Oxford, 1939), pp. 230-3, from MS. Porkington 10. Also ed., from MS. Lambeth 853, which lacks the second stanza, by F. J. Furnivall (E.E.T.S. 24, 1867), pp. 83-5. A sixteenth-century copy in Bodleian MS. Lat. misc. e. 85, ff. 81^r-82^r, omits the last stanza, and attributes the poem, or this copy of it, to one De Thomas Peny of Houghton.

> Owre lewying ys but one daye,
> Aȝeynst þe world þat euyre schal be (61-2).

Pope Gregory the Great related the five hours of the day mentioned in the parable of the Labourers in the Vineyard (Matthew 20, 1-16) to the Ages of man's life.[29] *Mane* corresponds to *puᴗritia, tertia hora* to *adolescentia*, the age of growing up resembling the way the heat of the climbing sun increases, *sexta* to *juventus*, resembling the sun in full strength, *nona* to *senectus*, resembling the sun descending, since in this age the heat of youth declines, and *undecima* to the age called *decrepita* or *veterana*. One recalls the imagery of Shakespeare's seventh sonnet, which compares the three ages of man with the passage of the sun across the heavens. In *The Hours of Man's Life* the seven ages are each allocated a stanza and correlated with an appropriate time of day. At 'the morrow-tyde' (17) the child is born, 'At myde-morroo-daye' (25) he plays and fights with other children, 'At vnder-day' he goes to school and disobeys his master; dubbed a knight at midday and crowned a king at noon he proudly indulges his lusts, but 'at myd-vndure-none' (57) his powers decline, and 'at ewynsong tyme' he is cold and decrepit (65). Similar imagery occurs in *The Mirror:*

> Þe sunne is past fer bi þe sowthe,
> And hiȝeth swiþe in to þe weste (347-8);
> It is past euensonge of my day (374).

Each age is contrasted with the old man's present regret for his sin: for instance, he was born unblemished, but 'Sethe in sin I have I-be' (22). The moral is similar to that of *Everyman*, the old man recognizing that

> When I am dede and layd in grawe,
>   Then no þing schall save me,
> But well and woo þat I done havfe (69-71).

Everyman itself is a powerful dramatic homily on the inevitability of death, in view of which preparedness is all. But a case has been made for regarding it as embodying, like its massive forerunner *The*

---

29. And to the Ages of the world: *Sancti Gregorii Magni XL Homiliarum in Evangelia* Lib. I Homilia xix, *P.L.* 76, 1153-9.

Castle of Perseverance, a survey of the Ages of man's life.[30] In *The Castle* Mankind begins as an innocent child guided by a good and a bad angel; he soon turns to the World and indulges in youthful follies that bring the Deadly Sins in their train; in middle age he repents and the Sins and the Three Enemies of Man fail to dislodge him and his attendant Virtues from the castle in which he has taken refuge; but as Age approaches he yields to Coveytyse, and dies apparently doomed but with the word 'mercy' on his lips (3007), which, after the debate of the Four Daughters of God, proves sufficient to save his soul as the Bad Angel is carrying it to Hell. Such a life-span is less obvious in *Everyman*, which begins with the message from Death which Mankind in *The Castle* receives only at the end of his life. Yet the decline of Everyman's fortunes as his friends desert him corresponds to the inadequacy of youthful fellowship and frivolities that leave his Good Deeds shackled, until subsequent repentance unlooses them and provides the more reliable companions that indicate his preparedness for the death that will introduce his soul to Heaven.

The brief dramatic dialogue *Of þe Seuen Ages* may be regarded as a link between such morality plays and *The Mirror*.[31] The conflicts of conscience that beset man at each age are allegorized by the argumentative figures of a Good Angel and the Fiend: similar figures occur in *The Castle of Perseverance*, *The Mirror*, *Dr. Faustus*, and, in an amorous rather than ethical context, Shakespeare's sonnet 144. The dramatic form dispenses with otiose descriptions of each age, which instead are indicated simply by the speaker's changing names: he is called þe Childe (twice), ʒouthe, Man, Age, þe Crepyl, and þe last Old Age. In each case, his speeches imply a moral attitude. Illustrations accompany the text. At each age except the first the protagonist is flanked by his contrasting attendants. Man waves a

30. *Everyman*, ed. A. C. Cawley (Manchester, 1961). *The Castle of Perseverance*, ed. M. Eccles, *The Macro Plays* (E.E.T.S. 262, 1969). Humanum Genus temporarily repents at forty (1575), and is presumably sixty (cf. 417) when he recounts the disabilities of old age (2482 ff.). Denis V. Moran, 'The Life of Everyman', *Neophilologus* 56 (1972), 324-9, traces Everyman's life from sensual youth to avaricious and finally repentant old age.
31. Ed., with facsimile of MS. B.L. Add. 37049, ff. 28ᵛ-29ʳ, by R. H. Bowers, 'A Medieval Analogue to *As You Like It* II. vii. 137-166', *Shakespeare Quarterly* 3 (1952), 109-12. Less satisfactorily printed by E. C. York, 'Dramatic Form in a Late Middle English Narrative', *M.L.N.* 72 (1957), 484-5.

battle-axe, Age clutches a purse, and the Cripple, like *Senectus* on the
Siena pavement, carries a rosary. The last Old Age lies dead in bed
while the Angel extracts the Soul from his mouth.[32] As in *The Mirror*,
the dramatic development, from sin to repentance, parallels the time
sequence from youth to age, the homiletic emphasis going to the
weightiest speeches, those on repentance, with which the dialogue
concludes. The irony that the Fiend is forced to report the salvation
that has defeated him drives home the moral message:

> Bot mercy has taken hym to grace
> For þᵗ he has lyfed in þis warld here
> And els in helle he hade had a place
> Emange fyre & fendes of vgly chere (57-60).

Dyboski says of *The Mirror*, somewhat disparagingly, that it
'possesses a certain interest as presenting a transitional stage midway
between the common Middle-English allegorical vision and the
early Modern English dramatic Morality'.[33] While the opening lines
of the second stanza refer to the poet dreaming, the poem is without
scenic content and does not establish a narrative framework by returning to the poet as *The Hours of Man's Life* does. Dialogue is
frequent, though not presented in dramatic form like the dialogue in
Of þe Seuen Ages.[34] Allegorical figures debate, especially when Man
is twenty, sixty and ninety. There are seventeen personifications in
six lines of one stanza (33-8), but only a few of these speak elsewhere
in the poem. The debates are of differing kinds: at twenty the Sins
and corresponding Virtues compete alternately for Man's attention,

---

32. Cf. the speech of the Aungell who conveys Everyman's soul to Heaven,
   Everyman 894 ff. There are other reminders of the morality plays. The Fiend
   uses a proverb that recurs in *Youth*, 607, ed. Peter Happé, *Tudor Interludes*
   (Penguin, 1972), p. 133: 'ʒonge saynt alde devell is an alde sawe' (9). The
   Angel warns 'Man (Bowers misprints 'Þan') hafe mynde of þine endyng day'
   (18), which is like the concluding admonition of *The Castle of Perseverance*:
   > Evyr at þe begynnynge
   > Thynke on ʒoure last endynge! (3647-8).
33. E.E.T.S. E.S. 101 (1907), p. xxx.
34. Some indication of dramatic form is attempted by the scribe of Pepys 1584:
   after line 16, in a red block inset without top, he writes 'The world answerth
   to the child and saith' (14ʳ), and occasionally names of speakers are placed
   in margins or centralized with red underlining.

at sixty Youth taunts Age, and at ninety Conscience argues with Despair.

As H. N. MacCracken pointed out, the early sixteenth-century morality *Mundus & Infans* is based on *The Mirror*.[35] The dramatist's adaptations reveal what he felt the poem needed to turn it into drama. Infans addresses the audience with a paraphrase of the opening lines of *The Mirror*:

The Mirror, 1-8	*Mundus & Infans, 28-35*
How mankinde dooþ bigynne	Now semely syrs, beholde on me
is wondir for to scryue so;	How mankynde doth begynne:
In game he is bigoten in synne,	I am a chylde, as you may se,
Þe child is þe modris deedli foo;	Goteningameandingretesynne.
Or þei be fulli partide on tweyne,	xl wekes my moder me founde,
In perelle of deed ben boþe two.	Flesshe and blode my fode was
Pore he come þe worlde with-	tho;
ynne,	Whan I was rype from her to
Wiþ sorewe & pouert oute schal	founde,
he goo.	In peryll of dethe we stode bothe
	two.

The playwright has simplified, most obviously in that he rhymes on four sounds instead of only on two, and has translated third person narrative into the first person speech of an actor facing an audience. The verbal differences are slight, but they have a noticeable effect on presentations and tone. As the Child in the play is addressing an audience, he inserts colloquialisms, 'now semely syrs', 'as you may se', which give his speech an easy familiarity in keeping with the conventionality of its content. He is saying simply 'Look, I'm a child, and you know what physically speaking that means'. But the word 'wondir' in the second line of the poem signals a different tone: 'Have you ever thought seriously about what it means to be human?'

---

35. *Mundus & Infans* was printed as 'a propre newe Interlude' by Wynkyn de Worde in 1522; see the facsimile ed. J. S. Farmer (Tudor Facsimile Texts, 1909). I quote the edition by J. M. Manly, *Specimens of the Pre-Shaksperean Drama* (1897, rpt. New York, 1967), I, 353-85. Ed., less satisfactorily and in modern spelling, E. T. Schell and J. D. Shuchter, *English Morality Plays and Moral Interludes* (New York, 1969), pp. 167-98. See H. N. MacCracken, 'A Source of *Mundus & Infans*', *P.M.L.A.* 23 (1908), 486-96.

The answer comes with grimly cumulative logic: conception is sinful, birth perilous, and the beginning and end of life sorrowful and poverty-stricken. At the price of the poem's powerful fourth line, the play finds room for an otiose reference to bridge the gap between conception and birth. That paratactic fourth line is evidently explained, in a physical sense, by the two lines that follow, but Furnivall's punctuation suggests that it should be linked with the preceding line, giving 'deedli' a moral force.

The Child in the poem sets out at birth on a pilgrimage 'to seke deeþ' (29): a familiar homiletic theme that recurs in the moralities.[36] A pilgrimage is a journey to a shrine; so too life, from a homiletic point of view, may be pictured as a progress to a spiritual end, in which death and the Judgement are inevitable stages on the way to the seventh age, which is 'in resurrectione finali'. Infans in the play alludes to the theme of death, but not of pilgrimage, in a quatrain that is a simplified and less powerful version of the fourth stanza of the poem:

The Mirror, 27-32	*Mundus & Infans, 36-9*
Naked out of the wyket of synne	
Of the perellis of streite passage,	Now to seke dethe I must begyn
To seke deeþ y dide bigynne,	For to passe that strayte passage;
Þat ilke dredful pilgrymage,	For body and soule that shall
Mi body & soule to parte a	than twynne
tweyne,	And make a partynge of that
To make a deuourse of þat	maryage.
mariage.	

The play uses fewer lines in this passage because it has simplified, not compressed, its original. As a physical description of birth 'streite passage' has objective force, especially in the context of

36. Cf. E. T. Schell, 'On the Imitation of Life's Pilgrimage in *The Castle of Perseverance*', *J.E.G.P.* 67 (1968), 235-48. For the pilgrimage theme see Rosemond Tuve, *Allegorical Imagery: Some Medieval Books and their Posterity* (Princeton, 1966), pp. 145 ff., and S. C. Chew, *The Pilgrimage of Life*. For the theory of 'the allegoric progress' see Angus Fletcher, *Allegory: the Theory of a Symbolic Mode* (Cornell, 1964), ch. 3 'Symbolic Action: Progress and Battle', pp. 147-80, especially pp. 151-7. See also Chaucer's *Balade de Bon Conseyl* ('*Truth*'), 17-20, and the notes in Robinson's edition, p. 861.

'wyket of synne'; applied to death as it is in the play, the same phrase becomes a commonplace. To the child in the play death remains a remote future event, but the lines in the poem bring it frighteningly close, for they show that the struggle of birth, both physically and spiritually perilous, is actually the start of that search for death which is what the grim journey of life inevitably entails. And the process is not merely physical, for it starts at the 'wyket of synne', and is a 'pilgrymage' to a spiritual destination.

Mundus & Infans deals with the problem of structure by perforce concentrating on significant moments of moral decision or conflict. The ages up to manhood are telescoped into a few brief monologues delivered while the youngster is under the tutelage of the World; youth and manhood are dramatized as a debate with Conscyence on the Deadly Sins and as a lively encounter with Folye; and Age is shown lamenting his youthful excesses and after repentance receiving belated instruction in the elements of the Christian faith from Perseueraunce. Effectively there are four scenes, the protagonist encountering in each a different allegorical figure, alternately a bad and a good one;[37] but he does pass through seven ages, more or less matching seven different names he goes by. He is Dalyaunce, Wanton, Lust-and-Lykyng and Manhode Myghty in the first four ages. During the course of the fifth, Folye changes his name to Shame. His last two names are Age, when he despairs, as Man in *The Mirror* does at ninety, and Repentaunce, when he learns all that is necessary to win Heaven, as the decrepit centenarian does at the end of *The Mirror*. But whereas the play draws out as much as possible that season when life is life indeed, in *The Mirror* Man reaches old age and has to face the prospect of death when the poem is only half over: the emphasis therefore falls on the theme of repentance, while the contrite sinner lingers on decade after decade to the last gasp of decrepitude.

The two stanzas describing the Child between seven and fourteen contain complementary advice from the Good Angel and the Bad; in the play Wanton's monologue is purely an expansion of the Bad

37. Concluding from the structure of *Mundus & Infans* that only two actors were available to play five parts, David Bevington, *From 'Mankind' to Marlowe* (Harvard, 1962), pp. 117 ff., argues, I believe unconvincingly, that the structure was pre-determined by casting restrictions, rather than shaped by artistic and thematic considerations.

Angel's advice. The period from fourteen to twenty (twenty-one in the play) features the opposing instructions of Reason and Lust: the former advises 'Goo to oxenford' (90),[38] the latter more alluringly advocates music, violent sports, and womanizing in the tavern with wild companions.[89] In the play Lust-and-Lykyng is much less specific, except on the subject of 'loue-longynge'.

When Man is twenty the Sins address him, each in two lines, then each in a stanza answered in turn by the corresponding Virtue. There is no narrative progress, the symmetrical speeches resembling a verbal ballet rather than a dramatic confrontation. Man himself does not speak till the next age, when Conscience reiterates the arguments against the Sins and Man scorns him. In the corresponding scene in *Mundus & Infans*, however, although Conscyence and Manhode are given alternate four-line speeches, the symmetry is both progressive and passionate. Conscyence forbids Manhode the company of each Sin in turn, Manhode growing angrier all the time; at last, with a neat twist for which there is no parallel in *The Mirror*, Conscyence disarms his adversary by unexpectedly permitting him to be covetous – but then he explains that he means covetous of well-doing. The 'debate' in *The Mirror* entails a detailed self-exposure of the nature of the Sins and Virtues, a familiar function of allegory;[40] but in the play description is entirely sacrificed to the dramatic form of the confrontation.

At fifty Man rejects Conscience's advice to 'use werkis of good

---

38. Most manuscripts give the age here as 'xx$^{(ti)}$' (89): Furnivall, ed. cit. p. vii, conjectures that xx is a mistake for xv. B.L. Add. 36983 has the apparently correct 'xiiij^e'.

39. The stanza concludes with a crux:
> And be to bemond A good squyer
> Al ny3t til þe day do dawe (95-6).

As a proper name, 'bemond' is not in *M.E.D.* or *O.E.D.* Furnivall says it is the name of a dog, and the reference may be to poaching; York suggests the word may be a form of 'beau monde'. C reads 'bemounde'. Perhaps 'be to bemond' was a scribal dittography in the archetype, and the original had 'be to þe mo(u)nde' (for 'le monde'). Then the concluding two lines of the stanza would summarize the worldly follies Lust is advocating. Add. 36983 avoids the crux, reading 'to sitte at tauerne alle in fere' (95).

40. Cf. the gloating self-revelations of the hags representing the Deadly Sins in Guillaume de Deguileville's *Pèlerinage de la vie humaine*: see R. Tuve, *Allegorical Imagery*, pp. 174 ff.

vertu' (324), and welcomes Coueitise instead, the traditional vice of old men.[41] But in his sixties he grows contrite as his physical powers decline, meekly accepting the taunts of Youth, who bids him 'Hange up þin hachet & take þi reste' (346).[42] The debate between Youth and Age is not an exchange of mutual recriminations: instead Youth, somewhat oddly perhaps,[43] becomes Age's moral counsellor, rebuking him for misspending his earlier years, and warning him that 'God wole haue rekenyng of al þis' (440).

Meekness's warning that Pride 'ȝeueþ but woo & wyssche(s) to wage' (138) has proved true of all the Sins, and Age complains 'Now haue y nouȝt but wisschis to wage' (381). After 392, L omits a stanza found in the four most complete of the other manuscripts, possibly because the next stanza covers what it says, and in fact starts by repeating its seventh line.[44] This next stanza is a cumulative list of the old man's misfortunes, each line ending with 'me' as object to the rhyming word. The old man finds himself forsaken by the false world, hated by the Sins he loved, accused before Conscience, and

41. Examples could be multiplied. Cf. Aristotle, *Ars Rhetorica*, ed. Ross, p. 103/14-15: αἵ τε γὰρ ἐπιθυμίαι ἀνείκασι καὶ δουλεύουσι τῷ κέρδει [their passions have slackened off and they are enslaved to gain]. Pope Innocent's old man is 'tenax ac cupidus' [grasping and greedy]: *Lotharii Cardinalis De Miseria Humane Conditionis*, ch. X (on old age), ed. M. Maccarrone (Padua, 1955), p. 16; also *P.L.* 217, 706. Chaucer's Criseyde knows that 'elde is ful of coveytise', and plans to bribe her father to allow her to return to Troilus: *Troilus and Criseyde* IV 1369 ff., ed. Robinson, pp. 455-6. In Medwall's *Nature*, I, 1243 and II, 989-92, ed. A. Brandl, *Quellen des Weltlichen Dramas in England vor Shakespeare* (Strassburg, 1898), pp. 73-158, Man sets little store by the counsel of Covetyse until he begins to grow old.

42. A conventional expression, occurring, e.g. in *The Owl and the Nightingale*, 658, ed. E. G. Stanley (Manchester, 1960, 1972), and in *Sir Gawain and the Green Knight*, 477, where it is used both figuratively and literally.

43. In *The Parlement of the Thre Ages*, ed. M. Y. Offord (E.E.T.S. 246, 1959), Old Age preaches to Youth and Middle Age. Anne Kernan, 'Theme and Structure in *The Parlement of the Thre Ages*', *Neuphilologische Mitteilungen* 75 (1974), 253-78, argues that the poem is a series of variations on the theme of mortality. For an attempt to find correspondences between youth, middle and old age and the Dowel, Dobet and Dobest sections of *Piers Plowman*, see John F. Adams, '*Piers Plowman* and the Three Ages of Man', *J.E.G.P.* 61 (1962), 23-41.

44. Hence, no doubt, the omission in P, by homoeoteleuton, of the last two lines of this stanza that is lacking in L. See the description of P in note 5 above.

awaited by fiends and hell-hounds. In two vivid metaphors he anti-
cipates the coming of death:

> Deeþ seiþ, my breed he haþ baken me;
> Now schakeþ he his spere to smite me (399-400).[45]

At this point, following Man's decline, contrition and expectation
of death, it is perhaps surprising that so much of the poem is left,
and that Man has yet four periods of life ahead of him, as if to draw
out as much as possible that season when repentance is repentance indeed. As a homiletic device the Ages of Man has the disadvantage of
seeming to invite the delay of repentance till old age (for why should
not *Juventus* have a rosary as well as *Senectus?*), otherwise the climax
would come too soon for dramatic convenience. But it would be a travesty in the manner of Jaques to suggest that the scheme of the Ages
unwittingly approves the Fiend's proverb 'ȝonge saynt alde devell';
more apposite is Gregory's interpretation of the labourers' enter-
ing the vineyard at the eleventh hour: 'Et si Deo vivere in pueritia
et juventute noluistis, saltem in ultima aetate resipiscite' [if you
weren't willing to live for God in childhood and youth, at least come
to your senses now your time is nearly up].

Two stanzas (449-64), of which the first looks like an uncancelled
draft of the second, since the second incorporates the ideas of the
first and adds more of the traditional signs of old age, describe Youth
and Age as two thieves, one stealing from and the other on the
ageing Man.[46]

> ȝougþe steeliþ from me, Y ȝeede up riȝte;
> Age steeleþ on me, Y bowe and ȝeelde (459-60).

P has 'I hokke & helde' [I bend and stoop]. Besides the crooked
back and the unsteady gait, other traditional signs of old age are
nervous irritability, cowardice and frigidity. For L 462 'Y wexe on-

---

45. Two stanzas later the author uses another, of special interest because it
recurs in *Hamlet:*
> God-is seruauntis in areest haþ þee take
> Til deeþ on þee haue doon bataile (413-4).

Here B.L. Add. 36983 reads 'seriaunt'. See M. C. Pecheux, 'Another Note on
"This fell sergeant, Death"', *Shakespeare Quarterly* 26 (1975), 74-5.
46. Cf. Horace, *Ars Poetica*, 175-6: 'anni venientes . . . recedentes' [the young
see the years as they come, the old as they go].

mylde' P reads 'cowardyse & unbelde' [timidity], and has Youth proudly fighting Man in the next line, where L reads 'ʒougþe steeleþ my corage To pleie & fiʒte'. Finally, what in P is simply another sign of old age, 'Age steleþ on me to suffre myche chelde', becomes in L the climax of the section: 'Age is so on me stoolen þat y mote to god me ʒilde' (464).[47]

At ninety the old man finds himself 'But skyn & boon' (492), deserted by his friends (like Everyman) and by the Sins he loved so well: he laments 'Now y am vndure Fortunes whele' (493).[48] At this age Conscience defeats Wanhope in the most dramatic of the debates in the poem, attacking him as 'þou dotid hoore' (561) when he misquotes Scripture in order to prevent Man from repenting, and because

> Þou wenest þi wickidnesse were moore
> Þan god-is goodnesse & his mercie (563-4).[49]

Man's sinful past continually returns to chide him. When the Sins (apart from Slouþe and Coueitise, whom Age favours) have announced that they have left him (505-20), when Conscience has defeated Wanhope, and when Man is calling for the Virtues, Conscience ungenerously reminds him 'þou flemed us from þee' (573), and Richelees presents instead his company: 'þe synnes þat þou louedist & seruedist' (576). However, in the last decade Good Hope comes to rescue Man from his six enemies, the World, his Flesh, Wanhope,

---

47. For the signs of old age see G. R. Coffman, 'Old Age from Horace to Chaucer: Some Literary Affinities and Adventures of an Idea', *Speculum* 9 (1934), 249-77.

48. For examples of the fusion of the theme of the Ages of Man with that of Fortune, see S. C. Chew in *Adams Studies*, pp. 167-8, and Rosemary Woolf, *The English Religious Lyric in the Middle Ages* (Oxford, 1968), p. 334.

49. The passage (537-68) is used in *Mundus & Infans*, 858-67, though without Wanhope's egregious misapplications of Scripture. The efficacy of divine mercy is the subject of *Merci passiþ riʒtwisnes*, a dialogue between Mercy and a sinner, ed. Furnivall (E.E.T.S. 24, 1867), pp. 95-100, from MS. Lambeth 853, and ed. Auvo Kurvinen, *Neuphilologische Mitteilungen* 73 (1972), 181-91, from MS. Porkington 10, which has six extra stanzas and where 'þe synner' is called 'Ryʒt'. The basic text is Psalm 144, 9, 'miserationes eius super omnia opera eius', a favourite: quoted, e.g. in *Piers Plowman* B xvii 312a (318∝ in the Kane-Donaldson edition, London, 1975), *Do Merci bifore thi Jugement* 40 (E.E.T.S. 24, p. 19), *The Mirror* 608, *The Castle of Perseverance* 3456a, *Mankind* 224 (E.E.T.S. 262, p. 161), and *Youth* 105-9.

Hell hounds, Fiends and Death (593-600).[50] After 624 P uniquely inserts three stanzas in which Man rejects each of the Deadly Sins. Having thus made his confession, Man asks for God's mercy to be sown among his seed, 'And Repentaunce my corne schal weede' (627). Then the Ten Commandments are the lock, and the Seven Works of Mercy and the Creed are the keys, to let him in at Heaven's gate.

Here B. L. Add. 36983 concludes uniquely with a four-line prayer that we may all have grace to come to Heaven, other manuscripts extending a similar sentiment over two stanzas (633-48). L and Pepys 1584 have a concluding stanza in a different rhyme scheme from the rest of the poem. The writer of L requests the reader to 'Praie for þe soule þat wroot þis tale' (651); the writer of Pepys 1584 is more specific: 'prey for þe soule of percivale' (f. 28ʳ).

Whatever precedents the lugubrious Jaques may have had for his jaundiced view of the Ages of Man, in none of which he saw any virtue or moral warning, they could hardly have included the comprehensive survey of the moral struggle between Conscience and Sin contained in the 'poem clepid þe seuene ages'. Jaques' speech on the Ages is intended to reveal something of his character, but *The Mirror's* purpose is unabashedly didactic:

> Now in þis mirrour loke ȝou soo:
> In ȝoure free wille þe choice lijs,
> To heuen or helle whiþir ȝe wille goo (638-40).

---

50. Good Hope is naturally the supplanter of Wanhope. In *Piers Plowman, the B Version*, ed. Kane and Donaldson (London, 1975), xvii 315, 'Good hope, þat helpe sholde, to wanhope torneþ'. In Skelton's *Magnyfycence*, 2309-24, ed. R. L. Ramsay (E.E.T.S. E.S. 98, 1906), p. 72, Good Hope, in a dramatic scene possibly based on a livelier comic one in *Mankind*, puts Despair and Mischief to flight as they are trying to persuade Magnyfycence to kill himself. In *Faerie Qveene* I ix 52 similar help is brought to the suicidal Redcrosse Knight by Una, but in the following canto (x, 21-2) Spenser appropriately allocates the task of rescue to Speranza.

A ROMAN THOUGHT

Renaissance Attitudes to History Exemplified in Shakespeare and Jonson

George K. Hunter

This paper will set out to discover what attitudes Tudor historians, translators of Roman history and some Elizabethan and Jacobean dramatists, held to the Roman past. One might suppose that these different groups had distinct aims, in that the latter were interested in Roman history mainly as a source of local colour or background to theatrical adventures where the former were in search of the facts of the case as they really occurred. Neither of these expectations is, however, fulfilled. The historians and the dramatists were both caught up by the pressure of the myth (as against the facts) of Rome, by the sense of the past as significant because of the values it has bequeathed to the present.

Some pressure of this kind is, in fact, a constant feature of historiography, and without it history-writing would probably be impossible. The facts of the past only acquire shape and order when the mould of particular questions forces out specific meanings. It is the historian's act of asking questions that determines the hierarchy of facts in the answers; and the historian, of course, asks the questions that the age (and the individual in the age) thinks relevant, largely because these allow the past to contribute to the present and be understood by it. The myth of the past forces the facts to dance attendance on the present's configurations, whether in confirmation or denial.

The exact nature of the pressure exerted by the myth of Rome on the historians and dramatists of the Tudor period is, however, rather different from that found in the modern world. Today, different kinds of questions about the past seem relevant, and different techniques for answering these questions have come into being (archaeological dating, economic analysis of surviving evidence, etc.). For the Elizabethans the prime material to work on was the patchwork of praise and blame of Roman achievement that the Roman historians had left behind them; and the principal problem was of fitting the norms of value that this implied into the value-confirming framework of the contemporary world.

The very word 'Roman' had a value-bearing content as well as
the more objective historical/geographical one. In *Antony and
Cleopatra* I.ii we are told of Antony, 'He was dispos'd to mirth; but
on the sudden/A Roman thought hath struck him'.[1] This would not
be a point worth making, were we dealing only with the geographical
sense of the word 'Roman'; Antony, as a Roman, must have 'Roman
thoughts' every time he thinks. But the word means more than this:
'Roman', as we easily recognize, carries the sense of a set of virtues,
thought of as characterizing Roman civilization – soldierly, severe,
self-controlled, disciplined. The point is highlighted in *Antony and
Cleopatra* by the co-presence of an Egyptian culture, thought of as
opposite. But the meaning does not require this underlining. In
Coriolanus, when the soldiers run away, Martius says they are,
'Though in Rome littered, not Romans' (III.i.239). The distinction
I am labouring could not be more clear.

This ethical sense of 'Roman' was transmitted to the Tudors, as
to the rest of Europe, and for century after century, in a series of
images of virtue held up as models or secular *mirabilia*, propagated
in tapestries and pictures, stained-glass, medallions, poems, speeches
of welcome and even plays. The earliest plays we hear of in the Tudor
court deal with precisely this range of figures – Mutius Scevola who
burned off the hand that had failed to stab Lars Porsenna, Alucius
who became Rome's ally when overcome by the magnanimity of
Scipio, Virginia who *'lively expressed a rare example of the virtue
of chastity . . . in wishing rather to be slain at her own father's hands
than to be deflowered of the wicked judge Apius'*,[2] and, of course,
Lucrece. What we are dealing with here might be called romantic
history or rather historical romance, familiar to us from tales of
Cavaliers and Roundheads or Saxons and Normans. But it is a
rather unusual kind of romance, a self-indulgent daydream of a
distant world of political simplicity, in which there was no space for
self-indulgence.

The romantic power of these images is in fact so great because
they are not simply daydreams; for they have a powerful claim (or

1. The edition of Shakespeare used here and elsewhere is that of Peter Alexan-
    der (London, 1951).
2. From the title page of *A New Tragicall Comedie of Apius & Virginia*, 'Im-
    printed at London, by William How', 1575. For the plays mentioned, see
    Appendix B.

seemed to have, on the evidence available) to be not only highly coloured but also true. This is why historians and playwrights could share so many assumptions about the Roman past. The idea of a small city-state which conquered the world, and did so because it had first conquered its own passionate weaknesses, has a great deal of apparent evidence to support it. Certainly ages like the so-called Enlightenment, which were contemptuous of the delusions of poetry and the romance of religion, remained enthralled by the spell of the togaed Senate and the lictor's *fasces*, and remained enthralled precisely because these were (or seemed to be) accurate images of a real piece of history, a real mode of social organization.

This seductive combination of political truth and aesthetic power has, I fear, faded from the modern scene. This is partly, I suppose, because the evident truth of Roman institutions as the sources of our own institutions has become less clear. Archaeology and Relativism have combined to detach the Roman world from our own one and to place it among other remote civilizations – Etruscan, Aztec, Chinese, for example – with an equal claim to *truth*, not only in the sense that 'it really happened thus' but also in the sense that their institutions are seen, like Rome's, as adequate responses to a particular set of circumstances and stimuli, and explicable in these terms rather than in any framework of teleology leading to our present situation, or in any framework of general evaluation. In modern terms, in short, the *truth* about the Roman past has become detached from our romantic and evaluative sense of its heroic achievements, the greatness of the shadow it has cast over succeeding ages. This is a divorce which has been arranged to benefit Truth, but (as in many divorces) the arrangement has had a markedly depressive effect on the discarded partner, the one that we may call Romance, but which earlier ages were willing to entitle *Greatness* or *Heroism*. Historical Truth has been freed to live in some kind of a liaison with Science, but Historical Romance has had in consequence to serve the stereotypes of shoddy wish-fulfilment, mothering a tribe of sentimental fictions from *The Last Days of Pompeii* to *Ben Hur* and *Quo Vadis*.

The Tudor and Stuart writers were innocent of these perils of relativism. The Roman past was to them not simply *a* past but *the* past, and, therefore, a subject necessarily evaluative, since it led to the present. Roman culture was not simply one competitor for attention among several, but supplied, in fact, the only possible range of meanings that would have attached to the word *culture*, if it had existed. The adequacy of national or modern culture seemed to be measurable, then, only to the extent that it could reproduce or rival the qualities of Roman culture. The combination of Romance and Truth in Roman history thus offered a set of evaluative norms by which the achievements of modern men and modern nations could be measured; indeed, the principal interest of history was that it provided a set of norms or ideals of conduct.

I have spoken of the modern divorce between the *truth* of a historical sequence, seen as quite separate from the world in which we live, and the *romance* of actions that are brought into an evaluative relationship with our own experience as models (either *horrenda* or *miranda*), and suggested that this divorce was not present for the Elizabethans. Strictly speaking that is correct. But there is a distribution of emphasis among Elizabethan and Jacobean writers that sets up interesting pointers towards the modern situation, and this is the real subject of my discourse. I wish to stress the point that the distinction in attitudes to Roman history which I perceive among English writers of the sixteenth and seventeenth centuries is one of emphasis only. This is important to my thesis because what I seek to derive my critical points from is the proximity of the alternatives and their capacity to overlap, rather than from any extremes of difference that can be set between them. A modern attempt to mediate between *Ben Hur* (say) and Theodor Mommsen would seem to be doomed to necessary failure, since the coherence that one demanded would necessarily rule out the coherence the other required. But Shakespeare's *Julius Caesar* and Ben Jonson's *Sejanus* are not only interestingly unlike (and unlike in ways that mark the polarity between *Truth* and *Romance*), but also interestingly like; the dialogue between these works (which I shall attempt to report at a later stage) is fruitfully open.

Julius Caesar and *Sejanus* (usually dated 1599 and 1603) occupy a crucial period of time, inside the great decade (1598–1608) when nearly all the best plays on Roman history were being written. On either side of this decade stretch developing attitudes which eventually create a gap in attitude as large as that between *The Mirror for Magistrates* and Thomas Hobbes – a gap between the attitude to history which sees it as determined by men (to put it crudely) and as (on the other hand) determined by events. It would no doubt be wrong to say that the Roman plays of the central decade (or so) are

great by the external reason that a competition or dialectic of alternatives was freely available at this point. But one can argue that the
passion and commitment that Shakespeare and Jonson were able to
bring to Roman history, and the human complexity they were able
to derive from it, depended on command of a range of vocabulary,
both truthful and romantic, then easy to use and elsewhere more
difficult to hold together.

A survey of sixteenth-century English translations of the Roman
historians provides, I think, a useful index to the way in which attitudes to the Roman past changed throughout the Tudor period (see
Appendix A). Such a survey throws up one central and, to me, always
surprising point – the point that though comment and translation
of Roman history was continuous from 1520 onwards, the major
Roman historians, Livy and Tacitus, were not translated till the very
end of Elizabeth's reign – Tacitus in 1591 and 1598, Livy in 1600.

Given the mouth-honour accorded to Rome, one would have
expected something else. But I think one can see why the complete
translation of these authors (or of what has survived from them)
posed particular difficulties for Tudor writers. Livy and Tacitus
(even in their truncated remains) offer us an overall interpretation
of the sweep of Roman history from Romulus to Vespasian, create
a pattern of organic rise and fall which not only separates the Roman
State from the modern world, but does so in terms of an ethic that
denies the official beliefs of the modern world as Tudor historians
were given to understand them. Livy and Tacitus are agreed (to sim-
plify grossly) that the characteristic virtues of Rome, those much-
prized ethical norms, *fides, pudicitia, libertas, concordia, disciplina,*
are essentially republican in their social context, and so are set
implacably against kingship, seen as the effeminizing degradation of
Eastern tyrants, the state towards which all single rule naturally
degenerates.

This was, of course, an attitude to rule quite counter to that which
the Tudor monarchs were assiduously promoting, and to which many
Humanist scholars were committed on theoretical as well as prudential grounds. It is impossible to be dogmatic about cause and effect,
but it is possible to hazard a guess that Tudor historians, so long as
they looked to the past for models of conduct that could be regene-
rated in the present, were inhibited from offering more than fragments of conduct, speeches, campaigns, lives, leaving the larger Livy
and Tacitus pattern to look after itself. Certainly this is what we find

when we list the English translations. Thus (to select, but not, I hope, to falsify – cf. Appendix A) the only English translation of Livy in the sixteenth century, Sir Antony Cope's *The history of the two most noble captains of the world, [H]anibal and Scipio, of their divers battles and victories, exceeding profitable to read, gathered and translated into English out of Titus Livius and other authors by Antony Cope*, 1544 (reprinted 1548, 1561, 1590), effectively turns a political process into an ethical lesson: as the printer tells us in his poem before the book, Hannibal lost the war because Scipio had the greater virtue:

THO. Berthelet on this history

Who so ever desireth for to read
Martial prowess, feats of chivalry
That may him profit at time of need
Let him in hand take this history
That showeth the sleights and policy,
The wily trains of witty Anniball,
The crafty deceipts full oft whereby
He gave his puissant enemies a fall.

Of worthy stomach and courage valiant,
Of noble heart and manly enterprise,
Of gentleness, of mind sure and constant,
Of government prudent ware and wise
Shall find according to his device
This prince Scipio, this mighty Roman,
Which all fon[d] pleasure ever did despise
In continence a lord and sovereign.

Lo thus may men plainly here behold
That wily wit, power, guise nor policy
Could Anniball ever still uphold
But that by Scipio's worthy chivalry,
His manhood, virtue and deeds knightly
He was subdued, there is no more to sayne;
And yet to speak as truth will verify
There was never found a better captain.

Chivalry is a recurrent word[3] in the prefatory matter of the translations of Roman historians, and I think one can see why. It is a word
which links prowess in the public field of war with inner or private
or personal virtue, implies, indeed, that these are two sides to one
coin. Scipio's public success was due to, or at least intimately connected with, his private moral qualities. This is an equation that any
impartial or extended survey of history would find it difficult to sustain; but in limited and specially selected contexts the point can be
asserted and pushed home in terms of present-day conduct. Cope
not only tells his dedicatee – King Henry VIII – that the translation
is appropriate to the present time of war:

> Wherefore well pondering the time of war to be now in hand
> as a thing so much needful for many considerations, I (for my
> poor part) thought that I should do not only to your highness
> acceptable service but also to all noble men and gentlemen of the
> realm great pleasure and commodity . . . (sig. a3),

but further tells the king that 'who so beholdeth the conduct of your
grace's wars in Spain, France, Britain [Brittany] and Scotland . . .
shall find the triumph thereof much more worthy of glory than any
that ever Livius wrote upon' (sig. a3ᵛ). The flattering implication
is clear: as with Scipio, Henry's virtue will cause him to win; and his
victory will prove the fact of his virtue.

A translation of a similar kind, with similar ethical and patriotic
motives, is Christopher Watson's version of Polybius, Book I:
*The histories of the most famous and worthy chronographer Polybius,
discoursing of the wars betwixt the Romans and Carthaginians, a rich
and goodly work containing wholesome counsels and wonderful devices against the incumbrances of fortune. Annexed an abstract of the
worthy acts perpetrated by King Henry V* (1568). What is in some
ways the most interesting part of this book is Watson's explanation
of how he came to write it: *To the questioners. Those which are
desirous to know the causes why I joined this abridgement of K. Henry*

---

3. See (for example) Golding's dedication of his *Trogus* (1570) to Edward de
   Vere: 'Great men idle read histories . . . for what can be a greater enforcement
   to chivalry', or Barclay's translation of Sallust's *Jugurtha* (c. 1520), dedicated
   to the Duke of Norfolk: . . . *a right fruitful history . . . right necessary unto
   every degree, but especially to gentlemen which covet to attain to clear fame
   and honour by glorious deeds of chivalry.*

V his life to this foreign history. He explains that after the labour of reading Aristotle, he sought recreation and thought that he might read histories for this purpose.

> So I raught to our English chronicles compiled by Edward Hall which by fortune lay open at that present in the life of King Henry the fift, where was noted in the margent, *the Oration of Henry Chickley Archbishop of Canterbury*, which oration I read over, and at the end a reply to the same, made by the right honourable Lord Rafe, earl of Westmoreland, a man of no less gravity than experience . . . [In Westmoreland's oration] There lacked no copy of examples, as of the Persians, the Africans, the Greeks, and especially of the Romans, by diverse other nations, yea of England and Scotland. When I had perused the mellifluous oration of this worthy orator and mighty magistrate I determined with myself to read some of the famous histories out of which he had picked such pleasant pearls, and especially, before the rest, that history intreating of the wars made by the Romans for Sicily and the city of the Samnites, out of the which he had collected the most firm and infringible arguments of his oration.

His translation is thus justified very clearly by the light it is thought to throw on Anglo-French rivalry, the traditional scene of English prowess, and the motive it supplies for military action in the present. As R.W. tells us in his poem *in laudem Histor. Polybij, Anglico lectori:*

> If famous facts
> Or worthy acts
> Rejoice thy daunted mind
> Polybius read
> Whereas in deed
> Good physic thou shalt find.
>
> . . . . .
> Of captains stout
> Which fought it out
> Their country to defend.

> Then virtue learn
> That thou mayst earn
> Such glories for to have
> As Momus sect
> Can not reject
> When thou art closed in grave.

The alternative to this fragmentation of Roman history into small and manageable ethico-historical vignettes is to find an over-all model which allows the historian to run counter to what I have described as the Livy-Tacitus or vulgate interpretation. This would seem to be the aim of William Fulbecke in a very curious book dated 1601 (by which date it is, I suppose, something of a Parthian shot): *An abridgement or rather a bridge of Roman Histories to pass the nearest way from Titus Livius to Cornelius Tacitus*, also known as *A Historical Collection of the Continual Factions, Tumults and Massacres of the Romans and Italians during the space of 120 years next before the peaceable Empire of Augustus Caesar*. For Fulbecke the expulsion of the Tarquins was a disaster for the Romans, who thereby changed gold for brass, 'and loathing one king suffered manie tyrants' (sig. B1). There is also, of course, good Christian reason for such recasting. Augustine had seen Rome as the city of fratricidal conflict, of Cain and Abel, Romulus and Remus, and from a medieval point of view represented most easily for us by Dante, the establishment of the Empire was a crucial stage in God's plan for a Christian world. But one must suppose that Fulbecke's most immediate motivation was the desire to make the progression of Roman history conform to the expectations of Tudor political doctrine.

Yet another alternative open to the Tudor translators of Roman historians can be represented by the work of W.B., probably William Barker, lately secretary to the Duke of Norfolk and in 1571 imprisoned in the Tower for his implication in the Ridolfi plot – from which he escaped by denouncing his late master.[4] Barker's background may help to explain the somewhat hysterical endorsements of monarchy that his *Appian* contains, as from a man trying to work his passage back into political favour; but it is only a hysterical form of the common assumption. Barker's choice of Appian almost made his point for him. Appian of Alexandria (fl. *c.* A.D. 160) wrote to des-

---

4. *Shakespeare's Appian*, edited by Ernest Schanzer (Liverpool, 1956).

102 GEORGE K. HUNTER

cribe the Romans as warriors. His history is a history of campaigns, in Spain, Libya, Macedonia, Syria, etc., and also of the civil wars in Rome (Books 13–17 of the 24 books he wrote). Barker only really seriously manipulates this material by putting the civil wars first; but notice what capital he is able to make out of it in the title-page: *An ancient history and exquisite chronicle of the Roman wars, both civil and foreign . . . in which is declared: Their greedy desire to conquer others. Their mortal malice to destroy themselves. Their seeking of matters to make wars abroad. Their picking of quarrels to fall out at home. All the degrees of sedition and all the effects of ambition . . . And finally an evident demonstration that people's rule must give place and princes' power prevail . . . With a continuation . . .* (to the Principate) (1578).

The notion that the Empire was the goal of the historical process and a safe haven for political virtue seems, however, to have had little effect on sixteenth-century playwrights. The animation of *Romanitas* in the theatre remained obstinately fixed on the ethical models that the Republic provided. Shakespeare's *Rape of Lucrece* of 1594 (like Heywood's play of the same title of *c.* 1607) condemns the Tarquins and exalts Collatinus and Brutus just as Livy does. Of the 29 Roman plays whose texts or titles are known to us before 1602, only six deal with the Empire, and of these six five (*Julian the Apostate* of 1566, *Titus and Vespasian* of 1592, *Diocletian* of 1594, *Julian the Apostate* (again) of 1596 and *Constantine* of 1599) are presumably (all have perished) stories of Christian triumph and pagan wickedness (like *Ben Hur* and *The Sign of the Cross*). The sixth (*Heliogabalus* of 1594) seems unlikely, given its hero, to have stressed the virtues of imperial rule. But again, we cannot be sure, for this play also has perished. (See Appendix B.)

Matthew Gwinne's Latin play *Nero* of 1603 (written for performance in St John's College, Oxford) and Ben Jonson's public theatre play *Sejanus*, also of 1603, seem to have been the first plays in England to treat the matter of imperial history in political terms. The coincidence of dates may point to the fact that by this time attitudes to Roman history had begun to change. To stick to the evidence supplied by English translations, Barker's translation of Appian in 1578 and North's translation of Plutarch's *Lives* in 1579 seem to mark the end of one phase of translating activity. The next English translations, Sir Henry Savile's rendering of Tacitus in 1591, completed by Greneway in 1598, and Philemon Holland's *Livy* of 1600,

belong to a rather different world, a world in which the centrality of
the single hero is increasingly being compromised by the sense that
success in politics has little or nothing to do with ethics.

What had happened, one may argue, is that England had begun,
at the end of the century, to catch up with currents of thought that
had been around in continental Europe for some time. The attitude
to historiography that we may associate with the names of Machiavelli, Guicciardini, Bodin or Lipsius only began to affect English
history writing in the fifteen-nineties. English translations again
supply an index of what seemed interesting to the decade and we may
note the cluster of titles such as Lipsius' *Politica* (trans. 1596), Bodin's
Commonwealth (trans. 1603), Montaigne's *Essays* (entered for publication in an English translation in 1595, and finally published in
1603), as well as Bacon's *Essays* of 1596, and Sir John Hayward's
'political history' of Henry IV (1599).[5] The new attitudes that these
titles imply were, of course, at this point still the expression of a
minority *avant-garde* taste. But Roman history was a particularly
sharp area of discrimination, and in this field the nature of the opposition declared itself with some rapidity, for Tacitus was the author
around whom much of the controversy turned. Diggory Whear
in his published lectures as the first Camden praelector in history at
Oxford[6] reports an exchange between Lipsius and Casaubon which
neatly sums up the role and importance of Tacitus. Lipsius supposed that Tacitus was an author who ought to be in the hands of every
prince, since he avoided *mirabilia* and legends:

> *Non ille Annibalis funestas Romanis victorias, non speciosam*
> *Lucretiae necem, non vatum prodigia aut Etrusca portenta recen-*
> *set, et quae alia sunt oblectandi magis quam instruendi Lectoris . . .*
> *Inveniens sub tyrannide adulationes, delationes, non ignota huic*
> *saecula mala . . . etc.*

Casaubon, on the other hand, thought Tacitus most unsuitable reading for princes and governors. His concentration on vices and petti-
nesses did not allow his history to form the proper basis of generali-

5. See S. L. Goldberg, 'Sir John Hayward, "politic" historian', *R.E.S.* vi (1955),
   233–44.
6. Diggory Whear, *De ratione et methodo legendi utrasque historias, civiles et
   ecclesiasticas dissertatio* (Oxford, 1633), cap. xxi.

zation about human destiny: *Historiam nihil aliud esse quam Philosophiam exemplis utentem.*

For Jonson and the English *avant-garde*, Tacitus offered an acerb and disenchanted observation of the gradual strangulation, under the Empire, of all those ethical wonders of Republican Rome that I spoke about at the beginning of my essay. What Giuseppe Toffanin, the Italian critic, has described as *il Tacitismo*[7] was already, of course, widespread in European political thought and flowed into England from many sources.[8] But all shared a sense that here was a view of history and life that was *plus propre* (as Montaigne remarked) *à un estat trouble et malade, comme est le nostre present.*[9] Even Tudor patriotism could not wholly stem the tide of disenchantment and scepticism, though for long enough the two attitudes preserved their strained relationship intact (as I have noted above). Was 'the State' an ethically neutral machine for self-perpetuating the possessors of power as Tacitus seems to imply and modern theorists repeated? Or was it a value-bearing institution laid down by God or Fate to protect *His* subjects? All the intellectual prestige of 1600 was on the former possibility, and Jonson and others clearly thought of Shakespeare and Plutarch as slow-witted provincials who hadn't caught up. If the former is the case, then the Empire (as against the Republic) becomes a suitable subject for a literature of satiric or tragic perceptions. Imperial history then becomes an appropriate cockpit for a display of individual destiny, only found real when the legends of a special Roman virtue crumble before *realpolitik.* Certainly the English stage shifts its emphasis in the seventeenth century. After Jonson's *Catiline* of 1611, seven out of the eleven known plays on Roman history deal with the empire (compare the figures for the sixteenth century, given above) – usually with its gloomier tyrants, and the same range of drama shows Jonson's influence predominant over Shakespeare's.

But in the decade around the turn of the century the balance of forces is more equal. The Jonsonian view of the distinction between himself and Shakespeare is clearly formulated, and easy to believe;

7. Giuseppe Toffanin, *Machiavelli e il 'Tacitismo'* (Padova, 1921).
8. See my essay 'English folly and Italian vice' in *Jacobean Theatre*, ed. J. R. Brown and B. Harris (1960), esp. pp.96ff.
9. *Essais*, III.viii. *Essais de Michel de Montaigne*, ed. Albert Thibaudet (Bruges, 1939), p. 913.

but it leaves too much unexplained. It is true that Shakespeare is closely dependent on Plutarch, and on one English translation of Plutarch, where Jonson, as the margins of his *Sejanus* amply inform us, had read, digested and reworked the whole of Silver Latin literature.

The stereotypes of Art and Nature misrepresent not only Shakespeare, but also Plutarch. The *Lives* are, of course, not histories, but their concentration on the ethical content of individual careers by no means repeats the Tudor praise of noble captains or ancient models of chivalry. Bodin certainly thought Plutarch too much a moralist to be a reliable historical witness, too quick with judgements, too much (as he says) a *principum censor*. He was particularly unimpressed by the method of parallelism as a technique of history: *Quid autem aliud est Agesilaum Pompeio quam muscam elephanto conferre?*[10]

Bodin's contempt, and the easy antithesis with Jonson, make it sound as if Shakespeare in reproducing or merely dramatizing Plutarch's *Lives* was falling back into the Tudor habit of setting up isolated deeds of the past as analogies to the present. Some critics have indeed argued this. But perhaps we should see Shakespeare as *using* Plutarch rather than as simply stumbling across him and thinking what magnetic images these were. Plutarch's point of view may be seen as precisely what Shakespeare was searching for at this point in his career, an escape from the assumption – necessarily implicit in the English histories – that personal qualities and political success are somehow interdependent. But before we accede to Bodin's view of Plutarch's *Lives* as an evasion of historical objectivity, we should remember that Plutarch was the favourite author of that idol of the *avant-garde*, Montaigne, who refers to him as 'the most judicious author of the world.'[11] Montaigne makes the same distinction between historian and moralist as Bodin, but entirely to the discredit of the mere historian: 'What profit is it . . . to read Plutarch? . . . [We read him] not so much to know the date of the ruin of Carthage as the manners of Hannibal and Scipio . . . not so much to know histories as to judge of them'.[12]

What the notion of Shakespeare's Tudor backwardness in choos-

10. See his *Methodus ad facilem historiarum cognitionem* (1566), Bk. IV.
11. *Essais*, II.xxxi.
12. *Essais*, I.xxvi.

ing Plutarch rather than Tacitus as his model conceals from our
understanding is that Plutarch's *Lives* do not offer us models of
personal-and-political praise and blame in the manner of the Tudor
historians, but rather a concentration on the inexplicable individuality of personal lives, seen together with the tortuousness of the process by which subjective traits become objective and politically significant facts. Plutarch resolutely asks private questions about public
men, and Shakespeare follows him in this, but neither blindly (he
had reached the point in his thinking where this was his own obvious
next question), nor without modification. Modification was indeed
inevitable. Plutarch wrote his *Lives* for an audience still living more
or less inside the political system and cultural assumptions of most
of his heroes. The political contexts of their public lives could,
therefore, remain implicit. For Shakespeare, however, creating
plays – i.e. coherent social worlds – for an audience with different
and indeed opposed political beliefs, meant making quite explicit
the nature of the alternative political possibilities that give the play
its definition, and the nature of the organization within which these
alternatives exist. Shakespeare's Brutus may be close to Plutarch's
Brutus, but the relationship of Shakespeare's Brutus to the whole
world described by the play has to be the invention of the playwright.

What Shakespeare offers us in *Julius Caesar* is, in fact, a highly
sophisticated piece of political thinking. If we compare this play to
some earlier Roman plays of the public theatre – Lodge's *Wounds
of Civil War* of *c*. 1588 or Shakespeare's own *Titus Andronicus* of
c. 1594 – or even to the academic *Caesar's Revenge* of *c*. 1595, we
notice at once the strength and stability that is implied of the system
within which the characters of *Julius Caesar* lead their mental as well
as their physical lives. In *Titus* the system for which Titus and others
suffer mutilation and death is hardly defined. The Roman myth
becomes a crucial factor at certain points, but elsewhere madness,
anger, family sorrow, the Goths, make us lose sight of it altogether.
Man is a political animal here only when the passionate drives of
his private life allow him to be so, but at the end of the play Titus's
private virtue and ethical constancy is given a political reward as if
this naturally follows. In *Julius Caesar*, however, the private life of
the individual is everywhere and everyhow intertwined with his
political role, as if there is no private action he can take that will
not cast an enlarged and distorted shadow into the entirely alien

and incommensurate dimension of political consequences. Shakespeare, like earlier Tudor writers, offers us for our admiration the ethical splendours of *Romanitas* in his central figure of Brutus; but like the later 'political' writers he shows us the ethical standards of *pietas, fides, pudicitia*, which Brutus and Portia display, inside a framework which forces it to seek expression in the enlarged focus of political action and then undercuts it by revealing the total irrelevance of ethics to political and historical development. In this way, *Julius Caesar* may be said to use as its basic dialectic the overlap of contrasting attitudes to Roman history that I have described above. The Empire, or 'Caesarism' as it is usually called, is seen to be inevitable and therefore in one way 'right'. In terms of the future, of predestination or necessitarianism, Brutus ought to be co-operating with the historical process. But Brutus in his opposition to all this is also 'right'. In terms of the present rather than the future, of ethical self-consciousness and free-will, he makes the right choice, and it is seen moreover as a choice which validates the past, the Republic, the original Lucius Junius Brutus, with his distrust and hatred of kingship.

Cassius and Brutus are said to be (respectively) 'the last of all the Romans' and 'the noblest Roman of them all'. What, then, are Octavian and Mark Antony? The play properly avoids asking the reductive question in this bald way. But an answer is to some degree implied by the action. 'The triumph of Caesarism', as it is usually called, controls the end of the play: it represents a force that men in the play cannot understand, however, though they can and, indeed, must respond to it, so that it is a shadow rather than a shape. The new world of the second triumvirate's proscriptions is clearly going to be a personally unpleasant world; but Shakespeare invites our attention to aspects of it other than the personal and ethical one. It is going to be a pragmatic world; it is going to work effectively, and the moral stance or personal nobility of those who direct it will not matter very much; the coming efficiency of the world will not be reduced by the fact that its directors have not invested a great deal of personal nobility in the system. The Roman Empire whose shadow lies over the deaths of Brutus and Cassius is seen as not only a political necessity but a Roman necessity. The focus of the play is not on what will come out of this dramatized slice of cataclysm, or on what the Roman Empire will be like, but rather on the way in which ethical integrity has become a tragic quality rather than a historical one, drawing its power from its capacity to fail magnificently, one might say – its power to make success and history look cheap and shallow. As Cleopatra remarks in a similar context: ''Tis paltry to be Caesar:/ Not being Fortune, he's but Fortune's knave' (*Antony and Cleopatra*, V.ii, 2–3). To this extent *Julius Caesar* may seem a reactionary or at least old-fashioned response to the new sense of history as itself a tragic destiny that was burgeoning in advanced circles in the 'nineties; but it is in fact an alternative novelty, rather than a rehash of the same old thing.

Looking at the route Shakespeare took into Roman history, through English history (he had been writing English history plays fairly continuously in the years preceding *Julius Caesar*), one can see that the Roman state offered him a *milieu* in which he could escape from the pressure of teleology – the pressure to make the English past lead up to the English present in which the theatre audience lives. He can hardly be said to assert in the Roman plays that history is a tragic destiny, but at least he has escaped from the necessity to allege that it is a happy destiny (comic in the Dantesque sense). He effectively escapes, indeed, from the necessity to make any long-term pronouncement on history at all. Plutarch allows him to concentrate on the presentness of the action rather than on its future consequences. Plutarch's *Lives* culminate inevitably in the great man's death and exert little pressure on us to enquire what happened next; and Shakespeare seems happy to endorse this folding back or self-sealing structure. Thus at the end of *Julius Caesar*, when the required praise of the dear departed has run its course Octavian concludes briskly with, '. . . Let's away/To part the glories of this happy day'. We may, if we wish, bring a sense of disillusioned irony to the *happiness* that is promised for the *parting* of these spoils. But the play does not ask us to do this. The sense of cadence, of conclusion, is too strong to allow the continuity of history to secure much of an effect.

In *Antony and Cleopatra* the historical sense that this is the end of the road, the closing of the book of the Civil Wars, is strongly felt. Octavian tells Agrippa (and us) that

> The time of universal peace is near.
> Prove this a prosperous day, the three-nook'd world
> Shall bear the olive freely.
>
> (IV.vi.5–7)

It is, however, characteristic of Shakespeare's tact that this is said nine scenes from the conclusion, and is referred to a battle which is inconclusive in itself, even though it does not contradict the truth of Octavian's *near*. The 'universal peace' is never energized in the play as any part of its dynamic; it is a blank wall erected against the end of the action, with little more content than 'lived happily ever after'. The actual end is concerned with the tomb and funeral service of the dead lovers; and our attention to *their* future has been phrased exclusively in the unhistorical terms of their behaviour in the Elysian Fields:

> Dido and her Aeneas shall want troops
> And all the haunt be ours (IV.xiv.53–4).

At the end of the action the army has become purely decorative: 'Our army shall/In solemn show attend this funeral,/And then to Rome'. Its action is phrased as a backward glance into the material of the play rather than a forward glance to new conquests. The future of Rome in terms of the Roman Empire is already in the play, one may say, as a counter-motive to the ethical qualities that are being dramatized inside its present time. The Empire is, as it were, already there in embryo in the character of the future Augustus. The conflicts that in history are extended as a sequence through time have been expressed by Shakespeare as telescoped into a spatial (rather than temporal) design bounded by the life-spans and the ethical outlooks of its central characters. Shakespeare, like Plutarch, is not writing history; he is, as Montaigne says of Plutarch, preferring judgement to knowledge.

Shakespeare's reluctance to expose fully the consequences of the actions of the present on the history of the future was no doubt one of the many aspects of Shakespeare's second Roman play that struck Ben Jonson as (in the manner of Bodin's judgement on Plutarch) an avoidance of the tragic truth of history. Shakespeare's *Julius Caesar* represents the tension between the romantic power of Roman ethics and the political knowledge that ethics could not eventually save the state; but the attitudes that emerged in Jonson's first Roman tragedy, *Sejanus*, of 1603, were not able to allow even that degree of balance between the two, let alone the concentration on ethics that appears elsewhere in Shakespeare. Jonson, more fully representative of what Hiram Haydn conveniently labels the Counter-

Renaissance,[13] seems to have seen ethics as bound to lose in any *true* description of public life. We do not know that *Sejanus* was aimed at *Julius Caesar*. We only know that Jonson remembered *Julius Caesar* for the rest of his life as a play containing Shakespearian absurdities.[14] Given the extent to which Shakespeare seems to have taken it upon himself to refashion Roman tragedy for the Elizabethan stage and to rescue it from mere romance on the one hand, and on the other hand from the static discussion form of Garnier closet drama – given this, we can hardly avoid supposing that Jonson determined to show that facile Johannes factotum the only Shake-scene of the Globe (and the rest of the world) what a Roman tragedy might really be like, if one had all classical literature and its commentators at command. At any rate Jonson seems to have shifted the focus of his play from the boys' companies, for whom he had hitherto written, and to have offered his new tragedy to Shakespeare's company. 'Not without mustard', one must suppose.[15]

The choice of the career of Aelius Sejanus for the subject of Jonson's play I take to point to the kind of significance Jonson hoped to extract from his piece. It is not, indeed, very hard to find the trigger of Jonson's intention in his principal source, Tacitus. At the beginning of the fourth book of the *Annals*, Tacitus looks back over the nine good years at the beginning of Tiberius's reign, in which imperial rule was still (as in Augustus's time) expressed through republican institutions, and notes that this suddenly changed in A.D. 23. The principate became a tyranny. 'And the cause and the beginning of the change,' Tacitus tells us, 'lay with Aelius Sejanus' (*Initium et causa penes Aelium Seianum*). An irreversible change has occurred and we are meant, I suppose, to sense the forward throw of that shadow on the next three hundred years of the Roman Empire.

In *Julius Caesar* the depressive ironies of history are well expressed: e.g. in that episode where the populace are so moved by Brutus's defence of the murder of Caesar that they shout out 'Let him be Caesar' (III.ii.50). To some extent this effect is reproduced in *Sejanus* when, Sejanus dead, the Senate welcomes Macro (the new Sejanus)

13. Hiram Haydn, *The Counter-Renaissance* (New York, 1950).
14. Ben Jonson, *Discoveries*, 'censura de poetis'.
15. Ben Jonson, *Every Man out of his Humour* (ed. Herford and Simpson), III.iv.86, and the commentators thereon.

as their deliverer from the old Sejanus. The similarity between the two plays is, however, a measure of their difference. For Shakespeare the mob's idiocy is a passing moment, serving to indicate the meaninglessness or at least difficulty of the context within which his principal figures try to realize their personal values. The values are not, however, effaced by the mob's incapacity to understand them or indeed anything that is happening. The capacity for personal nobility, for *Romanitas*, remains powerful and central, and the notion that the mob's innocence could be contained and controlled (rather than exploited) by good as well as effective men is never fully ruled out. The destructive violence of the mob after Antony's speech in the forum is represented by Shakespeare as arising from Brutus's miscalculation and Antony's opportunism rather than from any necessary law that makes historical development the prey of manipulators and places idealists among the failures. In the less deterministic work of *Julius Caesar* history seems to be made by human decisions, made inside present moments of time which *we* share with those making them. The mob violence at the end of *Sejanus* (seen in the moralized mirror of the Nuntius's speech) does not seem to involve any decisions; it is simply the visible lower end of a long chain of consequential manipulations. The mob cannot escape from the scenario that History has already written for it, its pre-determined role, any more than can the Senators or the informers or even the spider at the centre of the web, Tiberius himself. To be good exempts one, in neither play, from the pains of history; but Shakespeare allows his stoical suicides to express for future times the free Roman values of a present moment and an individual outlook that is fixed forever by the escape from flux and decay that suicide offers. But when in *Sejanus* Act III Silius kills himself rather than be censured by the Senate, we note the extent to which his gesture is made to seem pointless, and is sealed off from any consequential effect on history. His gesture has to be expressed as a defiance of the Senate, for the Senate is the 'front' organization he can see and refer to; but the Senate represents only, as he knows and as we know, a billboarding behind which the real power remains invisible and safe. So Tiberius can appear from behind the mask, wearing an air of injured innocence, and proclaim his personal sorrow at Silius's death: 'We are not pleased in this sad accident/That thus hath 'stalled and abused our mercy/Intended to preserve thee, noble Roman'. Silius's suicide simply allows his memory to be manipulated instead of his person. To avoid manipulation, the implication seems to run, you must opt out of history altogether, avoid having any point of view on any affair.

It seems clear enough that Jonson found this particular passage of Tacitus's *Annals* significant. It seemed to him to represent the hinge moment between defensible and indefensible kingship. He expects us to be interested in the historical process, so well described by Tacitus, by which the forms of liberty and open government are preserved intact, like the surface of worm-eaten veneered furniture, while the substance of political life is eaten away by the hidden forces of tyranny. The tragedy of the fall of Sejanus forms a complete story, but its general significance is that it is only one episode in the world created irreversibly by the rise of Sejanus. The manipulated impotence of both senators and plebs, who cannot take the chance offered when the new agent, Macro, is set up to replace the old one, Sejanus, extends our sense of what has happened to horizons well beyond A.D. 32. Unlike Shakespeare's Roman plays this is a dramatic action which relies for its full effect on a knowledge of the larger perspectives within which the Roman state is moving from freedom to tyranny, from manly independence to servile timidity. *Sejanus* is a difficult play to respond to if one does not have the Livy/Tacitus sense of the general sweep of Roman history already in one's mind, and especially if one brings to it the expectations of an action based on personalities of the Shakespearian kind.

This difficulty pales into insignificance beside that offered by Jonson's second tragedy, *Catiline*, of 1611. In fact, Jonson's central concerns in this play are the same as those in *Sejanus* – the slide of the Republican system of checks and balances towards the chaos of Civil war and the so-called 'rescue' operation of triumvirs and emperors. But the relationship between the particular episode that forms the substance of the play, the conspiracy of Catiline and its defeat by Cicero, and the use of this episode as an example of the way things are going, is more complex than in *Sejanus* and has, in general, been missed. The use of the ghost of Sulla as a prologue or *protatica persona* might, of course, be a warning. We may remember that the settling of Sulla's veterans was one of the triggers of discontent that fired the Catilinarian revolt.[16] Jonson, of course, does not use his prologue to narrate history, but to mimic the Senecan infernal

16. Sallust, *De Catilinae Coniuratione*, xvi.

prologue in which the crimes of the father are revivified in the fore-
cast actions of the son, but the personal relationship sketched has
clear enough historical roots:

> All that was mine, and bad, thy breast inherit.
> Alas, how weak is that for Catiline!
> Did I but say – vain voice! – all that was mine?
> All that the Gracchi, Cinna, Marius would;
> What, now, had I a body again, I could,
> Coming from hell.

We learn from ancient sources that Catiline had indeed been an
agent of Sulla's violences: *Quis erat huius* (Sullae) *imperii minister?
Quis nisi Catilina, jam in omne facinus manus exercens?*[17] but Jonson
has a still larger aim in view. It is not only their temperament and
personal contacts that associate Sulla and Catiline, but even more
their role as links in the great chain of dissidents and subverters of
Roman freedom. The dictatorship of Sulla is remembered (like the
power of Sejanus) as another of those hinge moments in the Roman
decline. As Sallust tells us (after relating the traditional republican
virtues): *Set postquam L. Sulla, armis recepta re publica, bonis initiis
malos eventus habuit; rapere omnes, trahere, domum alius alius agros
cupere; neque modum neque modestiam victores habere, foeda crudelia
in civis facinora facere.*[18]

So the revolt of Catiline is an episode whose true meaning
can only be seen in its historical context. This is more difficult
than in *Sejanus* because the apparent meaning of the plot (taken
in isolation) and the historical meaning are here at odds with
one another. On the surface *Catiline* is the story of a democratic
triumph, of a plot of subversion that failed, and Cicero is a trium-
phant hero. Even a little knowledge of Roman history tells us that
this is not the larger view; and Jonson weaves this point into his
narrative by his handling of Caesar and Crassus. He makes these
subsequent triumvirs into secret supporters of the plot (a point
Sallust and Suetonius deny), and when the plot fails they are seen to
be still too great to touch. Cato, as an absolutist of Republicanism,
seeks a showdown, but Cicero is seen to keep what is politically
possible in the forefront of his mind: *No violence. Caesar, be safe.*

17. Seneca, *De Ira* III, 18.
18. *De Catilinae Coniuratione*, xi.

The survival of Caesar and Crassus is undoubtedly intended to be, for the discerning reader, a reminder of what was to happen next: this conspiracy failed, but they didn't all fail, and Cicero's temporary triumph was only the prelude to a permanent defeat of Cicero and Cato and all they stood for. The individual, in *Catiline* as in *Sejanus*, believes himself to be making things happen, and in a limited sense he is; but the current of history moves in a more powerful sweep and will win in the end.

Both Jonson and Shakespeare see Caesar as the man of destiny, the man through whom the *Zeitgeist* breathed; but Shakespeare sees him in terms of particular successes and failures inside the large general polarizations of attitude that Roman history presented. The existence of *Titus Andronicus* shows us that these polarities of attitude, implied by the idea of Rome, existed for Shakespeare even when he was not following any Roman historian. *Titus* shows us Roman integrity, legality, inflexibility, chastity in one fictional family set against the self-indulgence, irresponsibility, lust and tyranny of another fictional group.[19] *Julius Caesar* offers us a more complex mixture of the alternatives than the *Titus*, since Julius is no mere tyrant and Brutus is no mere tyrannicide, but the same polarities remain the controlling elements of the conceptual diagram that the play contains. For Jonson, on the other hand, these Roman opposites are not so much simultaneously present alternatives within single minds in a single situation, but rather alternative ends of a historical process which carries Rome from one state to the other. He would have claimed (and virtually does claim) that this is 'truer' than Shakespeare. In the sense that History is a fair representation of the truth, one is obliged to endorse his claim. On the other hand, there is also the fair claim of a play to be an image of truth, in terms of what can be imagined to be seen and known as the internal experience of individuals rooted in a particular point of time.

It may be more instructive for us today to notice what Shakespeare and Jonson have in common rather than what separates them. Both see the same central issue in Roman history – the fatal collision of out-dated but real personal values with shallow but effective opportunism. For both of them the romance of *Romanitas* attaches to the traditional values of *fides, disciplina, pudicitia, libertas* – and for

19. See my 'Shakespeare's earliest tragedies: "Titus Andronicus" and "Romeo and Juliet" ', *Shakespeare Survey* XXVII (1974), 1–9.

both of them these values are 'placed' inside the minds of unsuccessful individuals hypnotized by the past and incompetent to change the future. The dialectic of free individual beliefs and external historical necessity commands both; but Shakespeare's preferences and techniques point towards the exaltation of the free and self-controlling individual. Jonson's techniques and preferences point him rather towards the necessities by which history crushes the individual and the present in order to extract the future.

APPENDIX A

Roman Historians translated into English 1520–1600

c. 1520　[Sallust's *Jugurtha,* translated by Alexander Barclay] *The ancient chronicle and famous history of the war and divers battles which the Romans had against the tyrant Jugurth, usurper of the kingdom of Numidy . . . a right fruitful history . . . both pleasant, profitable and right necessary unto every degree, but especially to gentlemen which covet to attain to clear fame and honour by glorious deeds of chivalry.*

1530　*Julius Caesar's Commentaries.* Newly translated into English as much as concerneth this realm of England.

1544　[Livy] *The history of the two most noble captains of the world,* [*H*]*anibal and Scipio.* Translated by Sir Antony Cope.

1550　*Herodian of Alexandria his history of 20 Roman Caesars. Relating the strange conjunctions and accidents of state that happened in Europe, Asia and Afrike in the revolution of 70 years. Interlaced with speeches, antiquities, court-passages, prodigies, embassies, sieges, surprises, battles, conquests and triumphs . . .* (etc.). Translated by N. Smith.

c. 1560　[Trogus/Justin] *The Orations of Arsanes against Philip, of the ambassadors of Venice . . . and of Scanderbeg praying aid of Christians against perjurious murdering Mahumet . . .* Translated by T. Norton.

1564　[Eutropius] *A brief chronicle wherein are described the original and the successive estate of the Roman weal.* Translated by N. Haward.

1564　*Thabridgement of the histories collected by Justine.* Translated by A. Golding. 'A work containing briefly great plenty of most delectable histories and notable examples worthy not only to be read but also to be embraced and followed of all men . . .'

1565　*The eight books of Caius Julius Caesar containing his martial exploits in Gallia.* Translated by A. Golding.

1568　*The histories of the most famous and worthy chronographer Polybius, discoursing of the wars betwixt the Romans and Carthaginians, a rich and goodly work containing wholesome counsels and wonderful devices against the incumbrances of fortune. Annexed an abstract of the worthy acts perpetrated by King Henry V.* [Book I only from Polybius] Translated by Christopher Watson.

1569　*A right noble history of the successors of Alexander taken out of Diodorus Siculus. And some of their lives written by the wise Plutarch.* [Books 18, 19, 20 of the *Bibliotheca,* together with Plutarch's life of Demetrius] Translated by Thomas Stocker [from the French of Claude de Seyssel].

1578　[Appian] *An ancient history and exquisite chronicle of the Roman wars, both civil and foreign . . . in which is declared: Their greedy desire to conquer others. Their mortal malice to destroy themselves. Their seeking of matters to make wars abroad. Their picking of quarrels to fall out at home. All the degrees of sedition and all the effects of ambition . . . And finally an evident demonstration that people's rule must give place and*

princes' power prevail . . . With a continuation . . . (to the Principate)
Translated by W.B.[arker].

1579 [Plutarch] *The lives of the most noble Grecians and Romans.* Translated
out of the French by Thomas North.

1591 *The end of Nero and Beginning of Galba. Four books of the Histories of
Cornelius Tacitus* . . . Translated by Sir Henry Savile.

1598 *The Annals of Cornelius Tacitus* . . . Translated by Richard Greneway.

1600 *The Roman history written by Titus Livius* . . . Translated by Philemon
Holland.

APPENDIX B

Elizabethan/Jacobean Plays on Roman Historical Subjects, up to 1611

Note: dates are from the Harbage-Schoenbaum *Annals;* extant plays are italicized, plays known only from titles are in italic capitals.

1564 R.B.		*Apius and Virginia*
1566		*JULIAN THE APOSTATE*
1574		*QUINTUS FABIUS*
1577		*MUTIUS SCEVOLA*
1579		*ALUCIUS*
1580		*SCIPIO AFRICANUS*
1580		*THE FOUR SONS OF FABIUS*
1581		*CAESAR AND POMPEY*
1581		*POMPEY*
1582 R. Edes,		*CAESAR INTERFECTUS*
1588 Lodge,		*The Wounds of Civil War*
1589		*SULLA DICTATOR*
1590 The Countess of Pembroke,		*Antonius* (from Garnier)
1591		*OCTAVIA*
1592		*TITUS AND VESPASIAN*
1593 Daniel,		*Cleopatra*
1594 Kyd,		*Cornelia* (from Garnier)
1594		*DIOCLETIAN*
1594		*HELIOGABALUS*
1594 Shakespeare,		*Titus Andronicus*
1595		*II CAESAR AND POMPEY*
1595 Anon,		*Caesar's Revenge*
1596		*JULIAN THE APOSTATE*
1598 S. Brandon,		*Virtuous Octavia*
1599 Shakespeare,		*Julius Caesar*
1599		*CONSTANTINE*
1599		*ZENOBIA*
1600		*JUGURTH*
1601		*HANNIBAL AND SCIPIO*
1602		*CAESAR'S FALL*
1603 M. Gwinne,		*Nero*
1603 Jonson,		*Sejanus*
1605 Marston,		*Sophonisba*
1605 Chapman,		*Caesar and Pompey*
1607 Alexander,		*Julius Caesar*
1607 Alexander,		*The Alexandrian Tragedy*
1607 Anon,		*Claudius Tiberius Nero*
1607 Heywood,		*The Rape of Lucrece*
1607 Shakespeare,		*Antony and Cleopatra*
1608 Shakespeare,		*Coriolanus*
1611 Jonson,		*Catiline*

SENSE AND INNOCENCE
Two Love Episodes in Dante and Milton

A. James Smith

Here are two celebrated portrayals of sensuous love, written four hundred years apart and spanning a European tradition of love poetry. What these episodes have in common is that both of them describe a kiss which leads on to physical fruition and is given a metaphysical consequence. In most other respects they are as dissimilar as two such sublime pieces of writing might be. The obvious difference between Dante and Milton is that they write so unlike each other, as if by contrary principles of poetic style, and I mean to ask what that contrast of styles has to do with such deeper disaccord as appears in their making opposite things of the kiss. For there's no doubt that something fundamental is at issue between the two poets here, which matters to our understanding of European love poetry if not of love itself. My purpose in this essay is to see what the disagreement between the two passages amounts to, and where it takes us.

(a)   Noi leggevamo un giorno per diletto
          di Lancialotto come amor lo strinse:
          soli eravamo e sanza alcun sospetto.
      Per piú fiate li occhi ci sospinse   130
          quella lettura, e scolorocci il viso;
          ma solo un punto fu quel che ci vinse.
      Quando leggemmo il disiato riso
          esser baciato da cotanto amante,
          questi, che mai da me non fia diviso,   135
      la bocca mi bació tutto tremante.
          Galeotto fu il libro e chi lo scrisse:
          quel giorno piú non vi leggemmo avante.
                                    (*Inferno* v, 127–38)[1]

1. *La Divina Commedia di Dante Alighieri, con il commento di Tommaso Casini* Vol. 1, *Inferno*, ed. S.A. Barbi (6th ed., Firenze, 1923), pp. 49–50.

(b)   So spake our general Mother, and with eyes
             Of conjugal attraction unreprov'd,
             And meek surrender, half imbracing leand
             On our first Father, half her swelling Brest   495
             Naked met his under the flowing Gold
             Of her loose tresses hid: hee in delight
             Both of her Beauty and submissive Charms
             Smil'd with superior Love, as *Jupiter*
             On *Juno* smiles, when he impregns the Clouds   500
             That shed *May* Flowers; and pressd her Matron lip
             With kisses pure: aside the Devil turnd
             For envie, yet with jealous leer maligne
             Ey'd them askance, and to himself thus plaind.
             Sight hateful, sight tormenting! thus these two   505
             Imparadis't in one anothers arms
             The happier *Eden*, shall enjoy thir fill
             Of bliss on bliss, while I to Hell am thrust,
             Where neither joy nor love, but fierce desire,
             Among our other torments not the least,   510
             Still unfulfilld with pain of longing pines;
                              (*Paradise Lost* iv, 492–511)[2]

I

The lines from the *Divina Commedia* are some of the first words spoken to Dante in hell by a damned soul and it matters that they are the confession of a lover. Dante and Virgil here confront the shades of Paolo Malatesta and Francesca da Polenta, a pair of adulterous lovers who were caught in the act and butchered by Francesca's husband. The lines are put into the mouth of one of the damned lovers, the woman as it happens, whom the compassionate poet has invited to tell the 'first root' of their love, how love passed from 'sweet sighs' in solitude to mutual avowals. She singles out the very moment of that fatal transition, which is evidently of consequence for Dante's poem, and prepares us to hear an impassioned account of it – 'I will tell you as one who weeps and speaks'.

In fact, it's the naked intensity of her speech we remark, as though

2. *The Poetical Works of John Milton*, Vol. 1, *Paradise Lost*, ed. Helen Darbishire (Oxford, 1952), pp. 85–6. Subsequent quotations are from this edition.

at times feeling is only just held in check by the formal order of the
verse itself. The simple, weighed words and lucid syntax – 'Ma solo
un punto fu quel che ci vinse' – caught up in that exquisitely natural
fall of the cadence, seem to put nothing between us and the swell of
the speaker's passions. So strong are the natural rhythms indeed
that a slight disturbance of them, even a momentary check, tautens
the voice with feeling. The whole twelve-line speech is held together
quite formally in a single dramatic impulse by the delicately pointed
phrasing of the *terza rima* pattern, each three-line stanza framing its
own little drama, yet each sweeping us on to that breath-catching
break across the stanza pattern at the moment which changed everything irredeemably. Dante has her throw in almost as an aside, load-
ing the fatal act with its consequences before it even arrives, the
momentous ambiguity of their eternal union: 'che mai da me non
fia diviso'. Lovers touchingly inseparable even in hell? Or damned
souls who must confront forever, and forever unfulfilled, the occasion of their ruin?

The climactic moment is singled out by the phrasing, which holds
the sense unresolved over the three-line stanza and piles it up on the
first line following, so that the whole sweep of the movement is
abruptly arrested and the voice held back in quivering tension. The
experience is powerfully rendered. Dante mimes Francesca's su-
preme moment for us there in the line as though he lived it; and one
can't but wonder at such tenderness, so close an imaginative involvement with an impulse he himself condemns to hell. But then
these mimetic textures involve the reader too, compelling us to realize
the sensations physically in our own lips, tongue, and throat:

> la bocca mi baciò tutto tremante.

It is all vividly there in the lingered-over labials, the sudden sharp
arrest at 'baciò', the pause in the voice; and then the whispered
drawn-out throbbing of 'tutto tremante', so tellingly picking up the
'amante' of line 134. Reading this with dramatic sympathy, you feel
the passion in your vocal cords.

Without any striving for emotional fervour, Dante comes as close
here as a poet can get to the creation of sensuous passion in words.
So the two discrete lines that follow fall almost as quick throwaway
observations after the lingering climax. But they are far from thrown
away. It must matter that Francesca's outburst against the book
breaks into the uncompleted story and precedes the simple massive
reticence of her final words, which is so dignified and moving in it-

self. 'Galeotto fu il libro e chi lo scrisse'. Bursting sibilantly off the
tongue, the line savagely turns back on her own tender recollection
and on the compassion it may have elicted. What follows needs no
drawing out, partly because it is already settled by that first fatal
contact of sense.

A feature of the telling is the way that Francesca is made to re-
enact for us the artless ambiguities of her motives, resolving them
only at the end when artlessness gives place too late to wilful mis-
prision. She and Paolo read together 'for amusement' of Launcelot's
affair with Guinevere, and particularly of how 'amor lo strinse',
how that pattern of chivalric adultery was constrained – as well as
beset – by love. They were alone, and 'sanza alcun sospetto' –
without fear of interruption or suspicion, but also unsuspecting as
yet the drift of their own feelings, as though the peril lay in the
situation rather than in themselves. The simple inversion in the
sentence describing their mutually suspended eyes, which holds back
the subject to the following line, picks out 'quella lettura' as the
surprising agent of their first timorous exchanges. It was the writing,
the story itself, which made them look into each other's eyes and go
pale; though we are left to ask whether that was because they amazed-
ly recognised their own case there or because the love story itself had
some hidden force in it to make people love. 'Ci vinse' suggests that
they weren't just overcome by the desire the story described, and
kindled (who wouldn't be overcome at such beauty as Dante renders
for us here!), but subjugated by it as by a power beyond their own
will.

Francesca's speech is a continual self-disclosure, typical of a poem
which places people quite precisely by the way they use words. We
see her hovering between the ecstatic memory of a first recognition
of love, such as circumstances had prompted, and the idea that they
had been betrayed into fatal love by a force beyond themselves which
had just put the circumstances in their way. The 'Galeotto' outburst settles all that, laying the whole error on others. Both book and
writer were pandars in bringing these lovers to their ruinous kiss;
just as Galehault in the story played the pandar when he persuaded
Guinevere to kiss the timorous Launcelot. She condemns the passion
which has brought such fearful consequences while wilfully laying the
fault of it at somebody else's door. Yet she can still close with that
simple line of understated recollection: 'quel giorno piú non vi leg-
gemmo avante'. The classic reticence has such effect here because it

puts the mind to what isn't said at all, the bliss with which she is not crowned:

> Nessun maggior dolore
> che ricordarsi del tempo felice
> ne la miseria.

The trouble is that Francesca's mind has nowhere to go beyond the memory of her 'tempo felice' of sensuous bliss, and her present experience of hell.

II

Milton's lines offer us a gravely beautiful picture, Dante's an impassioned drama. After Dante's manner of naked involvement with his subject, Milton's magisterial detachment – monumentality indeed – may seem chill. Such weighty locutions as 'So spake our general Mother' distance the actions they relate by keeping the reader's mind on general ideas and making him aware that something huge is being defined here. Dante's art really is to make art seem nature, as though word is feeling and syntax a plot of passions. Milton's artifice is on show, at least in that his sense partly depends upon our appraisal of the unexpected order in which he disposes his words. His writing gets much of its excitement from a continual play of syntactical artifice across the formal movement of the verse, purposeful inversions, dislocations, suspensions, extreme ellipses, and so on. Moreover, the diction itself has a marked intellectual life in the way it continually presents the simple gestures it describes in the character of general ideas. In fact, Milton's words never just describe. They are always developing ideas and attitudes and working to suggest a coherence between things.

The passage from *Paradise Lost* Book iv doesn't so much tell a story as present a situation. But the scene is dramatically realized, for we know of Satan's lurking presence within earshot of the human pair and our view of the garden and of them is punctuated by his avowals of destructive malevolence. The irony of our first seeing Eden and human innocence over Satan's shoulder shows up Satan's squalor without diminishing them; and there's nothing that calls for our pity in the picture of Adam and Eve which Milton offers us here, even though we know they will shortly fall and lose the delights they rehearse. The lovers themselves remain quite unaware that they are being spied on or have any cause for anxiety. There is no tension in their exchanges, which amount to a series of defining gestures such as must take on absolute value in a universe not yet subject to time. What's being defined here is right human love.

A little dramatic retrospect leads us into the lines describing the kiss. Eve has just told of her first encounter with Adam and how her early barren attachment to her own image, the one human thing she had then seen, was turned to yielding love and admiration of him. Everything in the passage that follows is controlled by the picture of attraction and surrender given us in its first three lines, and especially by the way this is put. The terms of Milton's depiction, such as 'with eyes/Of conjugal attraction unreprov'd', have a massive impersonalness not usually associated with loving glances, but they work rather to define and distance the affection than to mime it, and evidently what mattered for Milton was that they should be just. Eve's eyes draw Adam to her in undesigning conjugal love, blamelessly then because this is true married love, a 'meek surrender' of herself and not a mere use of sex or a self-indulgent abandonment. 'Conjugal attraction' singles out this sexual impulse from all others, such as wisdom must reprove; and in insisting that Adam and Eve were married it also implies a comment on the true nature of that bond.

The striking feature of the passage, though, is the way that everything that happens in it turns about the verb 'leand' in line 494, which the phrasing picks out and draws vividly across the line-end to 'our first Father'. All that precedes this verb qualifies Eve's leaning, and what follows describes its outcome. The simple act is thus invested with a meaning which we read partly in Eve's attitude and partly by what comes of it. This constant interweaving of sense and intelligence, act and its import, is one reason why actions which might seem voluptuous in themselves are yet so tenderly cool as Milton describes them. Even in the moment when the two bodies close thus unselfconsciously, Eve nakedly caressing Adam in sensuous pleasure, the little tag-phrase 'On our first Father' slips in to remind us that the end of these embraces is fruit, offspring, *us*, and that our existence is what justifies them.

Plainly the difference between the effect of this passage and of Dante's has to do with the distance Milton keeps from his characters and their attitudes. He doesn't involve us in intimate enactments of passion, but keeps the sense of archetypal events before us. Yet his writing certainly isn't frigidly remote. One of the notes of the passage is the way it balances monumentality and human intimacy, which it couldn't do without a distance, or without that curious alternation of Latinate and native diction whose impact so immediately suggests that the elevated and the familiar are at one here.

The beautiful description of their embrace seems pointedly placed to show us how much sense matters in human love. No one might suppose from these terms that the writer has been reputed an ascetic; less delicately controlled it's a voluptuary sensibility they'd display. Where decorous generalities would have been easy, though a mere apology for their sexual lovemaking in effect, Milton firmly insists on the physical actuality and its pleasure – 'half her swelling Brest/ Naked met his', that most sensuous 'swelling' not only describing the full breast but its movement against him. The soft nakedness of the encounter is carefully qualified, but not played down, by its concealment 'under the flowing Gold/Of her loose tresses'. Their unconsidered natural modesty here is different indeed from the modesty shame induces in them after their fall.

That description of Eve's hair strikingly shows how the diction of this poem evokes ideas as well as images, how far mind interpenetrates sense in Milton's writing. For 'flowing Gold/. . . loose tresses' does much more than tell us that Eve's hair was long, loose, and fair. 'Flowing Gold', for one thing, distinguishes this living wealth and sumptuous natural beauty from the barren stuff Mammon hoards and values. But these phrases also link Eve's beauty with the beauty of the garden, in which the reader has already encountered the 'vegetable Gold' of the fruits on the trees (iv, 219–20), and the 'crisped Brooks,/Rowling on Orient Pearl and sands of Gold' (iv, 237–8). That distanced brightness of pure natural life, sensuous without stirring sense, images true beauty and true wealth for us and implies a oneness in the natural cycle by which beauty is fruitful through love. The passage tells us that the end of beauty is not admiring contemplation but active love, and fruit; and 'loose tresses' just hints that pure beauty needs the regulation of something beyond itself even so.

Adam responds to Eve's half-embrace not out of desire but delight, however, and delight in her 'Beauty and submissive Charms' rather than in his own sensations. Delight in beauty is as carefully distinguished from passive admiration as from sexual arousal. What Milton has shown us in Book iv altogether is a creation delighting in

126   A. JAMES SMITH

its own right activity, delight being the active spirit in which nature works and the natural accompaniment of its proper functioning:

> The Birds thir quire apply; aires, vernal aires,
> Breathing the smell of field and grove, attune
> The trembling leaves, while Universal *Pan*
> Knit with the *Graces* and the *Hours* in dance
> Led on th' Eternal Spring.
>
> (iv, 264–8)

Adam's delight in Eve betokens a kind of pleased sharing in a general process of nature, which is more active and simply more human than the admiring contemplation neoplatonists speak of.

The focus of everything that happens in this sentence (lines 497–502) is 'Smil'd with superior Love', an action whose calm magisterial grandeur itself affirms a placing of sense. Formally, all the account of Adam's response to Eve's sensuous gesture is regulated by the idea of love, and of superior love at that, where 'superior' implies among other things the elevation of this loving impulse over any impulse we might now expect such an embrace to enkindle. Of course it is open to us to understand other kinds of superiority, such as that Adam's is a kind of love which fitted him to be the leading partner in their lovemaking, or that his is a higher love than hers because he comprehends love better, or even that his body was above hers as for the natural act of lovemaking. All these senses have place in the poem and the literal sense is a discreet pointer to the natural consummation of their human love which will shortly follow.

Lines 499b–502a work a curious sleight of syntax. We have the Ovidian simile coming in as a parenthetical parallel to Adam's superior love but then suddenly cut off as the main sentence resumes with the co-ordinate action, 'and pressd . . .'; so that syntactically Adam's kiss frames the cosmic fertility of Jupiter's delight in Juno: 'Smil'd . . . and pressd her Matron lip'. In fact, the only indication that we are to revert to the main drive of the sentence after '*May* Flowers' is the change of tense. The simile moves us into a universal present – 'smiles . . . impregns . . . shed' – from which we are abruptly switched back into the past of Adam's actions – 'and pressd'. Such witty artifice is the life of Milton's blank verse but this is a particularly pointed little switch. It reminds us that all this action of superior love is in the past, gone and irrecoverable; whereas the universal processes continue, though we are no longer in tune with them as

Adam was. The jar in syntax is a jar in sense too, bringing out a
fundamental meaning of the passage and the poem as it happens.

Another formal feature which shapes the way we read this sentence is the quite different stressing, and placing, of the two co-
ordinate phrases which describe Adam's action:

> Smíl'd with supérior Lóve, . . .
> . . . ānd prēssd her Mātron lip͡
> With kisses pure

The first phrase is quite sharply singled out, driven home, and em-
phatically cut off, whereas the second has a more even emphasis and
is drawn out as a coda, moving with a series of firm pressures rather
than the incisive weight of the first. The effect of the two actions
becomes pointedly unequal. That smile of superior love leads all the
rest; and the kisses themselves are subordinate to it in effect, coming
almost as a natural afterthought or consequence which needs no such
decisive emphasis. When Milton calls them 'kisses pure' we already
understand that these are not trembling climaxes of passion but the
innocent accompaniment of love, manifesting the universal spirit of
delight and fruitfulness.

The simile of Jupiter's smiling upon Juno which slips in so naturally here does more than embellish Milton's strikingly beautiful picture
of human lovemaking. One effect of the elegant transition to myth,
just at this point, is to take the human impulse up into a universal
process without making it impersonal or losing its spirit of delight.
It shows Adam's connubial love as the human repetition of the life-
giving interplay of the elements themselves, in a universe impelled
to generation by love and joy. The image of æther impregnating the
clouds and begetting spring flowers is sexual without being erotic,
and delicately points us to the true end of those human embraces
before we come to their consummation. Even the Botticelli-like
downpour of flowers suggests insemination and fertility, being most
like Botticelli in the way it transforms biological process into myth,
graceful yet pregnant. Milton's figure is boldly ambiguous. Do the
impregnated clouds literally rain down flowers, as if giving birth to
them? Or is it by metonymy that they are said to 'shed *May* Flowers'
in that they shed the cause of the flowers, those seminal rains of
April which quicken the dormant earth? Both senses, the sexually
direct myth and the bold rendering of spring growth in sexual terms,
come back upon the human lovers whose mutual exchanges promp-

ted this parallel. By such graceful means, and without the slightest indecorum, Milton shows us quite particularly what he takes to be the right end of love between human beings.

Part of the point of this little episode, though, is that for Adam and Eve it is no more than a casual passage of their day, which we happen to observe via Satan. Their lovemaking, as everything they do, has its fit time and place so that a kiss isn't a dramatic turning point for them or a spur to copulation. Yet they are still human lovers, whose embraces might strike us as staidly rendered by such a description as 'pressd her Matron lip/With kisses pure', which empties the kisses of passion. That is surely Milton's point, however. He needed a relatively neutral action, one that implies sensuous union and sensuous communion in pleasure as well, without passionate desire. The terms distinguish the act and the relationship here in fact – 'pressd', 'Matron', 'kisses pure'. They tell us that there is no compulsive demand in these kisses; indeed Eve is presented as passive under them, simply receiving Adam's imprints of love. This is a delight of sense to be distinguished absolutely from erotic contacts such as stir up feeling or release the pent-up force of illicit (and perilous) desire. In the full understanding which Milton has presented it is a natural part of a natural process whose only motives are delight and love.

As Milton describes it, Satan's torment of unappeasable frustration is worse than the suffering of Paolo and Francesca in hell. For at least they have lost all desire (it is externalized as the harassing wind that impels them) and keep only the perpetual double guilt of each other's presence, the guilt of the sin, and of their having landed each other in it. Yet there is nothing in their state that Satan might envy; and his jealous emparadising of the embrace of Adam and Eve (the grammatical boldness suggesting the force of his jangling passions) sharply points the contrast between Dante's placing of his lovers, and Milton's. The fulfilment of the love of Paolo and Francesca lands them in a hell of perpetual unfulfilment, as well as of perpetual self-reproach. But Adam and Eve are most truly fulfilled in each other's arms, and in sexual fruition. That is their sum of bliss, the consummation of their human state and their happier Eden.

It is true that Adam and Eve are innocents in an unfallen world at this stage, and that once they have fallen they become much more like Paolo and Francesca in their guilty play. They, too, will burn with desire, mastered by the peremptory demands of sense. Yet they are redeemable even then, if only because they never commit themselves wholly to the sensual sin as do Dante's lovers, or lose the idea of a happier condition than carnal appetite can allow them. A remark of Blake's to Crabb Robinson so exactly misrepresents the poem as to sharpen our sense of what Milton is really showing us here: 'I saw Milton in imagination and he told me to beware of being misled by his *Paradise Lost*. In particular he wished me to show the falsehood of his doctrine that the pleasures of sex arose from the Fall. The Fall could not produce any pleasure'.[3] No; but then the doctrine of *Paradise Lost* is that the true pleasures of sex arise from nothing else than love.

III

The contrast between the two portrayals of love is extreme. Dante offers us an adulterous affair to stand for sexual love and passion altogether, and he represents it as damned by the first contact of sense. Milton shows us a connubial love whose natural expression and highest human bliss is sense, physical fruition; and he takes it for our original created state in Eden, emparadising the lovers in itself. With all due qualification, there does seem a decisive difference of understanding here which the two poems make absolute as they develop, the *Divina Commedia* allowing no licit place to any senses save sight and hearing and moving to transcend even these, *Paradise Lost* affirming the value of even the supposed lowest of the senses, touch itself, when it is properly subordinate to love and reason. Plainly this is more than a local issue between Dante and Milton. The difference between them raises the whole question of the place of love and sexual pleasure in marriage, and possibly the question of the place of sensuous pleasure in the things of the world altogether. The shift from Dante to Milton is a shift to a modern understanding of love.

A comparison of the two passages raises more limited questions though. What are we to make of the paradox that it is Dante who puts his lovers in hell for their kiss, despite the fierce imaginative involvement with them his poetry itself betrays, while Milton, grave-

3. *Henry Crabb Robinson on Books and Their Writers,* ed. E. J. Morley (London, 1938), I, 330.

ly distancing and depassioning Adam and Eve, nonetheless represents their embrace as a paradise in itself? The *Inferno* episode may readily be taken for a prime case of a formal 'intention' belied by the inner truth of the poetry. A larger paradox is that it was Dante's rendering of sensuous love which mattered for Renaissance love poetry, not because the important poets knew the *Commedia* but because they shared some of Dante's fundamental preconceptions. A received understanding so alien to us, and so general, needs placing. To place both Dante's attempt to transcend sense in love and Milton's vision of a love which expresses itself through the mutual delights of sense would be to chart the course of European love poetry from the troubadours to Rochester.

FORM AND LANGUAGE IN ENGLISH
NEO-CLASSICAL POETRY

A. Cooper Partridge

Nature, reason and good sense dominated the thinking of French and English writers of the late seventeenth century. The trinity of excellences in their styles comprised harmony, rule and order, characteristics derived from the study of Latin Augustans, Virgil and Horace. The purpose of this paper is to inquire into some linguistic implications.

The English followers of Dryden differed from their Latin preceptors in one material consideration: the intervention of the scientific revolution, whose exponents were Descartes and Hobbes. Dryden's *Essay of Dramatic Poesy* (1668) was the earliest critical reconciliation of rationalism in the *Discourses on Method* (1637) with analytical representation in Aristotle's *Poetics*. Rationalism tended, however, to divert the poet from close observation to satire, leaving literary aspiration at the mercy of individual prejudice. A consequence of defining art as 'nature methodiz'd' was to inhibit the free imagination, and to place the emphasis in poetry on technique.

Nicolas Boileau, who translated Longinus's *Peri Houpsous* into French, offered the concept of the 'sublime' to replace the title's literal sense of *elevation;* but his contribution in *L'Art Poétique* (1674) was to make 'unimpassioned understanding' the watchword of neo-classical writing, both in French and English. Augustanism was fathered by Latin, rather than Greek, conventions.

John Dryden, not being a die-hard classicist, heralded a new phase in the classical revival; as a playwright, he saw much value in the expression of the emotions. Sympathy with his contemporary, Boileau, is evident in the following passage from 'Heroic Poetry and Poetic Licence', an apologia for the opera, *The State of Innocence and the Fall of Man* (1677):

It requires Philosophy, as well as Poetry, to sound the depth of all the passions; what they are in themselves, and how they are to be provoked: and in this science the best poets have excelled. Aristotle raised the fabric of his *Poetry* from observation of those things in which Euripides, Sophocles, and Aeschylus

pleased: he considered how they raised the passions, and thence
has drawn rules for our imitation. From hence have sprung the
tropes and figures, for which they wanted a name, who first
practised them, and succeeded in them. Thus I grant you that the
knowledge of nature was the original rule; and that all poets
ought to study her, as well as Aristotle and Horace, her inter-
preters. But then this also undeniably follows, that those things
which delight all ages, must have been an imitation of Nature;
which is all I contend. Therefore is Rhetoric made an art; therefore the names of so many tropes and figures were invented;
because it was observed they had such and such effect upon the
audience. Therefore catachreses and hyperboles have found
their place amongst them; not that they were to be avoided, but
to be used judiciously, and placed in poetry, as heightenings
and shadows are in painting, to make the figure bolder, and
cause it to stand off to sight.[1]

Dryden thus justified rhetoric as an aesthetic principle, emanating
from the imitation of nature; whatever the misconception, the view
does not invalidate two illuminating tenets of neo-classical writing:
that *human* nature is the dominant theme, and that 'elevation'
through figurative language implies the restraint of a judicious mind.
The celebrated Restoration imitator of Horace, John Oldham, who
died in 1683, warned Pope of the need for self-discipline:

> A Voice there is, that whispers in my ear,
> ('Tis Reason's voice, which sometimes one can hear)
> 'Friend Pope! be prudent, let your Muse take breath,
> And never gallop Pegasus to death;
> Lest stiff, and stately, void of fire, or force,
> You limp, like Blackmore, on a Lord Mayor's horse.'[2]

When Dryden claimed in 'Defence of the Epilogue' to *The Conquest
of Granada* (1672) that the language of his age was more refined than

1. John Dryden, *Of Dramatic Poesy and Other Critical Essays*, ed. George Watson (London, 1962), I, 200–1. References to Dryden's essays are to this
   edition.
2. 'Imitations of Horace' (1738), Book I, Epistle I, lines 11–16, in *The Twickenham Edition of the Poems of Alexander Pope*, Vol. 4, *Imitations of Horace*,
   ed. John Butt (London, 1939), p. 279. References to Pope's poems are to the
   appropriate volume of the Twickenham edition.

that of Shakespeare and Ben Jonson, he meant by *refinement* the avoidance of (a) archaic poeticisms, such as *ire* for *anger;* (b) redundancies and solecisms, whether of speech or syntax, including double comparatives (e.g. *more stricter*) and prepositions at the end of sentences; and (c) mean expressions, among which he numbered the plural of the copula, *be* for *are.* The last was a Northern dialect form of the present tense, which replaced Southern *be* in London English of the seventeenth century. Cultivation of an historical sense has made these objections seem trivial. But awareness of 'correct usage' was gaining ground, under the influence of the French Academy, to which royalist writers had been exposed during the years of the English Commonwealth. Positive aspects of refinement, such as phrase-making and decorum, Dryden acquired from Horace, rightly subjecting all novelty to the censure of custom. He specially disliked the intellectual snobbery of superfluous borrowings from the French.

Dryden regarded the cultivated tone of Restoration wit as the ultimate refinement in style, one feature of it being ingenuity of rhyme in the couplet form, which was not only in the heroic measure. Puns and other forms of word-play were, however, regarded as 'corrupters of Eloquence'. The burden of Dryden's disapproval arose from the dialogue of Jacobean comedies and tragicomedies.

The refinement of language was relevant to the progress of English poetry, because its advocates insisted on intelligibility and point as cardinal virtues. Criticism indicates, however, that some of the ideals of Dryden and Pope were imperfectly understood. Conscious of no inherent difference in the language of poetry and prose, they reacted sensibly to Thomas Sprat's rebuke of eloquence in the *History of the Royal Society* (1667), acknowledging 'luxury and redundance of speech . . . as a thing fatal to Peace and good Manners'. They chose 'positive expressions, clear senses, a native easiness',[3] as a *sine qua non*, although Sprat's accusations were not specifically directed to poets. But the real service of poetic refinement to the English language was the purification of syntax, achieved by confining poetic rhythms to manageable units. Schematic rhetoric was retained as useful in this style; what Dryden and Pope renounced was rhetoric as ornament, in which the tropes predominated.

3. Thomas Sprat, *History of the Royal Society,* ed. Jackson I. Cope and Harold Whitmore Jones (St Louis and London, 1959), pp. 111 and 113.

In the best neo-classical poetry there is less ambiguity of epithets than was customary with Elizabethan and Jacobean poets, and the verbs are strategically placed for semantic ends. This extract from *Religio Laici* (1682), a mature, discursive poem, shows that Dryden did not baulk at conventional adjectives, if they conveyed the purist's intention. Though the epithets appear jejune, there is no denying the vigour of the verbs, especially those that end the final couplet.

> The *tender* Page with *horney* Fists was *gaul'd;*
> And he was gifted most that loudest *baul'd* . . .
> *Plain* Truths enough for *needfull* use they *found;*
> But men wou'd still be *itching* to *expound* . . .
> This was the Fruit the *private* Spirit *brought;*
> *Occasion'd* by *great* Zeal, and *little* Thought.
> While Crouds unlearn'd, with *rude* Devotion *warm,*
> About the *Sacred* Viands *buz* and *swarm*[4]

By about 1680 the closed rhyming couplet had become the accepted vehicle of neo-classical verse. Pope perfected it, after the turn of the century, and the printers preserved most orthographical elisions, as illustrated in *gaul'd/baul'd, wou'd, Occasion'd* and *unlearn'd;* these were designed to ensure metrical regularity for the reader. Between the mid-seventeenth and mid-eighteenth century, the use of capital letters with nouns, and even with ecclesiastical adjectives (*Sacred*), was at its height. Straddled epithets (*rude* Devotion *warm*) were popularized by the epic poems of Milton.

In the use of generalized descriptive adjectives, the early Pope was more prolific than Dryden; his deliberate practice seems to have been to provide every noun with a suggestive epithet, preferably one approved by convention. This tendency was part of the Augustan campaign to shear adjectives of their dubious figurative associations. *Windsor Forest* (begun in 1704) teems with examples:

> With *slaught'ring* Guns the *unweary'd* Fowler roves,
> When Frosts have whiten'd all the *naked* Groves
> (125–6)

4. 'Religio Laici' 404–5, 409–10, 415–8, *The Poems of John Dryden*, ed. James Kinsley (Oxford, 1958), I, 321–2. Here and elsewhere, italics in extracts quoted are not original but are used to invite the reader's attention to the words discussed.

In rhymed couplets, the rhythmical movement determined the phrasing, and the diction tended to be unimaginative. Artificiality arose from the quest for compact, aphoristic expression, and the craftsman's desire to get the medial pause near the middle of the line, whenever antithesis or the syntax required it. To meet the demands of balance and emphatic rhyme, syntactical inversion was sometimes necessary, as in the third, seventh and eighth lines of the passage from *Religio Laici*.

The sustained simile of Greek and Roman epics was imitated by most neo-classic poets, both with heroic and comic effect. Dryden found the device in the *Aeneid*, which he translated, and Pope adapted long similes to a variety of uses. In the *Iliad* the poet's 'style of sound' has the pictorial felicity of painting:

> As thro' the shrilling Vale, or Mountain Ground,
> The Labours of the Woodman's Axe resound;
> Blows following Blows are heard re-echoing wide,
> While crackling Forests fall on ev'ry side.
> Thus echo'd all the Fields with loud Alarms,
> So fell the Warriors, and so rung their Arms.
> (Book XVI, 767–72)

In Pope's satires metaphor and metonymy were played down, and the extended simile became mock-heroic. Paradox, irony and climax crowd *The Dunciad* (1743); several shades of rhetorical ingenuity appear in the following lines:

> Around him wide a sable Army stand,   355
> A *low-born,* |*cell-bred,* |selfish, |servile band,
> Prompt or to *guard* or *stab,* |to *saint* or *damn,*
> Heav'n's Swiss, who fight for any God, or Man.
> Thro' Lud's fam'd gates, along the well-known Fleet
> Rolls the black troop, |and overshades the street,   360
> 'Till show'rs of Sermons, |Characters, |Essays,
> In circling fleeces whiten all the ways:
> So clouds replenish'd from some bog below,
> *Mount* in dark volumes, |and *descend* in snow.
> (Book II, 355–64)

Pope here castigates clerical journalists who dabble in politics. *Swiss* in line 358 is a reference to that country's widespread export of mercenaries. Particular attention should be paid to lines 356–7, 360–2, and 364, which are characteristic of Pope's rhythmical use of internal pauses, and pairing of words for satirical contrast. *Low-born* and *cell-bred* retard the rhythm effectively, to draw attention to themselves. The telling monosyllabic verbs *guard*, *stab*, *saint* and *damn* are given prominence by their semantic contrast. The incisive black and white finale has the cleanliness of a well-executed etching, clinched by the balanced opposition of the verbs *mount* and *descend* in the last line.

Epistolary poems, imitating Horace, display varieties of *wit* with some lexical imprecision. Among the many senses of *wit* are 'creative talent' and 'acuteness of mind'; the word seldom has the popular modern senses of 'witticism' or 'repartee'. Pope's conception of *wit* incorporates paradox and fallacy, especially if couched in dogmatic antitheses, as in the *Essay on Man* (1733):

> All Nature is but Art, unknown to thee;
> All Chance, Direction which thou canst not see;
> All Discord, Harmony not understood;
> All partial Evil, universal Good:
> And spite of Pride, in erring Reason's spite,
> One truth is clear, whatever is, is Right.
>   (Epistle I.x. 289–94)

Change to the inflected possessive (*Reason's*), to secure the terminal position of the rhyme-word *spite*, may be regarded as a syntactical weakness. But the reader should note the way in which parallelism aids the antithetical structure of the verse. Aphoristic economy confines the sense to individual lines, the copula being sparingly used until the last line, when *is* (three times) enforces the predications with powerful assertion. Five fallacious dogmas subsume the philosophy of Deism, which Bolingbroke transmitted to Pope in a series of epistles.

Appropriate diction was fundamental to Dryden and Pope, who developed their styles by the skill with which they rendered Virgil, Horace and Ovid for contemporary English readers. In forty years after the Restoration a tradition of urbanity and sophistication arose in the verse of Dryden and Oldham, and the fascination of the Elizabethan conceit was almost forgotten. Pope's letter to Walsh (Oct. 22, 1706) contains this: 'It is not enough that nothing offends the Ear, but a good Poet will adapt the very Sounds, as well as Words, to the things he treats of.'⁵ To demonstrate the principle of decorum, Pope produced the 'easy vigour' of lines 337–73 of *An Essay on Criticism* (1709), which simultaneously expose lack of phonic sensibility, 'low words', lazy adjectives and hackneyed rhymes. The poetic ideal is succinctly stated in the Preface to the *Iliad* (1715), in which Pope said of Homer's style: 'his expression is never too big for the sense, but justly great in proportion to it'.

Pope's diction now appears as the least mannered of the Augustans. He achieved perspicuity because he regarded himself as a skilled workman, investing common words with an amazing vitality and capacity for surprise. There is no poem to compare with *The Dunciad* for sustained satire, the motivating force being a sincere regard for poetry. The drawback of personal satire of this kind is the frequency of allusion, which compels a modern editor to endless annotation.

The eighteenth-century standardization of English owed more to the taste of Dryden, Pope and Swift than to any other group of writers. With Dr. Johnson's massive critical support, they stemmed the tide of Gothic ornament and the pseudo-sublime, threatened by the odes of Gray and Collins. They commended proper words, controlled syntax and the sober use of figures. In short, they habituated readers to the rigours of disciplined writing. Letter-writers, like Pope, whose missives were designed for publication, were regarded by Johnson as models for the 'common usage' of words.

The purification of diction, though enlightened, had the immediate effect of limiting the range of versification. A misconception of neo-classical poetic theory, the doctrine of 'kinds', required a special diction for the different verse forms (epic, elegy, satire, etc.); but the rhymed couplet, and the quatrain with alternate rhymes, staple measures of Augustan verse, made such distinctions difficult to preserve. After all, the tone of the language, as much as the choice of words, determines the relevance of the diction to the content. The generalized language of Augustan poetry reflects the desire to personify metaphor, when it is used at all, and to limit hyperbole as unscientific. But preference for common words did not inhibit periphrasis and, in lesser hands than Pope's, circumlocution. An instructive mark of 'generalization' is the frequency of functional participles, rather than adjectives of imaginative uniqueness. August-

5. *The Correspondence of Alexander Pope*, ed. George Sherburn (Oxford, 1956), I, 22.

an poetic theory suggested that what is *strong* is rational; what is *sweet*, fanciful, if not effeminate. The ideal of the English neo-classical poet was to convey much meaning in the fewest words, and those the least pretentious.

Pope planned his mature poems, as he did his garden at Twickenham. He pauses at each turning, by a sundial or bust, to illustrate, with a prudential maxim, a tenet of design. The thoughts, though dropped with apparent casualness, have the epigrammatic form of premeditations, as in the *Epistle to Burlington* (1731):

> Still follow Sense, of ev'ry Art the Soul,
> Parts answ'ring parts shall slide into a whole,
> Spontaneous beauties, all around advance,
> Start ev'n from Difficulty, strike from Chance;
> Nature shall join you, Time shall make it grow
> (*Moral Essays*, 'On the Use of Riches', 65–9)

Dissecting Pope's couplets is an intriguing exercise. Take this from *The First Satire of the Second Book of Horace Imitated* (1733):

> There S't. John míngles with my fri'endly Bówl,
> The Fe'ast of Re'ason|and the Flów of So'ul
> (*Imitations of Horace*, Satire II.1. 127–8)

Both lines have only four primary stresses, but the first pentameter has no internal pause. The stresses are invariably on words of significance, among which the sociable verb *mingles* is dominant in the initial line. *Friendly* personifies *Bowl* (a metonymic symbol for 'hospitality'), and exemplifies Pope's penchant for disyllabic predicative adjectives, ending in –*y*, or –*ful*. This syntactical arrangement has the convenience of throwing the monosyllabic rhyme word, pervasive in Pope, into bold relief.

The second line contains subtler evidence of artifice. The internal pause is in the middle of the line (after the fifth syllable), and so balances the antithetical elements metrically, as well as syntactically. Alliteration and assonance help to make the relationship memorable. Semantically, *Reason* and *Soul* are contrasted and combined in the person of St. John. *Reason* provides the intellectual pabulum of his mind; *Soul* the out-going enthusiasm, so infectious among friends.

Despite Pope's claim to precocity in the *Epistle to Arbuthnot*, line 128 ('I lisped in numbers, for the numbers came'), he was less a spontaneous than a calculating craftsman; but he was far from naive about the merits of parallelism. The syntax he displays is conceptual, rather than mechanical. Sometimes the schemes of rhetoric are not capable of precise labels, the verse being patterned by a natural inclination for grammatical orderliness. Disservice is done to the sense in citing individual lines, e.g.

> Who sees with equal eye, as God of all,
> *A hero perish, or a sparrow fall*
> > (*Essay on Man*, Epistle I, 87–8)

In the latter line we have the same antithetical balance as was observed above in the couplet on St John. William K. Wimsatt offers line 88 alone, as an instance of paradox.[6] The paradox resides, however, in the word *equal* of line 87, implying that a sparrow and a great man are of the same order in the sight of God.

Wimsatt quotes lines 105–6, Canto II of *The Rape of the Lock*, as an example of *Chiasmus* ('crossing of the two halves of a sentence structure'):[7]

> Whether the Nymph shall break Diana's Law,
> Or some frail China Jar receive a flaw.

But *Nymph/China Jar* and *break . . . Law/flaw* are correlated without syntactical transposition. The difference is that the Nymph is *active*, the Jar *passive*, *vis-à-vis* the verbs *break* and *receive* (a flaw). Pope is adept at juxtaposing trivial and heinous offences, with the same moral aplomb. His craftmanship in the mock-heroic was to exploit niceties of distinction, which the common man was likely to miss. To determine the figure of rhetoric, one has to interpret the sense in a copious context.

Antithesis through syntax is a game that may have pseudo-results. With couplets so loaded, the reader of Pope has to distinguish between paradox, antinomy and ambiguous alternatives. The difficulty of appraising patterns of words is not peculiar to Pope. Deployment of verbal skills, found in late metaphysicals such as Andrew Marvell, was carried furthest by Dryden in the seventeenth century, and con-

---

6. William K. Wimsatt, *Alexander Pope: Selected Poetry and Prose* (New York, 1951), Introduction, p. xxxviii.

7. Ibid., p. xxx.

tinued by Butler, Prior and Swift. All succeeded in generating energy, through structural diversification of the enclosed couplet; Pope saw the integrity of the individual end-stopped line as the ultimate economy. When invited to revise the verses of Wycherley, his reply to the author was as follows:

> Some I have contracted, as we do Sun-beams, to improve their Energy and Force; some I have taken quite away, as we take Branches from a Tree, to add to the Fruit.[8]

The vexed topic of neo-classic versification (including texture or metrical style), cannot be tackled without reverting to its French origins, and especially to Boileau. Pope summarizes his country's indebtedness in a few lines of the *Epistle to Augustus* (1737):

> We conquer'd France, but felt our captive's charms;
> Her Arts victorious triumph'd o'er our Arms:
> Britain to soft refinements less a foe,
> Wit grew polite, and Numbers learn'd to flow.
> Waller was smooth; but Dryden taught to join
> The varying verse, the full resounding line,
> The long majestic march, and energy divine.
> Tho' still some traces of our rustic vein
> And splay-foot verse, remain'd, and will remain.
> (*Imitations of Horace*, Epistle II.1.263–71)

Phonological implications, such as the theory of poetical elision, must now be considered. Denham, Waller and other poets regarded elision as part of literary progress in refinement. Critics and theorists, beginning with Bentley and Addison, debated the prosody of Milton. The main issues were *syllabism* (the syllable counting employed in Continental models), and *stress*, the latter concerned with the limits set on modulation by the principle of regularity. Dryden and Pope were syllabists, both referring to *numbers* when speaking of the art of metrical composition. In the *Essays*, Dryden several times mentions 'equality of numbers', as the soundest principle of English versification; 'barbarism', 'dissonance', 'discord' and 'harshness', were terms commonly used for departures from this norm after 1680. The new theories were fully enunciated in Edward Bysshe's *Art of English*

---

8. *Correspondence*, ed. Sherburn, I, 16.

Poetry (1702), which, in the improved third edition of 1708, held the field for two generations.

Some observations in Bysshe's influential treatise were very pertinent to neo-classical prosody. In heroic verse, the primacy is given to the position of accents and pauses. In a normal iambic line of ten syllables, the strongest accents should occur on the second, fourth or sixth; this makes for pauses after syllables anywhere from the third to the seventh; but the ideal positions are after the fourth, fifth and sixth syllables. The syntactical or sense structure should never end at a point in the line where a pause is forbidden, i.e. after the eighth and ninth syllable. Bysshe regards neglect of this rule as a principal cause of disharmony.

Bysshe advises the poet to avoid, wherever possible, the contiguity of vowels at the end of one word and the beginning of the next; if this is inevitable, the first vowel should be elided (e.g. *th*'other). He recommends the suppression of vowels in inflexional endings of weak preterites and past participles (e.g. *lov'd*); and also in the archaic second person singular of the present tense (e.g. thou *lov'st*). Bysshe regards both *riot* and *beauteous* as disyllabic words, and *victorious* as a trisyllable, condemning poets who indulge in syllable licence. So strict a syllabist is he that he disposes of trisyllabic feet by approving contractions such as *am'rous* and *t'amuse*.

Bysshe was not in favour of alliteration, and advised the sparing use of polysyllables in verse. An adjective at the end of a line is poorly placed, if the noun it qualifies has first place in the succeeding line. It should be noted that most of Bysshe's rules were broken by Milton, but they were observed by conscientious Augustan poets, though not by antinomian satirists. In lines 71, 74 and 78, Samuel Butler's verses *Upon Critics who Judge of Modern Plays precisely by the Rules of the Antients* (*c.* 1678) flout some of Bysshe's most cherished principles:

> An English Poet should be tryd *b*' his Peres
> And not by Pedants, and Philosophers,
> Incompetent to Judge Poetique Fury,
> As Butchers are forbid to *b*' of a Jury;   74
> Beside the most Intollerable wrong,
> To try their Matter in a Forrain Tongue
> By Forrain Jury men, like Sophocles
> Or *Tales* falser then Euripides;

When not an English Native dares appear   79
To be a witnes for the Prisoner[9]
(71–80)

Dr Johnson owned a copy of Bysshe's *Art of English Poetry* and some
of his Miltonic misconceptions were due to conservative prosody in
The Lives of the Poets, the Preface to the *Dictionary*, and *Rambler*
papers, Nos. 86, 88 and 90 of 1751.

In *Rambler* 86, Johnson calls a modulated line a 'mixed' measure,
and holds it inevitable in long poems, although it 'always injures the
harmony of the line, considered by itself'; many lines of Milton's
Paradise Lost, he claims, 'are more or less licentious with respect
to the accent'.[10] Inversion of stress is permissible in the first foot, and
a spondee or pyrrhic foot within the line; but not more than one such
licence is advisable in a single verse. On the other hand, he admits the
suitability of mixed measures for plays. Concessions are made
grudgingly because of the authority of Shakespeare and Milton; yet
he shows little appreciation of sense scansion, without which the
vigour and resource of both of these poets would be lost. In the
Dictionary of the English Language (1755), where he treats prosody
as a branch of grammar, Johnson, like Bysshe, disputes the validity
of trisyllabic feet (sig. N1^v).

Regarding elison (*Rambler* 88), Johnson dislikes the suppression of
the first of two contiguous vowels, common in Jacobean poetry, as
antiquated and 'unsuitable to the genius of the English tongue'. One
reason for disapproval is that it produces 'harsh cadences';[11] another,
that the loss of a vowel in elocution leads to sacrifice of a syllable
in the spoken, as well as the written, language. Johnson links with
this fault the opposite licence, the introduction of a redundant syllable, especially at the end of a line. In heroic poetry this facility tends
to make the verse rhythm prosaic, thereby confusing it with the mixed
measures of drama.

In the post-Renaissance era, the theory of elision cannot be di-
vorced from elocution; nor from the frequency of contraction in
colloquial speech, to which Swift objected in his proposals for an

9. Samuel Butler, *Satires and Miscellaneous Poetry and Prose*, ed. René Lamar
(Cambridge, 1928), p. 62.
10. *The Yale Edition of the Works of Samuel Johnson*, Vol. 4, *The Rambler*, ed.
W. T. Bate and Albrecht B. Strauss (Yale, 1969), pp. 90–1.
11. Ibid., p. 102.

English Academy. Cicero and Quintilian were concerned with the problem of metaplasms in the classical languages; those that passed into English prosody were the following:

1. *Aphaeresis,* loss of a syllable at the beginning of a word, e.g. *'till;*
2. *Apocope,* loss of a syllable at the end of a word, e.g. *approach'd;*
3. *Synaloepha,* loss of the first of two adjacent vowels, to avoid hiatus, e.g. *th'*other;
4. *Synaeresis,* shortening of two syllables into one, e.g. *ev'n,* endea*v'ring.*

The ready acceptance in England of syllabic verse, with the accompanying theory of contractions, was mainly due to the methodical exactness of French prosody, which was studied by the literate classes after the Restoration. In the mind of Dryden, the rules were not fictional theories, but dogmas to be applied by exponents of good taste and artistic principle. Dryden admitted into his nondramatic verse only such elisions and contractions as seemed refinements, in accordance with the received syllable limits. The vulgarisms of speech, against which Swift inveighed in his *Proposal for Correcting Ascertaining and Improving the English Tongue* (1712), played a minimal role in his system. English being regarded as a predominantly consonantal language, Dryden was wary of indiscriminate vowel-rejection, lest he should be guilty of harshness. A fair example of his mature versification is the following from *The Medall* (1682):

> Dríves down the Cúrrent with a *póp'lar* gále;   80
> And shéws the Fí'end conféss'd, |without a váile.
> He pre'aches to the Crówd, |that *Pów'r* is lént,
> But nót convéy'd to Kíngly Góvernment;
> That Cla'imes succéssive be'ar no bínding fórce;
> That Córonation Oáths are thíngs of coúrse;   85
> Mainta'ins the Múltitude can néver érr;
> And séts the Péople in the Pápal Cha'ir.
> The re'ason's óbvious; |*Ínt'rest néver lýes;*
> The móst have stíll their *Ínt'rest* in their éyes;
> The pów'r is álways the'irs, |and pów'r is éver wíse.   90
> Almíghty Crówd, |thou shórte*n'st* áll dispúte;
> Pów'r is thy E'ssence; |Wít thy Áttribute!
> Nor Fa'ith nor Re'ason máke thee at a stáy,
> Thou le'ap*st o'r* áll etérnal trúths, |in thy Pindárique wáy!

Áthens, |no do'ubt, |did ríghteously decíde,   95
When Phócion and when Sócrates were trý'd:
As ríghteously they díd those do'oms repént;
Stíll they were wíse, |what éver wáy they wént.
Crówds érr not, |though to bóth extrémes they rún;
To kíll the Fáther, |and recáll the Són.   100
                    (80–100)

Dryden uses the incisive language of debate, and satire assumes the
mantle of invective. The sense of the argument is enhanced by development in single lines, each of which is end-stopped. Stress and
pause provide the principal modulations of rhythm. Save in the
initial foot of 80, 92, 95 and 98, where the stress is inverted, all lines
have primary stresses on even-numbered syllables. Thirteen lines
have only four primary stresses, five have five such stresses, two have
six, and one (96) has only three. Line 99 is notable in opening with a
spondee, a device that retards the rhythm in order to give weight to
the maxim: *Crowds err not.*

The majority of the rhymes use strong monosyllables; polysyllables
(83 *Góvernmènt*, 92 *Áttribùte*) have the rhyme on the anticipated
syllable of secondary stress. In rising disyllables (91 *dispúte*, 95
decíde, 97 *repént*) the phonic element is either a long vowel, a
diphthong, or an emphatic short vowel. The masculine tone of
Dryden's couplet finds useful modulation in triple rhyme (88–90),
the last line usually being an Alexandrine.

Internal pauses are mostly orthodox: after the sixth syllable in
lines 81, 82, 90 (Alexandrine); after the fifth syllable in 88 (*obvious*
is a disyllable), 92 and 100; after the fourth syllable in lines 91, 95
and 98; after the third syllable in 99; and, exceptionally, after the
second in 95. The spectacular variation of line 94, with seven feet, has
the medial pause after the eighth syllable; the irregular technique
draws attention to verses reminiscent of Pindar. When the internal
pause is exactly in the middle of the line (88, 92 and 100), the break
is caesural in the French manner; invariably it marks a crucial turn
in the argument. An epigram *Int'rest never lyes* (printed in italics)
follows the pause in line 88; in 92 and 100 the pause serves as
fulcrum for balanced antitheses, the final line being a daring
paradox.

Modulation in Dryden is minimal, but shrewdly planned. The
iambic pentameter pattern is never obscured, and the variations are

designed, partly to avoid monotony, and partly to illuminate twists in the argument. Contractions that ensure regularity are rarely licentious, such as *pop'lar* (80, for *popular* 'of the people'). The metaplasms *confess'd* (81), *convey'd* (83), *try'd* (96), *Pow'r* (82, 90, 92), *Int'rest* (88), *shorten'st* (91), *leapst* (94), *o'r* (94), are conventional. Purists like Swift would, however, have objected to *reason's* (88), where the copula is colloquially contracted.

Dryden's argument is rhetorically emphasized by *ploce*, drawing attention to key words: *Crowd* (82, 91, 99); *Pow'r* (82, 90 twice, 92); *err* (86, 99); *Int'rest* (88, 89), *wise* (90, 98), *righteously* (95, 97). The seditious *Crowd*, in Dryden's eyes, invites pejorative senses for the synonyms *Multitude* (86) and *People* (87); the biblical allusions to *Almighty* (91), *Father* and *Son* (100), have the satirical effect of bathos, rather than of elevation. The *Medall* derides the Whig politician, Shaftesbury, who opposed Charles II's alliance with Catholic France, and instigated Monmouth's claim to the throne. The Earl was tried for high treason in 1681 and exonerated by a largely Protestant jury. London sympathizers rioted, and a medal was struck to commemorate the Whig victory. Phocion and Socrates were arraigned for similar offences and executed, though the Athenians afterwards repented.

Pope's suppleness in the colloquial idiom shows complete mastery of his medium in the *Epistles*, *Imitations of Horace*, the *Moral Essays*, and *The Dunciad*, written between 1730 and 1744. The following comes from the *Epilogue to the Satires*, Dialogue II (1738):

> Yés,|I am pro'ud;|I múst be pro'ud to se'e
> Mén not afra'id of Gód,|afra'id of mé:
> Sáfe from the Bár,|the Púlpit,|and the Thróne,   210
> Yet to'uch'd and shám'd by *Rídicule* alóne.
>   O sácred We'apon!|léft for Trúth's defénce,
> Sóle Dre'ad of Fólly,|Více, and Ínsolence!
> To a'll but He'av'n-dirécted hánds deny'd,
> The Múse may gíve thee,|but the Góds must gu'ide.   215
> Rév'rent I to'uch thee!|but with hónest ze'al;
> To rówze the Wátchmen of the Públick We'al, . . .
>   Ye tínsel Ínsects!|whom a Co'urt mainta'ins,   220
> That co'unts your Be'auties ónly by your Sta'ins,
> Spín all your Cóbwebs o'er the Éye of Dáy!
> The Múse's wíng shall brúsh you áll awáy:

Áll his Gráce pre'aches,|áll his Lórdship síngs,
Áll that makes Sa'ints of Que'ens,|and Góds of Kíngs, 225
Áll,|áll but Trúth,|dróps de'ad-bórn from the Préss,
Líke the lást Gázette,|or the lást Addréss.
                        (208–17, 220–7)

Pope here achieves a flexibility and variety unmatched in the earliest works. Dialogue enabled him to relax his rigid monosyllabism and Gallic regularity of stress. Even the invocations in lines 212–16 and 220–2 are divertingly relevant to the ridicule.

Pope contracts and expands the rhythm by varying the heavy beats, within the limits of four to seven. Eight lines appear to have four primary stresses, eight have five such stresses, and two (224 and 226) have six and seven respectively. Trochees or spondees modulate the first foot of lines 208–10, 213, 216, 222, and 224–7, these ten inversions in eighteen lines being a high proportion for Pope. In 224 and 227 spondees occur in the second foot, and in 226 in the third. The rhythm is also modulated sporadically by pyrrhic feet. Only two trisyllabic nouns are introduced, *Ridicule* (211) and *Insolence* (213); the two compound epithets *Heav'n-directed* (214) and *dead-born* (226) are effective, because unusual.

The only enjambed line is the first (208). Internal-pause variation occurs after the fourth syllable in lines 208, 210 and 226; after the fifth syllable (i.e. midway) in 212, 213, 215, 216, 220, 224 and 227; after the sixth syllable in lines 209 and 225; and after the seventh syllable in 210. There are unconventional pauses after the first syllable in lines 208 and 226, the latter to separate iterative uses of *All*.

The rhymes contain long vowels or diphthongs in all but three couplets and are generally monosyllabic. Vowel modulation is more sensitive than Dryden's, harmony being the principal end for which Pope strove. Pope shared the views of Johnson (*Rambler* 90) (a) that the fourth and sixth syllables of the line should be well sounded; (b) that a pause concluding a period should be made upon a strong syllable. He stressed *Gazette* (227) on the first syllable, favouring a pronunciation current in London and, according to the *Oxford English Dictionary*, approved by Dr Johnson.

Though the technique of Pope was modelled on Dryden, his iambic line in the Horatian epistles has greater verve and individuality. Swift in 1731 wrote admiringly:

> In POPE, I cannot read a Line,
> But with a Sigh, I wish it mine:
> When he can in one Couplet fix
> More Sense than I can do in Six.[12]

The unobtrusive use of rhetorical figures in the *Epilogue* passage should be noted:

Tropes

Metaphor: 212 *sacred Weapon* (Ridicule), 220 *tinsel* Insects, 222 *Spin all your Cobwebs*, 223 *The Muse's wing shall brush*, 226 *drops dead-born from the Press*

Personification: 214 *Heav'n-directed hands*, 222 *Eye of Day*

Simile: 227 *Like the last Gazette, or the last Address*

Schemes of Words

Epanaphora (repetition of a word at the beginning of successive sentences): *All* in lines 224–6

Epizeuxis (contiguous repetition for emphasis): 226 *All, all*

Ploce (sporadic repetition of key words): 208 *proud*, 209 *afraid*, 209/215/225 *God*, 211/216 *touch*, 212/226 *Truth*, 215/223 *Muse*, 227 *last*

Alliteration: Prominent in lines 214, 215, 217 and 226

Metaplasms: 211 *touch'd, sham'd*, 214 *Heav'n, deny'd*, 216 *Rev'rent*, 222 *o'er*

The vogue for this orthography was moribund by 1740.

Schemes of Thought

Ecphonesis: 212 *O sacred Weapon !*, 220 *Ye tinsel Insects !*

Paradox: 221 *counts your Beauties only by your Stains*

Antithesis (juxtaposed contrasting ideas): 215 *The Muse may give thee, but the Gods must guide*

Symmetry is the basis of Pope's style. Balancing of parts in the line, involving a medial pause as fulcrum, is not predominantly antithetical. The most important element is *parison* (clausal, phrasal or ideational counterpoise), which is not always perfect, e.g. in lines 209, 224, 225 and 227. Seldom did Pope emulate Dryden in modulating by means of triplets and Alexandrines.

---

12. 'Verses on the Death of Dr Swift', 47–50, *The Poems of Jonathan Swift*, ed. Harold Williams (Oxford, 1937), II, 555.

These professional poets represent the neo-classical style at the pinnacle of achievement. The common aims they shared were clarity, simplicity and the animation of rational ideas; smooth rhythm and strong rhyme; native vigour of language that avoids laboured expressions. Both adapted versification to topics they favoured, the manners of men in a politically activated society. Their only expressed passion was for decorum, which produced few inelegant phrases. They advanced no formal ideals that they could not put into practice.

On the debit side, there is the inevitable sameness of a technique that compresses the sense into ten highly-charged syllables. The self-imposed limitation of the heroic line, visualized as a dichotomy of parts, was crippling to imaginative talents, and to Dryden and Pope themselves. Their enduring contribution to refinement was to give the language of poetry urbanity and argumentative ease. In so planning, they produced poems consisting of lively precepts and critical animadversions; but these were so heterogeneous and disparate, as to be deficient in organic wholeness. Dryden's apologetics, and Pope's assumed humility in the face of great predecessors, were symptoms of the undoubted limitations of neo-classical poetry.

PLAIN AND CONTORTED SPEECH IN
EMMA

Mary C. Penrith

Critical views, from those of Archbishop Richard Whately in 1821[1] to those of Professor Norman Page in the 1970s,[2] seem to affirm R. W. Chapman's claim that Jane Austen 'is one of the greatest, because one of the most accurate, writers of dialogue of her own, or any age'.[3] It was Chapman who began the trend for the non-literary or barely literary examination of Jane Austen's work, and his successors have attempted in a variety of ways to define the nature of her 'accurate' dialogue and 'verbal felicity'.[4] However, a great number of these studies have either been limited by their linguistic approach or, when amalgamated with literary insights, have generally been impressionistic. Few critics of Jane Austen, therefore, seem to have gone beyond what might be called the initial or intuitive stage of criticism. This is by no means to decry the value of intuitive literary studies, to which Miss Mary Lascelles' major work, *Jane Austen and her Art*,[5] bears notable testimony. Nevertheless, the origins of even the most crucial impressions have often been glossed over with few real attempts at objectivity or precision. For example, Miss Lascelles writes:

> [Jane Austen] was discovering that only certain kinds of elaboration were disagreeable to the ear – those that go against the grain of the language. The sentence that makes a double bend where it had better have run straight is of this kind . . . And her *hollow* people have a taste for double negatives . . . As her touch grows surer and lighter she allows her tiresome talkers to em-

1. Unsigned review of *Northanger Abbey* and *Persuasion, Quarterly Review* 24 (Jan. 1821), 352-76; rpt. B. C. Southam (ed.), *Jane Austen: The Critical Heritage* (London, 1968), p. 98.
2. *The Language of Jane Austen* (Oxford, 1972); and *Speech in the English Novel* (London, 1973).
3. Appendix I to *Sense and Sensibility*, ed. R. W. Chapman, 3rd ed. (London 1933), p. 389.
4. Virginia Woolf, 'George Eliot', *The Common Reader*, First Series (London, 1948), p. 216.
5. London, 1939.

bark on sentences that are too elaborate for their powers, and *stick* – as Mr. Elton and Mrs Clay do in their complimentary speeches (pp. 88–89).

The problem with figurative critical descriptions, as Spencer and Gregory comment in *Linguistics and Style*, is that such terms 'tend to conflate statements about language with statements about the effects produced by language, and . . . have a habit, like many critical terms, of sliding out of their accustomed place in the framework of literary description if too carefully scrutinized'.[6] By means of a closer, linguistic examination of Jane Austen's writing, however, it seems possible to substantiate intuitions such as those of Miss Lascelles. Some work of this nature has been done, such as Howard S. Babb's *Jane Austen's Novels: The Fabric of Dialogue*,[7] but a comprehensive methodology has still to be proposed that is analytically delicate and yet sufficiently comprehensive to allow the description of the variations of language in her novels. That such an approach is practicable I shall attempt to demonstrate by a brief examination of a small area of Jane Austen's writing – the direct speech in *Emma* – and by a consideration of the possibilities that this analysis raises: that there is a correlation between linguistic varieties and the moral values of the speakers; that personalities as diverse as Mrs Elton and Harriet Smith share certain qualities of language and hence of attitude; that in the early stages of the novel they also share these attributes with Emma; and that there are identifiable linguistic parallels to Emma's social and moral development. Not only does stylistic analysis suggest these possibilities, but it seems to offer a means of identifying both their sources and their likenesses to other structural patterns in the work.

At the very centre of this novel is Emma herself, distinguished from her fellows not by a radically different character, but by her ability to change and mature. Like the structure of *Hamlet*, that of *Emma* concentrates on the protagonist so that every minor character or idea is related directly to the centre. We expect, therefore, that dialogue, which constitutes a large part of the novel, should reflect such a structural relation. It is evident that the presentation of character and of comedy, both allied to speech, serves this end. In

6. John Spencer (ed.), *Linguistics and Style* (London, 1964), p. 92.
7. Ohio: Archon Books, 1967.

the traits of those surrounding Emma, nearly all her attitudes and faults are taken to unacceptable extremes: Frank Churchill, for example, extends her abuse of imagination, Harriet Smith her ignorance of feeling, and a norm of rationality and moderation is consequently made desirable. The comedy follows a similar pattern: Mrs Elton, for example, in taking Emma's snobbish and domineering tendencies to extremes, exposes them to discriminating ridicule. Likewise, the speech presents a variety of idiolects that exaggerate certain features of Emma's language, implying by their extremity the existence of some ideal that they are violating.

Furthermore, as well as definitions of ideal speech by its negative opposites, there are positive and explicit recommendations of a particular kind of language. Firstly, certain authorial comments relate linguistic plainness to superiority of character. In Chapter 51, for example, we read:

> ... it was in plain, unaffected, gentleman-like English, such as Mr Knightley used even to the woman he was in love with ... (E, 448).[8]

Plain language is being allied here with 'gentleman-like English', and the implicitly contrastive 'unaffected' refers indirectly to the many varieties of false, and hence faulty, speech that have already been deployed. Secondly, it is notable that the merits of plain language as a definable idiolect are attested to only by speakers who have already been established as morally sound. Mr Knightley, the foremost of these, says in Chapter 49:

> 'I cannot make speeches, Emma:' – he soon resumed; and in a tone of such sincere, decided, intelligible tenderness as was tolerably convincing. – 'If I loved you less, I might be able to talk about it more. But you know what I am. – You hear nothing but the truth from me ... ' (E, 430).

The plainness of language such as this can be discovered not only in moral terms but also in linguistic forms: the manner in which a speaker observes or deviates from plain language seems to be directly relevant to his moral stature, contraventions of moral and linguistic norms being in equal ratio. An examination of the lexical and syntac-

8. Page references are to R. W. Chapman's edition of *Emma* (London, 1933); chapters have been numbered consecutively.

tic patterns in a few representative samples of dialogue seems to support the contention that Jane Austen has ordered her choice of idiolects so as to signify values through linguistic forms. In the brief analysis below, string A allows for the inclusion of lexical patterns and string B for some of the syntactic structures; and the whole is a tentative identification of Jane Austen's conception of the ideal of plain language.[9]

S_1 A I cannot make speeches, Emma
    B I make speeches, Emma
S_2 A If I loved you less
    B I love you
S_3 A I might be able to talk about it more
    B I talk about it (i.e. my love for you)
S_4 A But you know what
    B You know [me]
S_5 A I am
    B I am [thus]
S_6 A You hear nothing but the truth from me
    B You hear the truth from me

In this short statement by Mr Knightley it seems possible to trace a correlation between the linguistic patterns and the ideas that are being asserted; and its position in the novel and the importance of the situation (his first declaration of his love for Emma) give it crucial prominence.

S_1 is a statement, its use of the vocative allowing an overt balance between addresser (initial *I*) and addressee (final *Emma*); and it introduces a negative (*cannot*) that is developed in succeeding sentences.

S_2 is embedded in S_3, but is foregrounded, thus drawing attention to the negative by the consequent stress on *if* and *less*, and linking it to the negative of S_1. The equal balancing of pronouns *I* and *you* makes more explicit the addresser-addressee relationship referred to in S_1. Stress and semantic progression seem to complement the syntactic patterns here.

---

9. In the analyses that follow I have not aimed at representing deep structure. Rather, I have isolated the various sentences which may be said to occur in the utterance in order to illustrate some of the syntactic complexity of the passages.

S_3 continues the conditional element in *might*, which, in association with *if* and *less* (S_2) and the negative of S_1, is related by syntactic similarity to verb phrases that involve ability (*can*, S_1, *able*, S_3). From these structures a pattern of contrast and progression seems to develop. The *more* of S_3, for example, contrasts in stress and in lexis with the *less* of S_2, suggesting some kind of weighing and judgement. This evidence of linguistic equilibrium seems to substantiate the impression of Mr Knightley as a 'rational' man.

Similar inferences seem possible from other structures. The verb phrases of ability, namely *can* and *able*, change to stative verbs, *know* (S_4), *am* (S_5) and *hear* (S_6). This syntactic development is allied to the particular collocations of the lexical items in these sentences. The item *speeches* (S_1) in collocation with *can* and *make* suggests artifice but is contained within a structure with a negative transformation. The item *talk* (S_3) is similarly in collocation with *might* (possibility) and *able* (ability) and derives an implied negative from both the *if* and *less* of S_2 and their contrast with *more* (S_3) which in turn collocates with *talk*. Collectively, these patterns suggest that Mr Knightley recognizes the nature of artifice and illusion (which has played a major part in the events of the novel), but rejects it.

At this point the negatives do not disappear but, as has been noted above, the verb phrases change to those involving stative verbs. *Know* (S_4) collocates implicitly with [*me*], *am* (S_5) with *I*, and *hear* (S_6) with *truth*. There seems, thus, to be a syntactic contrast between S_1-S_3 and S_4-S_6 that also serves as a background for lexical contrasts such as those between *speeches* and *talk*, on the one hand, and *me* and *truth*, on the other. The relation of the negative in S_6 (*nothing but* the truth) seems to establish *truth* as absolute because of the restricted collocation of this quasi-idiomatic legal formula. The surface negative, therefore, serves as an emphatic positive, expressing solemnity and judgement.

As well as embodying transitions in the verb phrases and collocations, S_4 marks the beginning of a change in the pronominal pattern. The *I-Emma* (S_1), *I-you* (S_2), *I-it* (S_3) order reverses to *you-*[*me*] (S_4), then to *I-*[*thus*] (S_5) and finally to *you-me* (S_6). The central point of the change seems to be *But* (S_4), which is given orthographic prominence by its position at the beginning of a sentence. The balance of the pronouns in this passage suggests the speaker's conception of the equality of the addresser and addressee (which later con-

versation makes explicit), a status that Emma has earned during the
course of the novel. As J. F. Burrows demonstrates,[10] the relationship between Emma and Mr Knightley alters as she grows in awareness, developing from that of child and parent, to sister and brother,
to friends, to lovers. Only at the last stage has Emma achieved full
adulthood, and the consequent responsibility of judgement, and
so only then can she and Mr Knightley have real equality.

As a whole, the syntactic balances of this extract suggest stability
by their two-part contrasts and equivalences. As well as the balances
within sentences (for example, *I-Emma*) and contrasts between a
part of one sentence and a part of another (for example, between
less and *more*), there is a larger scheme of equilibrium that gives a
kind of symmetry to the six-sentence extract. The two contrastive
elements fall into equal parts: sentences 1 to 3 all contain modality
and either explicit or implicit negation that reaches a peak in the
extra stress given to it by the over-positive *more* of S_3; and sentences
4 to 6 similarly gain cohesion from an opposite tendency towards
conciseness evident in the deletion in S_4 and S_5, and the positive
stress of S_3 is repeated in an even stronger form by the surface negative of S_6.

Although each sentence has some kind of transformation applied
to it, Mr Knightley's statement is achieved in a relatively simple
sequence: no sentence has more than one other sentence embedded in
it; and the basic forms of all the sentences fit the expected SPO(C)
pattern of standard English syntax. All the transformations applied
to the basic sentences seem to aim at precision and balance. Syntactically and lexically, the structure of the speech seems to represent a conception of the equality of the addresser and addressee;
to establish by its contrasts and equivalences a relatively specific
definition of 'truth'; and to realise its ostensible objectives through
an observable order and equilibrium.

Language such as this may be described as 'plain' not only because,
negatively, it is unembellished by modification or by complex embedding, but also because, positively, its semantic simplicity leads
readily to what appears to be a relatively clear matching of surface
structure to deeper levels. Furthermore, in terms of the contrasts in
Emma, plain language seems to serve in the novel as the norm of ideal
speech. In such a situation, it is easy to see how Mark Schorer,

10. *Jane Austen's Emma* (Sydney University Press, 1968).

for example, could write 'the author (or, if you wish, Knightley)'.[11] Although this confusion of roles is questionable, Professor Schorer's impression seems to result from the way in which Mr Knightley performs part of the narrator's discriminatory function in upholding both the moral and linguistic ideals of the novel. Whenever Mr Knightley deviates from the standard, as he does when his jealousy of Frank Churchill influences his behaviour, his lapse is also a fault of judgement. In like manner, those whose judgement or intentions are consistently faulty, such as Mrs Elton and Harriet Smith, regularly stray from plain language. The particular nature of the deviations seems to be identifiable and significant: the two extracts that follow may be said to be typical of the speakers; intuitively we would attribute them to Mrs Elton and Harriet; and linguistically we can specify the origins of some of the impressions that contribute to our conceptions of these characters.

(a) *Mrs Elton*:

> 'My dear Miss Woodhouse, a vast deal may be done by those who dare to act. You and I need not be afraid. If *we* set the example, many will follow it as far as they can; though all have not our situations. *We* have carriages to fetch and convey her home, and *we* live in a style which could not make the addition of Jane Fairfax, at any time, the least inconvenient . . . ' (E, 283).

S_1 You are my dear Miss Woodhouse
S_2 they may do a vast deal
S_3 they dare to act
S_4 You and I need not be afraid
S_5 If *we* set the example
S_6 many will follow the example
S_7 they can follow the example thus far
S_8 though all have not our situations
S_9 *We* have carriages
S_{10} [our] carriages fetch her [from] home
S_{11} [our] carriages convey her home
S_{12} *we* live in a style
S_{13} it could not make the style the least inconvenient at any time
S_{14} X adds Jane Fairfax

11. 'The Humiliation of Emma Woodhouse', *The Literary Review*, II, 4 (Summer 1959), 547-63; rpt. Ian Watt (ed.), *Jane Austen: A Collection of Critical Essays* (Englewood Cliffs, 1963), p. 105.

By no means all the characteristics of Mrs Elton's speech that this passage illustrates can be considered here, but a brief look at her language suggests that it could be going 'against the grain of the language' in its elaboration; and she seems to have 'a taste for double negatives', for example in S$_{13}$, where both *the least* and *at any time* reinforce a point that could be made more simply.

Many of her sentences could be said to 'make a double bend': there is considerable and complex embedding, passivization, and an unusual choice of word order that is reinforced by orthographical stress markers. S$_6$, for example, has both pre- and post-modifying sentences embedded in it (S$_5$, S$_7$ and S$_8$); the compounded S$_{10}$ and S$_{11}$ are embedded in S$_9$, the head word of which is the stressed *we*; S$_{13}$ is embedded in S$_{12}$; and S$_{14}$ is embedded in S$_{13}$. The last of these embeddings, which is accompanied by nominalization, suggests a covert relation between *it* and *Jane Fairfax* that may be related to the speaker's attitude. Furthermore, the co-ordinating *and* linking S$_9$ and S$_{12}$ seems to function also as a subordinator (such as *and so*), so that the relations between sentences S$_9$ to S$_{14}$ are complicated.

Surface word order and stress markers seem to complement the syntactic structures. For example, the *you and I* of S$_4$ is implicit in the structure of S$_1$ and is made overt in the three stressed uses of *we*. Lexical contrasts point to the speaker's assumption of an equality between addresser and addressee that is socially inappropriate at this point (Emma and Mrs Elton are on different social levels, and in any case are new acquaintances). *They dare* (S$_3$), for example, is in syntactic and lexical relation to *you and I-not-afraid* (S$_4$).

Language such as this can scarcely be said to 'run straight'. The elaboration of syntax and stress suggests that social and linguistic conclusions could be drawn from them, correlating with the social attitudes that the rest of Mrs Elton's behaviour expresses: Mrs Elton has a preoccupation with elaborate trimmings, both in language and in dress; she has inflated ideas about her social importance; she is self-interested; and she is inclined to regard others (such as Jane Fairfax) merely as a means of exercising her imagined supremacy.

(b) *Harriet Smith*

'To be sure. Yes. Not that I think Mr Martin would ever marry any body but what had had some education – and been very well brought up. However, I do not mean to set up my opinion

against your's – and I am sure I shall not wish for the acquaint-
ance of his wife . . . ' (E, 31)

S_1 To be sure
S_2 Yes
S_3 I [do] not think [it]
S_4 Mr Martin would ever marry any body
S_5 any body has not had some education
S_6 any body has not been very well brought up
S_7 However, I do not mean [it]
S_8 I set up my opinion against your's
S_9 I am sure
S_{10} I shall not wish for [it]
S_{11} I become acquainted with his wife

The pronominal patterns of this extract also seem to reveal the
social attitude of the speaker, the six occurrences of the first person
pronoun in subject position suggesting Harriet's growing self-
assertiveness. The structures that do not contain this form seem to
differ from plain language in other ways as well: S_4, S_5 and S_6 differ
in aspect; and S_1 and S_2 are not strictly sentences, being verbless,
recurrent features in Harriet's speech that stress her eagerness to
please and are perhaps no fuller semantically than an orthographic
capital letter.

The possibility that S_1 and S_2 are phatic utterances is supported
by the fact that they are contradicted by the negation of S_3 (which is
foregrounded by the inverted word order). S_3 and S_5 together con-
stitute a double negative, which is intensified by *ever* but is also
contradicted by the speaker's desire to please (S_1 and S_2), with the
consequence that the denials appear to be more strongly expressed
than felt. A double negative such as this is what Miss Lascelles
attributes to Jane Austen's '*hollow* people', and, like Mrs Elton
in S_4 and S_8 of her utterance, Harriet seems to have a tendency to
use negative structures (as in S_7 and S_{10}).

Another characteristic that Harriet shares with Mrs Elton is
nominalization at a socially significant point. In Mrs Elton's sentence
(S_{14}) Jane Fairfax tends to be reduced to the status of an object
(*it*, S_{13}) in a structure that may be more revealing than the speaker
realizes; and in Harriet's use (S_{11}) nominalization seems to be a
means of converting a process to an abstraction, so obscuring from
the speaker herself something that she does not wish to acknowl-

edge. Harriet's stubborn regard for Robert Martin thus reveals
itself in spite of what she says or of what Emma chooses to infer.
The structure of Harriet's sentences is different from that of
Mrs Elton's. Although there is a certain amount of embedding, it is
less intricate. Both S_5 and S_6 are embedded in S_4, but the relation
between S_5 and S_6 is co-ordination and both are post-modifiers.
Similarly, S_9 is co-ordinate with S_7. In each instance of co-ordination, however, there is a graphological pause mark that suggests
some kind of effort on the part of the speaker in making these
additions. It is an effort because Harriet instinctively rebels against
what she is stating, but her naïveté is such that she herself is unaware
of her 'dishonesty'. Harriet gives other unconscious revelations of
her mind: in S_6 the superlative *very* suggests an implicit comparison
that is possibly between the hypothetical wife and Harriet herself;
and in S_9 her pause serves to emphasize the lack of logic in the co-
ordination with S_7. In a significant way, then, Harriet seems to
'*stick*', giving credence to Miss Lascelles' claim that a study of
structure can reveal deeper levels of meaning.

Direct speech such as that in the two extracts examined above is
only one of the forms of language deployed in *Emma*, and it seems
to fulfil specific functions. For example, the reader's initial encoun-
ters with characters generally take place through direct speech,
whereas free indirect speech serves to epitomize a speaker's linguistic
idiosyncrasies and so to keep him relatively static in the total scheme
of the novel. Mrs Elton's monologue when strawberry-picking, for
example, is an implicit source of reference for her later speech and
actions. Notably, not all the speakers are epitomized in this way, the
exceptions being those who prove themselves capable of growth and
change. Emma in particular goes through a whole range of linguistic
diversity, none of her speeches immobilizing her as she advances
towards maturity and self-knowledge. The following brief analysis
of two contrasting speeches, one from near the beginning of the
novel, the other from near the end, illustrates in general terms the
degree of change that takes place in Emma's language – a linguistic
change that seems to parallel her maturational development.

(a) ' . . . A young farmer, whether on horseback or on foot, is
the very last sort of person to raise my curiosity. The yeomanry
are precisely the order of people with whom I feel I can have
nothing to do . . . ' (E, 29)

S₁ A young farmer is the very last sort of person
S₂ A young farmer is on horseback
S₃ A young farmer is on foot
S₄ Such a person does not raise my curiosity
S₅ The yeomanry are precisely [that] order of people
S₆ I feel [it]
S₇ I can have nothing to do with [it] (i.e. the order)

The embedding in this utterance is complex, S_2, S_3 and S_4 all being embedded in S_1; and S_7 being embedded in S_6, which in turn is embedded in S_5. There is a tendency towards negatives, overt in S_4 and S_7 and implicit in S_1.

The items made prominent by structure and by stress seem to be significant: *a young farmer* (S_1), *sort of person* (S_4), *the yeomanry* (S_5) progress in their degrees of generality and show little consideration of Robert Martin himself. The nominalization in *curiosity* (S_4) suggests that Emma is distancing the experience. The intensifiers *very* (S_1) and *precisely* (S_5), in combination with forms of the verb 'to be', make the structures resemble absolute statements and support our impressions of Emma's dogmatism and bossiness.

The collocational patterns of these items involve forms of the personal pronoun: *is-very-last* (S_1) relates to *my* (S_4); and *are precisely* (S_5) to *I* (S_6, S_7), suggesting that Emma regards herself as the source of authority.

Beneath the generalizations there seems to be a contradiction between statements and opinions that reflects Emma's confusion of reality and illusion. Furthermore, her speech seems to repeat some of the characteristics noted in the language of Mrs Elton and Harriet: negatives, complex embeddings, nominalization, and a pronominal pattern that concentrates on the first person. These linguistic similarities and the inferences that can be drawn from them suggest that the speakers share certain social attitudes and weaknesses of character, such as a desire to dominate, an avoidance of uncomfortable truths, and excessive self-interest.

(b) Emma to Mr Knightley about Frank Churchill's letter:

'You do not appear so well satisfied with his letter as I am; but still you must, at least I hope you must, think the better of him for it. I hope it does him some service with you' (E, 488).

In this extract we see a reversal of some of Emma's former attitudes, and also significant changes in her language. The only negative in this speech is qualified by the intransitive *appear* (S_1) and the consequent acknowledgement that illusion is possible. The verbs *hope* (S_4, S_6) and *think* (S_3) complement the conditional structure, the interpolated *hope* (S_4) modifying the imperative possibilities of *must* (S_3) towards simple futurity (*must*, S_5). Lexically the structures are complemented by items related to assessment: *so* (S_1) and *as* (S_2), *the better* (S_3), *at least* (S_4) and *some* (S_7). No longer is Emma uncompromisingly dogmatic.

The embeddings in this speech also tend to moderate the strength of the opinion that is expressed. The pronominal pattern differs markedly from that of extract (a): *you* (S_1) is in contrastive balance with *I* (S_2); *you* with *him* (S_3); *I* (S_4) with *you* (S_5); and *I* (S_6) with *him* and *you* (S_7). These suggest Emma's new conception of balance and proportion between the addresser and addressee in their relation to the object. The evidence for Emma's judgement, the letter, is in a final position in S_3 (*it*), and the reversal of *you-for it* (S_3) to *it-with you* (S_7) stresses the importance she places on Mr Knightley's reasoned approval.

The contrasts between extracts (a) and (b) seem to be considerable, and to indicate that changes have taken place in both the surface and deeper levels of Emma's language, and hence in her linguistic and social relations to those around her. At the start of the novel her egoistical qualities predominate as she attempts to dominate the minds of others; towards the end she is shown to have achieved an understanding both of herself and of those around her that enables her to perceive her true social and moral position.

What is particularly notable about Emma's deviations from plain language and her later observance of the norm is that they are not peculiar to her idiolect, as, for example, Mrs Elton's deviations are to hers. Instead, Emma's dialogue has links with the whole spectrum of language presented in the novel. Like Mrs Elton, she is inclined to make dogmatic statements, to Harriet in particular ('There can be no doubt of your being a gentleman's daughter' E, 30), and she generalizes wildly ('A man always imagines a woman to be ready for anybody who asks her' E, 60). Her use of the first person pronoun is obtrusive in her summing up of Robert Martin's letter (E, 51), and when she is trying to bend Harriet to her will in refusing Robert

Martin (E, 53), she uses the first person pronoun with all the insistence that Frank Churchill does (E, 250-51).

> 'Not for the world', said Emma, smiling graciously, 'would I advise you either way. You must be the best judge of your own happiness. If you prefer Mr. Martin to every other person; if you think him the most agreeable man you have ever been in company with, why should you hesitate? You blush, Harriet. – Does any body else occur to you at this moment under such a definition? Harriet, Harriet, do not deceive yourself; do not be run away with by gratitude and compassion. At this moment whom are you thinking of?' (E, 53).

The repetition in this speech of *you*, like Frank's and Mr Elton's, is aggressive in its frequency. Furthermore, Emma's deviations from the SPO(C) pattern are noticeable, the complement often being foregrounded; many of the verbs are conditional or imperative; interrogative structures are prominent; and there are a number of negatives. Although this speech is apparently advice, these characteristics seem to preclude the balance that would be expected to accompany judgement. When Emma is trying to persuade others to do what she thinks they ought to do, her syntax resembles Mr Elton's most closely in its neglect of the SPO(C) pattern. The first intimation is her repetition of his inversion in her reply to his compliment:

> ' . . . Skilful has been the hand.'
> 'Great has been the pleasure, I am sure . . . ' (E, 43)

Like Frank Churchill, Emma expresses insincere agreement with a 'very true' (E, 55), and throughout her speeches can be found evidence that, like Frank, she is not regarding facts but 'considering exteriors and probabilities' (E, 83).

In short, it is evident that Emma's deviations from plain language are not unique to her, and that she shares linguistic attributes with the Eltons, Frank Churchill, Jane Fairfax, Mr Woodhouse, Harriet Smith, and even with Miss Bates, though in Emma's speech the same characteristic is generally in a milder form. Dialogue in *Emma* therefore functions structurally in the same way as the comedy: through a series of interrelations and contrasts, Emma is placed securely at the centre of the novel, the only character to be illumined by everyone else.

Structurally, Emma's linguistic and moral likenesses to the residents of Highbury are most heavily weighted at the beginning of the novel, diminishing as her affinity to Mr Knightley increases. As the dialogue illustrates, Mr Knightley stands in contrast to many faulty speakers, demonstrating by his own example how plainness and sincerity may be practised and that they can be attained by Emma. Emma's progress towards Mr Knightley and her goal increases in moral seriousness as the deeper implications of the dialogue emerge, so that what we may at first accept as merely commonplace and undiscriminating praise of a 'plain style' gradually becomes manifest as a confrontation between fundamental honesty and deception. Mrs Elton tries to deceive others, Harriet Smith deceives herself, and Emma learns to discard such dishonesty in favour of the linguistic self-consciousness that is a realization of moral integrity. Mr Knightley, therefore, by maintaining the attitude that only through a critical appraisal of language can we discover truth, presents one of the most important lessons that Emma and the reader have to learn.

Because of the complexity of the relations of Emma's idiolect, we cannot generalize about its character. At each point we need to look as much at the speech of her fellows as at her own. As she grows in self-knowledge, so her linguistic relation to them alters, and never at any point can her idiosyncrasies be as densely or exclusively represented as theirs are. Indeed, the changes that take place in her idiolect show her discarding idiosyncratic markers, so that by the end of the novel she has come close to a self-effacing language free of generalizations, elaborate syntax, excessive negatives, fragmented utterances, verbless sentences, overworked pronouns, and all the other features that have come to represent divergencies. What remains is the plain language of morality:

'... My Emma, does not every thing serve to prove more and more the beauty of truth and sincerity in all our dealings with each other?' (E, 446).

WALT WHITMAN PASSES THE FULL-STOP BY . . .

Mark Kinkead-Weekes

No one will get at my verses who insists upon viewing them
as a literary performance, or attempt at such performance,
or as aiming mainly toward art or aestheticism.[1]

Now I reverse what I said, and affirm that all depends on the aesthetic
or intellectual
And that criticism is great – and that refinement is greatest of all.[2]

> Do I contradict myself?
> Very well then I contradict myself,
> (I am large, I contain multitudes.)[3]

There is need, of course, for opposite stresses; and there is something
refreshing about the very openness of Whitman's contradictions: the
gross egotism and the eager democracy, the defiances and the need
to embrace every thing, the pleasure in attitudinizing and the awareness of pose. The draught of fresh air that still blows through his
pages comes also from his determination to have nothing to do with
the merely 'literary' and to have the courage, instead, to trust his
voice to take him freely and organically to original forms of utterance. The first vital challenge of his poetry is that we have to throw
away our normal critical toolkits – the equipment tends not to fit.
Yet there is need also to emphasize how much of Whitman remains
blab yawp and belch; how right Pound was when he told his father
that he could not read *Leaves of Grass* 'without swearing at the author
almost continuously';[4] how right Lawrence was to denounce the
inability to imagine the otherness of the other, which makes so many

---

1. 'A Backward Glance O'er Travel'd Roads' in Walt Whitman, *Leaves of Grass and Selected Prose*, ed. S. Bradley (New York, 1966), pp. 486-7. All subsequent quotations, except where otherwise stated, are from this edition.
2. 'Says', *Leaves of Grass, Inclusive Edition*, ed. E. Holloway (New York, 1927), p. 481, §7, ll. 2-3.
3. 'Song of Myself', Section 51, op. cit., p. 76.
4. 3rd June 1913, *The Letters of Ezra Pound*, ed. D. D. Paige (London, 1951), p. 57.

of the embracing gestures unbearably facile.[5] Whitman's attitudinizing frequently masks unwillingness to examine what he is saying. Might it not have been better if he had 'let it all out' less and discriminated more? – since letting it out can as easily be a sign of flatulence as of liberty. I must also confess to being rather weary of hearing so much from critics, especially American ones, about Whitman's *attitudes*, which strike me on the whole as sadly flabby. (Indeed, it could well be argued that America is now paying for the failure to examine the inadequacies of large Whitmanesque gesturing.)

There has on the other hand been significantly little effort to establish what it is that makes Whitman a great and a revolutionary *poet*, an extraordinary user of words and discoverer of form, though in far fewer poems than is generally admitted. On the Alexandrian library test I think that 'Song of Myself' could be allowed to perish without excessive grief, provided that 'When lilacs last in the dooryard bloom'd', 'Out of the cradle endlessly rocking', and 'Crossing Brooklyn Ferry' were preserved; and it is only a little teasing to suggest that we can 'get at' what makes these his major poems far more surely by looking at Whitman's syntax than at his sentiments.

The real significance of many of Whitman's attitudes is their disconcerting implications for the making of poems. The one point that several critics do seem to raise about the poetics of 'Song of Myself' is the insistence not only on organic form but also on democratic syntax. The voice not only has to be free to take its way wholly independent of preconceived formal organization and careless of structure, finding its own; but, also, nothing that it says can be intrinsically any more important than any other thing. So, continuously, half-lines may equally celebrate opposites; and, more significantly, the syntax has to be radically co-ordinative rather than subordinative. This reaches a democratic extreme in those passages where each line has become an independent as well as an equal unit.

I believe a leaf of grass is no less than the journey-work of the stars,
And the running blackberry would adorn the parlors of heaven,
And the tree-toad is a chef-d'oeuvre for the highest,
And the pismire is equally perfect, and a grain of sand, and the egg of
                                        the wren,

5. *Studies in Classic American Literature* (New York, 1923).

And a mouse is miracle enough to stagger sextillions of infidels,
And the cow crunching with depress'd head surpasses any statue,
And the narrowest hinge in my hand puts to scorn all machinery . . .[6]

But it is not merely that the lines are equal, so that the syntactical
relation between them can only be 'and'; it follows also that the
order of the lines cannot be important. I have in fact misquoted:
the first line is where Whitman put it, but not one of the others is in
its textual place in relation to those that precede and follow. Yet
few readers will have noticed because there is really nothing *to*
notice.

   One can play the same game with the sections of the work to some
extent, though not so much. They do fall into groups thematically
like an extempore sermon, but different critics give equally plausible
classifications, all of which are very approximate. The sections are
often 'poems' on their own, and one can play ducks and drakes a
good deal with their ordering before one makes any real difference.
This has its bearing, of course, on the theme of the poem and its
revolutionary and experimental nature; but the trouble is that the
organic and democratic impulses, carried to such lengths, tend to
produce flabby formlessness in the work as a whole. There is no
need for the poet to question whether any bit of it is doing any work,
and the Song becomes an anthology, of distinctly uneven quality,
where the good is often neutralized by being cocooned within the
flabby. Similarly the more democratic one's syntax, the more likely
one is to produce catalogues in which there is little real imaginative
life, for in art (whatever may be true politically – and it is very naive
to conflate different kinds of activity) quality depends on exploratory
discrimination.

   How above all is such a poem to end? It cannot *conclude*, with
any sort of climax or finality, without playing its premises false. In
one sense, of course, Whitman went on writing it through the various
editions from 1855-1892, so that it kept on being the song of himself. In another sense he kept passing the full stop by, so that the
poem goes on far too long. Even so there had to be some sort of
ending, however arbitrary, and the solution is a neat one, achieving
a final relation of the poet and the reader that is yet not concluded.
'I stop somewhere waiting for you'. The poem thus openly proclaims

---

6. 'Song of Myself', Section 31, op. cit. p. 50.

that its formal ending is merely arbitrary; but this is also the deeper
thematic point about time and the human life which the poem pro-
jects into the future, where Walt is still alive, not so much under our
boots as on the page as we read, kept going by that present participle. There is a 'point' but no full stop.

Only, the poetry carries little imaginative conviction because its
statements so often remain assertions rather than creations which
can command the suspension of disbelief. The tone of the last line
is clever and jokey, with a fine full ring, and a nice ambiguity about
our deaths as well as our gift of renewed life to the poem and the
poet, but one isn't inclined to take it very seriously. There is, however,
in that continuous present participle, an indication of how radically
Whitman may be committed to writing in not merely the present
tense, but the continuous-present, projected forward beyond the
apparent 'end'. This seems to me a major feature of his best work,
and a very significant one. I propose now to consider seriously the
ways in which the three major poems achieve form, and discipline,
and conviction, in banishing the full-stop and making the poem a
grammar of eternal life, achieving a triumph over the threat of death
and finality in the *poetry*, the structure of the poetic language, not
merely 'what it says'.

'When lilacs last in the dooryard bloom'd' (1865/6, 1871) is
probably the most accessible of the three, because Whitman achieves
a primary order and organization (which 'Song of Myself' so notably lacked) through the structural imagery of the lilac, associated with
on-going life, the star that is associated with the death of Lincoln, and
the song of the hermit thrush – and we are quite familiar with that
kind of organization. It is, therefore, no accident that in a representative collection of essays on Whitman,[7] this is the only poem of the
three that gets fairly full treatment, by Charles Feidelson in 'Whitman as Symbolist'. Yet in trying to discover how the poem finally
brings together its different modes of apprehension, we may find
that symbolism is less important than syntax.

Since the poem proceeds by re-writing itself again and again, extending itself each time, but circling back into itself having taken in
more, there is a sense in which the whole is already present in embryo
in the first short section.

7. *Twentieth Century Views of Whitman*, ed. Roy Harvey Pearce (Englewood
   Cliffs, 1962).

When lilacs last in the dooryard bloom'd,
And the great star early droop'd in the western sky in the night,
I mourn'd, and yet shall mourn with ever-returning spring.

Ever-returning spring, trinity sure to me you bring,
Lilac blooming perennial and drooping star in the west,
And thought of him I love.

The first three lines are set firmly in the past tense, but then project an eternity of mourning into the future. Lincoln is dead. The language carries an odd suggestion that 'last' in 'Where lilacs last . . . ' could mean 'for the last time', and though it clearly doesn't mean that, the 'ever returning spring' merely brings a recurrent springing up of past grief. There is no present life. But the next three lines contain what the first three leave out, though they also leave out what those contain. Now the tense is the present, with not only the lilac 'blooming perennial' but the drooping star's continuous presence also allied with a continuity of love. And, though we don't notice this until afterwards, the poetry has not merely juxtaposed two different modes of being and feeling, but is already beginning to mediate between them, and contain them in a more inclusive medium. Already we cannot take the star as 'symbolic' of death or the lilac of life, one confined to the past and the other to the present and future; for the essence of what has happened is that each is beginning to participate in the mode of the other.

   The next three sections then take up each of the elements we have met, and extend them. The fallen star is mourned anew, but the exclamatory mode of the grief now, which may strike one at first as objectionable apostrophe, suddenly reveals its point in its syntax. There are no verbs, hence there can be no sentences, only clauses. Nothing can be done; there can be no shaping into meaning; only cries of loss, grief, obscurity, helplessness. In contrast the verse for the lilac swells out, the growing thing *stands*, and the present participles proclaim its continuous and active life. (But is the poet's action as he breaks the sprig of lilac a death-action or a love/life-action? We shall see . . .) In the fourth section we are given a surrogate for Whitman's poetry in the song of the hermit thrush which contains, in the present, both death and life. Growing, breaking, warbling, bleeding, have been associated with one another more firmly than before.

   In sections five to nine the poem is rewritten again. Now the spring of continuous life out of winter, and the mournful cortege of death, are visually and dramatically juxtaposed. Through a spring landscape (which yet reminds us how it has sprung from death, violets from gray debris, grains of wheat ambiguously from 'shrouds') there is suddenly threaded the passing of Lincoln's coffin. Immediately the process is then reversed: the funereal pomp of the great procession passing sonorously through the land is suddenly brought up against the poet, bestowing his gift of lilac as an explicit fusion of life and love with death. It is not for that coffin only; for Whitman is determined to offer in gift and song the reminder of the burgeoning life of spring for all deaths. In section eight, however, finality is allowed its say, in the memory of how the great star 'Concluded, dropt in the night, and was gone'. Only, it had manifestly not gone, for there it is a month later, 'sailing the heaven', and the poem is conceiving a new awareness, therefore, of what the star 'must have meant'. Already, as the bird's song is taken up again in section nine, the poet hears and understands; but he is not yet ready to give the understanding full expression, for he has not yet included enough. The process of the poem reveals itself as a cumulative delaying, which allows the potential reconciliation which has been present since the first section to keep announcing itself, but continually holds it back in order to get more into it, more resonance. The poem is prevented from developing in a straight line; above all it is prevented from coming to an end. In that sense, already, we can see how its form is its theme; for the poem is preventing Lincoln's death from becoming final, in preventing itself from becoming finalized.

   In sections ten to twelve the poet completes the elegiac formalities, composing an American elegy for the dead leader, decking funeral song and chamber. From east and west, sea and land, the winds are summoned to fuse with the poet's living breath, perfuming the grave. He creates American genre pictures of life for the dead man, of sunset in April, but also of the cyclical life of the sun. In singing for death he creates life through the senses. Once more, in section thirteen, the bird sings on. Once more, but for the last time, the poet hangs back, held by the star and the lilac.

   In section fourteen the final rewriting begins by plunging us back into the past tense; and the poet is ready to announce now, in the recreated context of the approaching summer, but under the cloud of the long black funeral trail, his possession of both the 'thought' and the 'knowledge' of death. Between them, as between companions, he finally moves to hear the hermit thrush's song. The distinction between 'thought' and 'knowledge' requires no abstract formulation – Whitman merely expresses in a figure what the movement of his poem has been all the time. Between potential conception and actual realization, each stronger with each rewriting, the poem has moved from the beginning. And now the birdsong is permitted to voice its with-held syntactical secret: that death's rhythm is, no less than life's, *a continuous present and not a full stop.*

> Come lovely and soothing death,
> Undulate round the world, serenely *arriving, arriving,* [my italics]
> In the day, in the night, to all, to each,
> Sooner or later delicate death . . .

Death is part of a continuous cycle, and must be celebrated along with life, even joyfully. One retorts, of course, that the lyricism is facile and sentimental, finding it simple to see death 'universally', and call it pretty names, because the eyes are closed to actual human experience. Is death 'lovely and soothing', 'delicate', 'cool-enfolding', 'soft', 'floating . . . bliss' to the dying or to the bereaved? Fortunately Whitman himself has just proclaimed that 'thought' must go hand in hand with 'knowledge'; so the conceiving of death's universal rhythm has to be fused with a realization of the 'debris' of the dead and the suffering of those who remain. Lyricism is stilled into a silent nightmare vision of a civil war battlefield. (He had of course been to the front to search for his brother and had been a volunteer army hospital nurse from 1862-1864.)

> I saw battle-corpses, myriads of them,
> And the white skeletons of young men, I saw them,
> I saw the debris and debris of all the slain soldiers of the war.

Yet he will not have the reverse sentimentality either. By dying, the dead no longer feel the tragedy of the full-stop and the past tense; it is the living who carry the full weight of these.

> But I saw they were not as was thought,
> They themselves were fully at rest, they suffer'd not,
> The living remain'd and suffer'd, the mother suffer'd,
> And the wife and the child and the musing comrade suffer'd,
> And the armies that remain'd suffer'd.

This section is perhaps still too visionary; it lacks the quiet factual horror of his letter to his mother on March 29th 1864;[8] but it saves the poem which, without it, would be as sentimental as the song of the thrush taken alone. Yet the full-stop after 'suffer'd' is as half-a-truth as the rhythm of death as continuous present. What end can the poem attain that is not sentimental or partial?

The answer is to create a poetry that encompasses all that has gone before, beginning with letting go, ending; but remarshalls all into a unique form which can not only make the full-stop on which we have just ended only a phase to be passed by, but can also convincingly retrieve what is past and make it infinite. It works like the winding and unwinding of a spool so that neither movement is the whole, and I think my insistence on syntax justifies itself, since this is how it is done. (The 'symbols' of lilac, star and bird are revealed as only the means to a marvellously creative syntactical end.) First Whitman circumvents that full-stop by 'passing', apparently in farewell, going back through his poem from the end to the beginning, enacting a process of continual separation. He takes leave of each element in the complex whole, one by one, 'passing', 'ceasing' – yet each element as it is passed is there to us in the continuing life of present participles. But finally there is a retrieving out of the night whose achievement is even stranger; for the memory of the elements is woven together and projected in that form we refer to precisely as the infinitive.

Yet each to keep and all, retrievements out of the night,
The song, the wondrous chant of the gray-brown bird,
And the tallying chant, the echo arous'd in my soul,
With the lustrous and drooping star with the countenance full of woe,
With the holders holding my hand nearing the call of the bird,
Comrades mine and I in the midst, and their memory ever to keep,
                                    for the dead I loved so well,
For the sweetest, wisest soul of all my days and lands – and this for
                                    his dear sake,
Lilac and star and bird twined with the chant of my soul,
There in the fragrant pines and the cedars dusk and dim.

8. *The Collected Writings of Walt Whitman. The Correspondence Vol.* 1, ed. E. H. Miller (New York, 1961), pp. 204-5.

The poem nominally 'ends' with the word 'dim' and a full-stop; but its form proclaims the opposite, centering on the infinitive 'to keep'. There is no verb – 'twined' is a past participle – because what is 'infinitive' must be neither present past nor future, but a mode secured beyond all. 'Passing . . . I leave . . . I cease . . . yet each and all *to keep . . . there . . .* ', this is the poem's achieved grammar of eternal life. The meaning is enacted in the language, fully formed and controlled, where 'Song of Myself' orates and attitudinizes. 'Lilacs' is a revolutionary poem for which we have to find an uniquely appropriate critical approach. I know no other poem like it.

Or rather, I do: 'Out of the cradle endlessly rocking' (1859, 1881), which is indeed in some ways even better. For if one had to formulate a limiting criticism of 'Lilacs' it might well be that, for Whitman, it is still too 'symbolic'; in his terms almost too 'literary'. The three 'symbols' are appropriate and are handled tactfully, but they have a certain initial arbitrariness, a sense of being imported into the poem as machinery, whereas the sea, the mocking bird and the child are concretely fused in an actual memory, and the eliciting of their interaction is more spontaneous and organic than the elaborate tour-de-force of 'Lilacs'.

Once again the poem is adumbrated in potential at the beginning, and then rewritten and extended. This time, however, instead of beginning even apparently in a 'symbolic' way, Whitman starts with a splendid oratorio interweaving the senses and the tenses in music. The first energy is a gathering movement in the language, done this time by the prepositions. From all directions, out of, over, down from, up from, out from, from under, borne hither, the various elements of the remembered scene are gathered together. The weaving is done in terms of sound (the sea rocking, the mocking-bird's shuttle); of light (the interplay of moonlight and shadow); of inner and outer space (the boy on the beach, and the inner movement of the heart responding to the notes); and of time (the man in the 'now' of the poem fusing with the boy in the past). The past is created as a repository of energies, still going on in present participles within the past tense, and capable of being tapped and brought bodily into the present, uniting with the 'words' the experience had already given rise to. The past becomes actively present and the poet aspires to unite the here with the hereafter.

From those beginning notes of yearning and love there in the mist,
From the thousand responses of my heart never to cease,
From the myriad thence-arous'd words,
From the word stronger and more delicious than any,
From such as now they start the scene revisiting,
As a flock, twittering, rising, or overhead passing,
Borne hither, ere all eludes me, hurriedly,
A man, yet by these tears a little boy again,
Throwing myself on the sand, confronting the waves,
I, chanter of pains and joys, uniter of here and hereafter,
Taking all hints to use them, but swiftly leaping beyond them,
A reminiscence sing.

The second section of the poem proceeds to orchestrate the memory
of boy and bird – with the sea only as murmurous background – by
playing the boy's language against the bird's song. Here again,
watching the tenses will show the curious way in which, as they are
interwoven, each is transformed into the mode of the other. The
boy begins in a subtly 'imperfect' past. 'Once' secures pastness
from the start, but the poetry emphasizes, in the repeated 'every day',
the continuous being of the nesting birds and the continuous activity of the boy 'peering, absorbing, translating'. Suddenly one realizes
that there is no finite verb ('crouched' being, again, a past participle).
Meanwhile, the first birdsong is a tremendously confident present
imperative: 'Shine! shine! shine! . . . Singing all time, minding no
time,/While we two keep together'. With the disappearance of the
she-bird, however, the boy's tense hardens into the perfect; but the
bird's song becomes more tentative: 'Blow! blow! blow! . . . I wait
and I wait *till you blow* my mate to me' (My italics). Now, however,
the boy's language begins to turn from the past into the present;
the past tense changes back into the-present-in-the-past, done in
participles; and that becomes infinitive and 'now'.

> I, with bare feet, a child, the wind wafting my hair,
> Listen'd long and long.
>
> Listen'd to keep, to sing, now translating the notes,
> Following you my brother.

Conversely, in a beautifully modulated process too long to quote, we
hear the confidence in continuity ebbing away in the birdsong, revealing a greater and greater tentativeness, breaking the rhythm,

getting softer and more despairing, till eventually the full impact of
loss locks home in the past tense.

> Loved! loved! loved! loved! loved!
> But my mate no more, no more with me!
> We two together no more.

The two complementary processes are enacted in the language. In
the birdsong we are made to *experience* how the living present cannot
be held, but turns agonizingly into the past with the inescapable
fact of death. Conversely, in the 'translation' we experience the opposite process as the past is made to live so vividly again that it becomes a mode of present energy. As the birdsong dies away, the
language surges into continuous activity, rendered in a powerful
series of present participles, and out of that concentration of energies
the poet is born. The bird has become a daimon – 'demon', wakening
inspiration for a thousand songs, but also arousing torment. Out of
the intuition of grief and death poetry starts to life, but the process
is then projected into an endless future, with the realization that he
will never cease perpetuating the bird, will never escape the cries of
unsatisfied love, 'the sweet hell within,/The unknown want'.

And it is in answer to the pain of that – which is *always* the present
projecting the future, unable to cease or be satisfied, unable to achieve
the rest of the past – that the sea (which has been murmuring in the
background all the time) is at last allowed to sound through.

Whereto answering, the sea,
Delaying not, hurrying not,
Whisper'd me through the night, and very plainly before daybreak,
Lisp'd to me the low and delicious word death,
And again death, death, death, death.

I do not think that 'delicious' is as damaging as the lapse into sentimentality at the corresponding point in 'Lilacs'. For, in context, the
sound and rhythm of the language in these lines *is* tranquillizing,
with something of the whisper of sea on sand that all men find soothing; and not only has the pain of loss already been secured, but we
have just been made to realize, also, how intolerable it would be to
banish the past tense and live without death. Yet what the sea
whispers is not the bird's tragic apprehension of the past as finished;
any more than it is the boy's sense of an unfinishable present and
future. The next lines ensure that we hear sound and sense aright,

not only whispering, but with the spaces between the words that
show the secret meaning. The rhythm of death is, even more clearly
than in 'Lilacs', a cyclic recurrence of that which gives rest again,
and again, and again, like the 'shsh' of wavelets on the shore or the
soothing of a mother at the cradle, but rocking endlessly.

Hissing melodious, neither like the bird nor like my arous'd child's
                                                                heart,
But edging near as privately for me rustling at my feet,
Creeping thence steadily up to my ears and laving me softly all over,
Death, (pause) death, (pause) death, (pause) death, (pause) death.

All the poet has to do, finally, is to 'fuse' birth and death in a series
of paradoxes. What the weaving together of birdsong, responsive
song, and sea song has achieved is a sense of how the intuition of
death both brings the poet and his poetry to life, and soothes the
ache of endlessness with finality, which is yet endlessly recurrent.
The sea is both aged crone and sweet-smelling mother. There is also
a hidden paradox in the syntax of the ending;

That strong and delicious word which, creeping to my feet,
(Or like some old crone rocking the cradle, swathed in sweet garments,
                                                            bending aside,)
The sea whisper'd me.

for the delay caused by the parenthesis, especially if the lines are
read aloud, ensures that the last line echoes in the mind on its own,
as well as in its grammatical relation to its predecessors. One can see
how this curious effect would have been spoilt if Whitman had
written 'The sea whisper'd *to* me', for though the sea does whisper
to him, it also in another sense whispers *him*, into poetic being, and
the 'me' is not yet finite, though the poem has happened. Moreover,
Whitman has also invented a new tense, the past-present, for the
experience is apparently in the past, a memory, yet it is equally
obviously happening now, when the poem finally comes into existence, – as it ends.

If one were still to carp a little, it would be because death continues
to be seen in a context which takes the sting out of it, though there
is less damaging sentimentality than in 'Lilacs'. (There is also, however, less to counteract it of the tragic stature of the civil war, or indeed the death of Lincoln). Whitman certainly never focuses on
what it is like to die. Nevertheless, the talk about 'delicate' or 'de-

licious' death is not merely a question of Whitman failing to make himself realize what death is and means with sufficient resonance. At least part of the trouble is that he is not really interested in death, but is using it notionally in order to explore the ability of poetry to connect past and future. If one were now to draw up a recipe for a poem that would be even better, even less question-begging than 'Out of the cradle', it would be one in which the poet no longer needed to talk of death in order to achieve his dance of the tenses. And, since the superiority of 'Out of the Cradle' to 'Lilacs' rests on the absence of symbolic manipulation, it should be a poem still more 'everyday', still less exotic and contrived. I am describing what I take to be Whitman's finest poem.

'Crossing Brooklyn Ferry' is a deeply democratic poem in the sense that it springs naturally and unforced from the experience of anyone who has ever crossed on a big-city ferry – a marvellously complex and convincing work built out of the very ordinary. From the beginning it is concrete and specific, set matter-of-factly in space and time: the flood tide, the sun half an hour from setting, the hundreds of people sharing the experience, the people who will cross years hence. The poem seems to grow spontaneously, unmanipulated, with no showing off of the poet, or his powers, and yet from the start there is a quiet declaration that the 'usual' may be more extraordinary and meaningful than one supposes.

The second section allows the setting and the crowds to sustain the individual poet. He and all the other individuals are alone, 'disintegrated', yet part of the 'scheme'; his actions in walking the streets and being borne on the flood are 'similitudes' of both past and future; they have happened before and will happen again; and this gives them a glory in their ordinariness for they connect him with 'certainty of others'. The tense breaks into the future, in the calm and naturally justified conviction that others *will* do and see just as he does and sees.

In the third section Whitman enacts just this in enacting the crossing. In closely observed visual detail he brings the scene alive: the gulls wheeling above in the last of the sunlight, the low sun aureoling the reflection of his head in the water, the haze on the hills, the shipping coming in from the bay, the activity in the docks, the light fading, the fires from the foundry chimneys casting flickering lights on housetops and the chasms of the streets. There seems little to say about this section except to point to the vividness, the con-

viction that this is just what he saw, and what one would see essentially oneself. Difference of place and date are insignificant.

So when he declares his love for Brooklyn and Manhattan, and the
stately river, it is matter of fact; and we accept equally his feeling for
the others crossing with him, for the affection of the whole portrayal
includes them. We can even accept quite simply that imagining the
future the same as his present has brought him 'near' to those who
will look back on him – ourselves – because he looked forward to
them. 'The time will come, though I stop here to-day and to-night.'
This gives a strange yet simple feeling, for of course the time has
come and Walt Whitman has stopped . . . in a sense.

But in a sense this is not so. In the fifth section the poem begins to
stir and grow curiously. For it was with the body that is now dead –
as he foresaw, putting himself into the past – that Walt Whitman was
himself in his personal identity, 'struck from the float'. It was in his
body that he was what he had called in another poem a simple
separate person. And it was also through the physical imagination
that he is able to enter past and future. In the sixth section he writes
a self-analysis quite free from posturing and attitudinizing; simply
emphasizing how it was his life in the body that gave him the ordinary experience of humanity, the evil as well as the good, the friend-
ship and the reticence. (Perhaps Whitman's homosexuality adds a
level of meaning here, but one would distort by emphasizing it,
because he is stressing the common experience of all human
beings.)

In the seventh section he springs a comic surprise; telling us that
he has considered us seriously before we were born, and teasing us
with the thought that he may be looking at us, and enjoying it, as
we read. And in the eight section, after reminding us of his evening
scene in not only its beauty but its human relationship, he insists
that something has happened, while we were not looking. The 'play'
immortality is suddenly revealed in a truer mode.

What is more subtle than this which ties me to the woman or man that
                                              looks in my face?
Which fuses me into you now, and pours my meaning into you?

We understand then do we not?
What I promis'd without mentioning it, have you not accepted?
What the study could not teach – what the preaching could not ac-
                        complish is accomplish'd, is it not?

It *is* accomplished – that annihilating of time that is immortality, that fusion of present past and future that has been the subject of all three poems, but that this one has achieved so quietly that one hadn't even noticed.

Away back in the third section, as Whitman subtly placed future 'crossers' in the present and himself in the past ('Just as you feel . . . so I felt'), he had made us identify with the scene as happening to us 'now'. It manifestly does happen as we read, the experience of crossing the ferry, and he is with us as we cross in his crossing. We experience from moment to moment the turning eye, and the movement of the ferry from the near side to the far side coming near, and the fading of the sun into the dark. More subtly still, within the scene itself, Whitman has provided us with common optical illusions which themselves enact, in miniature, the whole strange intersection of time that is the central experience of the poem. 'Just as you stand and lean on the rail, yet hurry with the swift current, I stood yet was hurried.' The passenger stands apparently still on the spot, but is being carried from one side of the river to the other; stands apparently steady in the present, yet is being carried momentarily from the past into the future. As he looks up the gulls seem to float motionless; but they are moving and he is moving, as the slow drift away finally shows. The reflected face in the water is even more significant. The 'centrifugal spokes of light' that aureole the face happen because the sun is shining past a moving object onto moving water; and yet the face appears to the observer on the boat to be still, whereas in fact it is moving fast. The face Whitman gazed at each split second was gone from the water the next, but another was there in its place . . . and it was still there when he wrote the poem in 1856, and revised it in 1881, and it is still there when I am reading it now, and will be there when you read it in the future. The poetry marvellously creates an experience which is pluperfect before the poem, perfect in the poem, present and manifestly happening as we read, and available in the future. Moreover, we are always *crossing* Brooklyn ferry in the poem; we never get to the other side, finish it all off, say 'that's done'. Whitman has connected his past, his present, and our future in which he is clearly immortal, in the poetry.

So he has earned the right in the final section to celebrate the crossing again, and all the things he 'saw', in that continuous present tense and imperative mood that are his favourite modes of expression, because the limitation of finite time is abolished and control is as-

sured. 'Flow on', he cries, 'flow and ebb . . . frolic on . . . drench . . .
cross . . . stand up . . . throb . . . suspend here and everywhere, eternal
float of solution . . . gaze . . . sound out . . . live', and so *on*. The rich
vitality is urged on into continuous active life; and the imperative
takes place both in his time scheme and in ours. Lastly, he celebrates
what enabled him to bridge present past and future: the bodily
senses which made his experience both his then and ours now, and
the lastingness of the world of appearances. These are spiritual too,
for it is they that have linked Walt Whitman in immortality with us.
By the final paragraph, for the first time in any of the three poems,
the dominant pronoun has become 'we', with an inevitability quite
unforced by exhortation. 'What the study could not teach – what the
preaching could not accomplish is accomplish'd, is it not?' If he was
at fault so very often in confusing poetry with oratory, in this poem
he has created rather than harangued. He has realized a fusion of the
tenses through the senses, and in doing so has been able (of all things
for Whitman!) to be subtly reticent, and to make the achievement
good before proclaiming it.

HARDY AND RESPECTABILITY[1]

Ronald P. Draper

According to Robert Gittings, Hardy adopted the curious scheme of having his own autobiography published after his death as if it were a biography written by his second wife in order to 'silence future writers'. 'Probably the most powerful motive' for this secrecy, says Gittings, 'was some sort of snobbery'. A little further on, however, he qualifies this:

> Yet snobbery is too sweeping and easy a dismissal for Hardy's purpose. In early life he had to fight the massive social stratification of the Victorian age. Finally he broke through from one class to another; but one can only guess what violence this did to his own nature. To shut the door on a social past from which he had escaped became a compulsion in his later life. Nor were his motives merely those of social and class distinction, though these were powerful in the years when he was struggling for recognition, and he still remembered and resented them deep into the twentieth century. This strange record also reveals Hardy's reverence for learning. The gulf between someone with whom he could talk freely in an educated way, and one of his own background, who, however full of simple wisdom, could literally not speak the language which Hardy had acquired, haunted his mind. In novels, he might extol the instinctive rightness of the peasant; in life, he always sought the company of the educated. Again, one can only guess the conflicts this caused.[2]

One is reminded of the dialogue in *Sons and Lovers* between Paul Morel and his mother:

> 'You know,' he said to his mother, 'I don't want to belong to the well-to-do middle class. I like my common people best. I belong to the common people . . . from the middle classes one

1. This paper was read to the third annual Conference of University Teachers of English in Scotland, held at the University of Edinburgh, November 1975.

2. Robert Gittings, *Young Thomas Hardy* (London, 1975), p. 4.

gets ideas, and from the common people – life itself, warmth.
You feel their hates and loves.'

'It's all very well, my boy. But, then, why don't you go and
talk to your father's pals?'

'But they're rather different.'

'Not at all. They're the common people. After all, whom do
you mix with now – among the common people? Those that
exchange ideas, like the middle classes. The rest don't interest
you.'

'But – there's the life –'

'I don't believe there's a jot more life from Miriam than you
could get from any educated girl . . . It is *you* who are snobbish
about class.'

And the narrator comments:

> She frankly *wanted* him to climb into the middle class, a thing
> not very difficult, she knew. And she wanted him in the end to
> marry a lady.

> (*Sons and Lovers*, Chapter 10)

These are characters from a work of fiction, granted; but I think
this particular passage has the ring of autobiographical truth, and
we probably don't do too much damage if we think of it as a dialogue
taking place between David Herbert and Mrs Lawrence. The important qualification, however, would be that Lawrence, the adult
writer, sees the paradox better than Paul, the young Lawrence within
the fiction, does. It is echoed at the opening of *The Rainbow* in the
contrast between the intense blood-consciousness of the male
Brangwens, which yet produces a narrowness, and the wider social
and intellectual aspirations of their womenfolk.

The actual Lawrence did go on to marry a lady, though one very
different from the kind Mrs Morel envisages, and one who did not
bother unduly about respectability (indeed, she shocked Lawrence
himself sometimes). Hardy, too, married a lady – at any rate Emma
Lavinia, sister-in-law of the rector of St Juliot, North Cornwall, so
regarded herself; and Hardy, coming back from Lyonnesse with
magic in his eyes, seems to have thought her 'better connected and
more intellectual than she was to prove'.[3] Both marriages produced

3. Op. cit. p. 137.

their strife, but whereas Lawrence blazoned his in prose and verse
and invited his readers to look that he and Frieda had come through,
Hardy did his best to inhibit looking, and left us to guess that Emma
and he had *not* come through. Both also had prior affairs with girls
of their own class educated via the late-nineteenth century pupil-
teacher system, but, again, Lawrence's presentation of the Paul/
Lawrence – Miriam/Jessie Chambers relationship is in striking contrast to the reticence of Hardy about Tryphena Sparks.

Hardy, was, of course, a very old man when he laid his strange
plans for his biography. As a young novelist he seems to have been,
at least initially, less reticent. The text of the unpublished *The Poor
Man and the Lady* has been lost (though parts of it may have been
used in *Under the Greenwood Tree* and *An Indiscretion in The Life
of an Heiress*), but Hardy tells us that it was supposedly written
'By the Poor Man' and he calls it 'a striking socialistic novel'. It
was read by the publisher's reader for Chapman and Hall, no less
than George Meredith, who 'strongly advised its author not to 'nail
his colours to the mast' so definitely in a first book, if he wished
to do anything in literature; for if he printed so pronounced a thing he
would be attacked on all sides by the conventional reviewers, and
his future injured.'[4]

Hardy would seem to have taken this advice, but the anti-respect-
ability streak remained in his work, and after he became a successful
novelist (i.e. roughly speaking, after the publication of *Far From
the Madding Crowd*, 1874), it grew stronger rather than weaker.
The later tragic novels especially are full of indignation against the
self-satisfied narrowness of a society which holds inflexibly to its
conventional moral judgements and keeps its class barriers high;
but the sharpest criticism is reserved for the liberal detachment from
these standards which exists only on the surface, leaving the springs
of action controlled by the theoretically outmoded convention, for
this reveals how deeply chilling respectability's grip can be. Thus,
in *Tess of the d'Urbervilles* Hardy writes, 'Within the remote depths
of [Angel Clare's] constitution, so gentle and affectionate as he was
in general, there lay hidden a hard logical deposit, like a vein of
metal in a soft loam, which turned the edge of everything that at-

4. Florence Emily Hardy, *The Life of Thomas Hardy, 1840–1928* (London, 1962,
    reprint of 1972), pp. 57–61. (This biography was originally published in two
    volumes covering 1840–1891, pub. 1928, and 1892–1928, pub. 1930.)

tempted to traverse it'. It is this which is especially inimical to Tess, and makes Angel's sardonic 'I wish half the women in England were as respectable as you . . . It isn't a question of respectability, but one of principle!' (Chapter 36) a peculiarly painful comment on his own class, education and respectability.

In an extreme moment Jude Fawley exclaims: 'It takes two or three generations to do what I tried to do in one; and my impulses – affections – vices perhaps they should be called – were too strong not to hamper a man without advantages; who should be as cold-blooded as a fish and as selfish as a pig to have a really good chance of being one of his country's worthies' (*Jude the Obscure*, Part 6, Chapter 1). This is, no doubt, excessive, but it only carries to excess what appears as a recurrent theme in many of Hardy's novels, the idea of failure as more worthy than success. Its purest examples are Giles Winterborne and Tess, but Michael Henchard also exemplifies it (though we must not make the mistake of thinking that Farfrae, because he is the successful rival, is therefore as deplorable as Dr Fitzpiers *vis à vis* Giles). Gabriel Oak partly exemplifies it, but not entirely, for his virtues have something to do with his ultimate success. All are common men made uncommon by their innate qualities rather than by birth, education or wealth, Henchard's moderate wealth being the temporary product, and only the temporary product, of these qualities which equally produce his ruin.

This failure is also seen in the context of the failure of an old way of life, that 'defeat of agricultural life by nullifying urban forces', to quote one of Douglas Brown's formulations of it,[5] which has suffered some overstatement, but which *is* a valid part of the Wessex novels. In recording this changing society, however, Hardy did not deceive himself. As R. J. White says,

> . . . he never suffered from the delusion that 'things are not what they used to be', largely because he knew in his shrewd old country-dweller's way that they never are. Nor did he idealise a way that was departing. He came from a stratum of society which has always lived close to poverty and loss, suffering and rough weather, a part of society that has never had much time for the luxury of lamentation or the pleasures of nostalgia.[6]

5. Douglas Brown, *Thomas Hardy* (London, 1954). Extract reprinted in *Hardy, The Tragic Novels: A Casebook*, ed. R. P. Draper (London, 1975), p. 160.
6. R. J. White, *Thomas Hardy and History* (London, 1974), p. 5.

The crude, lumpish element in country life is seen for what it is; and among his tragic protagonists the destructiveness of Henchard's passions, or the fatal passiveness into which Tess lapses at crucial moments, are understood with almost Nietzschean insight (though in other respects Hardy is a very un-Nietzschean writer) as weaknesses that reveal a decadence in the old provincial ways. Consequently, Hardy does not, in *Tess of the d'Urbervilles*, for example, despite his defiance of conventional moral judgement (Tess 'a pure woman'), declare war Lawrentian-fashion on conventional respectability in the name of natural, and often lower-class, vigour. As Tony Tanner says, there is a strain in *Tess of the d'Urbervilles* which would make Tess a victim of man-made laws which are absurdly out of tune with Nature. 'But', he goes on, 'it is an important part of the book that we feel Nature itself turning against Tess, so that we register something approaching a sadism of *both* the man-made *and* the natural directed against her'.[7]

The implication of this is that nature arrested is potentially as destructive as the obviously inimical man-made forces symbolized by the threshing-machine which makes Tess its victim at Flintcomb Ash. Simple oppositions are rejected. Hardy may write the Wessex novels, as he says in the General Preface to the 1912 edition, 'in order to preserve for my own satisfaction a fairly true record of a vanishing way of life', but he refuses to sentimentalize. This is particularly clear in his important essay, 'The Dorsetshire Labourer' (1883), passages from which are often quoted in connection with *Tess* (published eight years later, in 1891). There the 'annual migration' of Lady Day is described as wearing 'an aspect of jollity', and mobility is seen as better for the labourer than stability: 'Whenever the habitually-removing man comes into contact with one of the old-fashioned stationary sort, who are still to be found, it is impossible not to perceive that the former is much more wide awake than his fellow-worker . . .' Disturbance is seen as involving both loss and gain; 'They are losing their individuality, but they are widening the range of their ideas, and gaining in freedom'. As for the outsider's literary nostalgia for vanishing country ways, 'It is too much', says

7. Tony Tanner, 'Colour and Movement in *Tess of the d'Urbervilles*', *Critical Quarterly*, 10 (Autumn 1968). Reprinted *Hardy, The Tragic Novels*, p. 204.

Hardy, 'to expect them to remain stagnant and old-fashioned for the
pleasure of romantic spectators . . .'[8]

The Lady Day removal in *Tess* proceeds in a very different way and
has tragic consequences; but the circumstances of Tess and her family
are what account for this. The removal is certainly not the basis for a
generalization about mobility as such – though some general comment is made on 'depopulation' as it affects life-holders and copy-
holders, with a sardonically authorial comment on 'statisticians'
who call it 'the tendency of the rural population towards the large
towns', meaning, says Hardy, 'the tendency of water to flow uphill
when forced by machinery' (*Tess*, Chapter 5). Nor does Hardy regard the kept woman as necessarily the tragic figure that Tess is
represented as being when she is the mistress of Alec d'Urberville
at Sandbourne (Chapter 5). For example, the mock-ballad-style
poem, 'The Ruined Maid' (written as early as 1866), presents a quite
different view of the kept woman:

'O 'Melia, my dear, this does everything crown!
Who could have supposed I should meet you in Town?
And whence such fair garments, such prosperi-ty' –
'O didn't you know I'd been ruined?' said she.

– 'You left us in tatters, without shoes or socks,
Tired of digging potatoes, and spudding up docks;
And now you've gay bracelets and bright feathers three!' –
'Yes: that's how we dress when we're ruined,' said she.

– 'At home in the barton you said "thee" and "thou",
And "thik oon," and "theäs oon," and "t'other"; but now
Your talking quite fits 'ee for high compa-ny!' –
'Some polish is gained with one's ruin,' said she.

– 'Your hands were like paws then, your face blue and bleak
But now I'm bewitched by your delicate cheek,
And your little gloves fit as on any la-dy!' –
'We never do work when we're ruined,' said she.

– 'You used to call home-life a hag-ridden dream,
And you'd sigh, and you'd sock; but at present you seem
To know not of megrims or melancho-ly!' –
'True. One's pretty lively when ruined,' said she.

8. Extract reprinted *Hardy, The Tragic Novels*, pp. 42–4.

> – 'I wish I had feathers, a fine sweeping gown,
> And a delicate face, and could strut about Town!' –
> 'My dear – a raw country girl, such as you be,
> Cannot quite expect that. You ain't ruined,' said she.[9]

One explanation of such differences is offered by Hardy himself in a comment of October 1888: 'If you look beneath the surface of any farce you see a tragedy; and, on the contrary, if you blind yourself to the deeper issues of a tragedy you see a farce'.[10] However, I do not think that in 'The Ruined Maid' Hardy is exactly blinding himself to the deeper, tragic issues. What that poem has to say is really very sensible, even if it doesn't say all there is to be said. The way in which it has its say, its style, is also very different from that of *Tess;* and this is not just a matter of the difference between sardonically humorous poem and tragic novel. Important stylistic differences exist side by side within the novels themselves. A formally polysyllabic, syntactically complex style, reminiscent of late-Victorian public utterances, rubs shoulders with a plainer, more energetic style (which some have seen as ballad-like in its simplicity); and this contrast is echoed in the different styles of Hardy's dialogue, varying between the educated, often rather stilted language of respectable characters and the more naturally rhythmical speech and blunter vocabulary of dialect speakers. The oscillation between these two is often taken as indicative of the lack of touch typical of the 'autodidact', but it can more reasonably be seen as a balancing of the tensions out of which Hardy's work springs.

David Lodge, who has given the most intelligent attention to Hardy's language, comments:

> There is the Hardy who can recreate dialect speech with flawless authenticity, who shows how closely he is in touch with the life of an agrarian community through being in touch with its idiom; and there is the Hardy speaking to 'the quality' in orotund sentences of laboured syntax and learned vocabulary, the Hardy who studied *The Times*, Addison, and Scott to improve his style... to regard the second Hardy as a regrettable excrescence superimposed upon the first, 'true', Hardy would be mistaken.

9. *The Collected Poems of Thomas Hardy* (London, 1930, reprint of 1974), pp. 145–6.
10. *The Life of Thomas Hardy*, p. 215.

For while one aspect of the novelist's undertaking in *Tess* demands a quality of immediacy, of 'felt life', achieved through
his empathetic identification with his characters, particularly
his heroine – in other words, the voice of the first Hardy – other
aspects demand a quality of distance, both of time and space,
through which the characters can be seen in their cosmic, historical and social settings – in other words, the voice of the second Hardy.[11]

This close-up and long-shot view of the variation in Hardy's style is
excellently put, but it does not, I think, account fully for the impression created by the novels as a whole. Hardy does not appear to be
engineering all his effects quite so deliberately as this, even though a
good deal of what he does is consciously measured, most obviously
when he juxtaposes dialect and non-dialect speech, or action and
reflection. Transcending this technical deployment is the sense of a
mind living in two worlds which it connects, but doesn't quite inte-
grate. As John Bayley argues, Hardy does not have the organic
unity of experience that would make him yield to the sort of criticism
that we associate with F. R. Leavis:

> Hardy's [intelligence] is deeply and radically divided. And it is
> this division, more than anything else, I suspect, which has led to
> his subordination in the fictional hierarchy of such a critic as
> Leavis, who makes something of a fetish of the unified and or-
> ganically 'whole' creative intelligence, locating its prime exem-
> plar in Lawrence. Hardy will not fit into such an image of
> unified creative power, but it is his strength that he will not do
> so, not his weakness.[12]

'Deeply and radically divided' seems to me to be putting it too
strongly, but that Hardy lacks this particular sort of 'unified creative
power' is true, and I agree with Bayley that this can be viewed as
strength rather than weakness. Hardy is most truly himself when he
allows images from a wide range of his experience to stand side by
side, contradictory perhaps, but each demanding sympathy. That
they are not necessarily fused into a new whole does not make them

11. David Lodge, 'Tess, Nature and the Voices of Hardy', in his *Language of
    Fiction* (London, 1966). Reprinted *Hardy, The Tragic Novels*, p. 169.
12. Introduction to the New Wessex (hardback) edition of *Far From the Madding
    Crowd* (London, 1975), p. 31.

less an enrichment of the reader's own experience; they can indeed be the more liberating because of their power to suggest new perspectives without demanding commitment to a new judgement.

One can see this in Hardy's poetry, 'a persistent characteristic' of which, as Kenneth Marsden observes, 'is the use of juxtapostition; an event, opinion or scene is given and is followed by another which contradicts or substantially modifies the first . . .' One of the poems Marsden mentions is 'The Convergence of the Twain', saying, however, that it belongs to a group which 'lack the clear juxtaposed *structure*, but are subtler versions of the same technique'.[13] What arrests one at the beginning of this poem is the weird picture of the Titanic, the acme of technology and luxury, which 'couches' (with its double suggestions of crouching like a beast and lying as a human being on a couch)

> In a solitude of the sea
> Deep from human vanity.

The sea-worm crawling 'Over the mirrors meant/To glass the opulent' intensifies this effect of mocking disparateness, which is summed up in the question of stanza 5, with its monosyllables surrounding a typically ponderous polysyllabic word, 'What does this vaingloriousness down here?'[14]

No doubt the passengers of the *Titanic* were all very respectable people; certainly it is the trappings of respectability on which Hardy focuses in this poem. But – perhaps, in an indirect and very bizarre way, drawing on his own experience of courtship and marriage – Hardy sees a 'sinister mate' being prepared for '*her*'. The conventional feminine for ship comes to life here, and the human analogies take on grim suggestiveness in phrases like 'the smart ship grew/In stature, grace, and hue' and 'The intimate welding of their later history', till finally the 'august event' of the collision becomes a ghastly wedding of misallied partners in a 'consummation' which does not join, but 'jars two hemispheres'. ('Twain', it might be added, is poetic diction for a pair of lovers which Hardy used for himself and his first wife, for example in 'After a Journey'. Recalling an

---

13. Kenneth Marsden, *The Poems of Thomas Hardy* (London, 1969), pp. 106 and 107.

14. *The Collected Poems*, pp. 288–9.

earlier journey that unexpectedly led to their marriage, he asks the
now 'thin ghost' of his wife what she has to say of their past:

> Summer gave us sweets, but autumn wrought division,
>   Things were not lastly as first well
>   With us twain, you tell?[15])

The consummation resulting from the weird conjunction, or marriage, celebrated in 'The Convergence of the Twain' is an ironic one;
like Hardy's own marriage it is also, one might say, a barren one,
producing no imaginative offspring to fuse the qualities of the par-
ents, but nevertheless jarring the mind into a strange new awareness.
I think much of Hardy's work is like this; and for the rest of this
paper I would like to attend to one or two examples, from the fiction,
which illustrate this point in different ways.

From very early on in his writing career Hardy saw marriage in a
jaundiced as well as a joyful light. This ambiguous view is the key
to the early, and nowadays unduly despised *Under the Greenwood
Tree* (1872). The cause of its neglect is not far to seek. There are
elements of coyness and prettiness in this novel which make most
readers a bit uncomfortable at times. Geoffrey Grigson suggests,
without producing very convincing evidence, that Hardy was 'rather
ashamed' of it and that his attitude towards his rustics is patronizing.
Hardy, he maintains, 'was too much the victim still of what had been
his own social grade in the village, of what was his own situation
vis-à-vis John Morley and Macmillan and middle-class culture, and
the prospect of marrying into a middle-class family'.[16] In my own
experience, however, it is not this supposed patronizing of the rustics
which is tedious in *Under the Greenwood Tree*, so much as the semi-
jocular manner in which Hardy describes the courting of Fancy by
Dick:

> It followed that as the spring advanced Dick walked abroad
> much more frequently than had hitherto been usual with him,
> and was continually finding that his nearest way to or from
> home lay by the road which skirted the garden of the school.
> The first-fruits of his perseverance were that, on turning the

15. Op. cit., pp. 328–9.
16. Introduction to the New Wessex (hardback) edition of *Under The Greenwood
    Tree* (London, 1975), pp. 17–21.

angle on the nineteenth journey by that track, he saw Miss
Fancy's figure, clothed in a dark-gray dress, looking from a
high open window upon the crown of his hat. The friendly
greeting resulting from this rencounter was considered so valuable an elixir that Dick passed still oftener . . .

(Under The Greenwood Tree, 'Spring,' Chapter 1)

But to regard this as the dominant tone of the novel is a mistake.
Fancy and Dick are set in the context of a rustic community which is
tolerant and sympathetic towards young love, but sceptical of its
vision of life and disillusioned about its duration. Marriage and the
prosaic reality of everyday domestic life are as much the book's
subject as courtship and the innocence of youth (quite apart from the
fact that Fancy is not all that 'innocent'). Fancy's step-mother is a
slightly mad house-proud woman whom Geoffrey Day resignedly
tolerates. Dick's mother, Mrs Dewy, is a more sensible and con-
siderate woman, but her marriage, too, has long passed the romantic
stage, a point which Hardy emphasizes by contrasting Dick's state
of mind after dancing with Fancy at the Christmas party and Mrs
Dewy's attitude to 'the dirty plates, and knives and forks, and dust
and smother' which remain to be cleared up:

> Dick wondered how it was that when people were married they
> could be so blind to romance; and was quite certain that if he
> ever took to wife that dear impossible Fancy, he and she would
> never be so dreadfully practical and undemonstrative of the
> Passion as his father and mother were. The most extraordinary
> thing was that all the fathers and mothers he knew were just
> as undemonstrative as his own.

('Winter', Chapter 8)

Under The Greenwood Tree owes much to pastoral convention. In
pastoral fashion the little points to the big, and the inner rural world
echoes the outside world. Thus Mr Penny, the shoemaker, knows a
man by his shoe-last and the character of Fancy Day by her shoe.
The schoolgirls' singing in competition with the gallery, instead of
being its respectful followers as tradition demands, is a serious
disturbance in this quiet backwater; and the subsequent replacement
of the Melstock 'quire' by Fancy's organ-playing becomes, in this
sense, a major social upheaval. Even honey-taking has its larger
resonances: as Geoffrey Day shakes the bees out of his shirt and hair,

the rest looked on, comments Hardy, 'with a complacent sense of being out of it, – much as a European nation in a state of internal commotion is watched by its neighbours'.

The effect of this pastoral device is charming and reassuring. Where such things are disturbances, disturbance is not greatly to be feared; the trials of the rustic can be viewed indulgently as those of a child are. (To that extent Grigson may be right to talk of 'patronizing'.) But as courtship has its marriage context, so conventional pastoral has its more sombre side. Mr Perry's shoe-making view of the world also points to a man drowned in Parkmaze Pool whom he knows by 'the family voot', and the pastoralism of the bees, though it returns as a reassuring fertility motif on the wedding-day of Fancy and Dick, also brings with it, in the episode of the smoking of the bees, reminders of death and economic necessity:

> 'Those holes will be the grave of thousands!' said Fancy. 'I think 'tis rather a cruel thing to do.'
> Her father shook his head. 'No,' he said, tapping the hives to shake the dead bees from their cells, 'if you suffocate 'em this way, they only die once: if you fumigate 'em in the new way, they come to life again, and die o' starvation; so the pangs o' death be twice upon 'em.'
> 'I incline to Fancy's notion,' said Mr Shiner, laughing lightly.
> 'The proper way to take honey, so that the bees be neither starved nor murdered, is a puzzling matter,' said the keeper steadily.
> 'I should like never to take it from them,' said Fancy.
> 'But 'tis the money,' said Enoch musingly. 'For without money man is a shadder!'
>
> ('Autumn', Chapter 2)

The seriousness of this can, of course, be misleadingly exaggerated. This is not the way that solemn moral reflections are made. The pastoral can still be enjoyed as delightful play, presenting the naive for the pleasure of a sophisticated audience; but in such a way that overtones of the real world cannot escape being heard. The art of such fiction is to preserve the pleasure to be had from dallying with Innocence while keeping in mind the realities of Experience.

This is done in the courtship story itself. The course of true love never did run smooth, and here the roughness comes from that characteristically Hardyan theme, the dissatisfaction with rustic

modesty and coarseness which the refining effect of education
generates in a clever young woman's mind. The Parson Maybold
episode is somewhat peremptorily handled (it may be a late addition
of Hardy's), but it accords with the temptation that is always present
to Fancy – to put vanity and tasteful appearance and artful adorn-
ments above instinct and the old, tried ways of the community into
which she was born.

Grigson maintains that the title of the novel is not from the song in
As You Like It, 'but from the broadside ballad of "Under the Greenwood Tree" '.[17] Given, however, the quotation incorporated in the
song of the nightingale at the end (' "Tippiwit! swe-e-et! ki-ki-ki!
Come hither, come hither, come hither!" ') this seems unlikely.
The final chapter, with its title 'Under The Greenwood Tree', seems
a deliberate summation of that mingling of the sympathetic and
critical, the enchanting and the disenchanted, which Hardy seems to
have found in *As You Like It*. The description which opens the chapter offers the ancient tree at the end of Geoffrey Day's premises as a
presiding pastoral symbol. It has pastoral modesty ('no great pre-
tensions to height'), and also the pastoral fertility ('Many hundreds
of birds had been born amidst the boughs of this single tree'). At
the same time it includes degeneration and corruption ('fungi' grow
in 'the cavities of its forks' and moles and earthworms are about its
roots). What is contained in miniature in this first paragraph is
echoed in the whole chapter, itself a miniature of the novel. The
dancing and the union of old and young reflect the harmony appropriate to the close of a comedy, but discords persist. Fancy's vanity
keeps Dick waiting, and we learn that her step-mother is not at the
wedding, but petulantly cleaning out drawers and dusting her second-
best china. Mrs Penny remarks, 'Well, 'tis humps and hollers with
the best of us'; and the tranter comments grimly on the time that is
to come, when the couple will have grown-up children and perhaps
little money to feed them with:

'I tell ye, neighbours, when the pinch comes,' said the tranter:
'when the oldest daughter's boots be only a size less than her
mother's, the rest o' the flock close behind her. A sharp time
for a man that, my sonnies; a very sharp time! Chanticleer's
comb is a cut then, 'a believe.'

17. Ibid., p. 20.

Finally, the scene of Fancy and Dick's driving home expresses
contradiction between Dick's innocent belief that they have no
secrets and Fancy's sly concealment of the truth about Parson
Maybold. To the first mood the nightingale's song is a sweet pastoral
accompaniment; but it is a mocking cuckoo-like comment on the
second.

However, I don't want to seem to be claiming that Hardy is a great
comic writer on the level of Shakespeare, or that *Under The Greenwood Tree* is a masterpiece. A work in the same mode which comes
nearer to achieving that status is 'The Romantic Adventures of a
Milkmaid' (1883 – eleven years after *Under The Greenwood Tree*).[18]
Here Fancy Day has been transformed into Margery the milkmaid.
She has lost some of her coquettishness and taken on the softer, passionate quality that Tess of the d'Urbervilles is to have eight years
later, but she is still reluctant to settle down with her Jim (the stolider,
more prosaic character that Dick Dewy has now become), and she is
even more fascinated, indeed dazzled, by the social superiority represented in Baron von Xanten than Fancy was by Parson Maybold.
Maybold, however, was a minor figure in *Under The Greenwood Tree*,
very possibly an afterthought, whereas the Baron is a major figure
in 'The Romantic Adventures of a Milkmaid'. He exercises some of
the supernatural power of the fiddler in 'The Fiddler of the Reels':[19]
'Margery always declared that there seemed to be some power in the
stranger that was more than human, something magical and com-
pulsory, when he seized her and gently trotted her round' ('The
Romantic Adventures of a Milkmaid', Chapter 3).

This imaginatively heightened, ballad-like quality, is balanced by
more familiar, everyday material. The Baron may be a pre-Lawren-
tian symbol of the subconscious sexual appeal of 'otherness', and
in his suicidal broodingness a figure of dark Byronic glamour, but
he is also dazzlingly attractive in Margery's eyes quite simply because of his association with social refinement and beautiful fur-
nishings. There is a very precise inventory of the attractive items
he gives Jim to help him to win back Margery's affections:

Pair of silver candlesticks: inlaid work-table and work-box: one
large mirror: two small ditto: one gilt china tea and coffee

---

18. To be found in the collection entitled *A Changed Man* (London, 1913).
19. 1893. In the collection, *Life's Little Ironies* (London, 1894).

service: one silver tea-pot, coffee-pot, sugar basin, jug, and dozen spoons: French clock: pair of curtains: six large pictures.

(Chapter 7)

The effect of these is deflatingly comic, but Hardy does not scoff. What makes the story so successful is its mixed tone which enables the reader to enter sympathetically into the adolescent girl's feelings, but also to see them as, in fact, no more than romantically adolescent and bound in the end to give way to a more sober view of reality. The Baron himself, though sorely tempted by the prospect of elopement with a pretty, willing young milkmaid, sees that it would be not only immoral, but impractical. In Hardy's more formally didactic style he tells Margery, when persuading her to marry Jim, that 'marriage is a life contract, in which general compatibility of temper and worldly position is of more importance than fleeting passion, which never long survives' (Chapter 12). In the end the 'skittishness' of Margery is balanced by the long-suffering, good-natured pedestrianism of Jim, without either being devalued, and 'romantic adventures' give way to domesticity – though if the Baron were to command her again, Margery says, 'I believe I should have no power to disobey'.

The remarkable thing about 'The Romantic Adventures of a Milkmaid' is that it makes the trappings of respectability glamorous, mainly because that is what they are for the adolescent girl – the scene in which she first sets eyes on her balldress, shoes and gloves is pure 'Cinderella' – but also partly, I suspect, because that is what they were for Hardy. At any rate his imagination certainly stretches to include the glamour of aristocratic life viewed from below and outside. When he attempts to view it from within, as he does in *The Hand of Ethelberta* (1876), the result is a willed and laboured performance. Its interesting scenes are those which – in Hardy's own words – showed 'servants were as important as, or more important than, their masters; wherein the drawing-room was sketched in many cases from the point of view of the servants' hall'.[20] Curiosity is there, but imaginative zest is wanting, perhaps because Ethelberta is not placed in a position where she can be dazzled as Margery is.

As a young woman supposedly making her way by her poems and story-telling talent and yet also a kind of Jamesian fortune-hunter,

20. Hardy's 1895 Preface. Wessex edition (London, 1912), p. vii.

Ethelberta is in a queerly compromised position. She is neither
tempted by respectability like Margery, nor capable of developing
into a prototype-Sue Bridehead 'new woman'. Her logical position
would be with her brother Sol who tells her bluntly:

> 'Berta, you have worked to false lines. A creeping up among the
> useless lumber of our nation that'll be the first to burn if there
> comes a flare. I never see such a deserter of your own lot as you
> be!' (Chapter 46).

If Hardy had put Ethelberta on the same side of the social fence as
her brothers he might have been able to work that earlier 'socialistic'
vein which gave rise to *The Poor Man and the Lady*. As it is, *The
Hand of Ethelberta* is an interesting attempt to present a satirical view
of respectability from within, but one which goes off at half-cock.

Notwithstanding that fight against 'the massive social stratification
of the Victorian age' to which Gittings refers,[21] or possibly because
of the very nature of that struggle which involved resentment against
social barriers and the feeling that some of the things he most valued
lay on the other side of them, comparatively little in Hardy's fictional
work is simply anti-respectable. A few short stories such as 'The
Son's Veto', or 'For Conscience' Sake', or 'A Tragedy of Two
Ambitions',[22] are single-minded in this way, but they are stories
which clearly do not engage Hardy's imagination very intensely.
The divided attitude is more typical and seems to produce more
powerful imaginative effects. The one exception is perhaps *Jude the
Obscure*. It would be easy to say that singlemindedness is there
Hardy's undoing, but in fact I don't quite feel that; and possibly
the reason is that, for all its animus against orthodoxy and respectability, the novel is built out of a series of antitheses ('Christminster
academical, Christminster in the slums; Jude the saint, Jude the sinner; Sue the Pagan, Sue the saint; marriage, no marriage; &c., &c.'[23])
which involve the exercise of a kind of corrosive sympathy even for
experiences that are anathema to the author.

However, a more representative work, as I see it, is *The Mayor of*

21. See quotation at the beginning of this paper.
22. 'The Son's Veto' (1891), 'For Conscience' Sake' (1891), and 'A Tragedy of
    Two Ambitions' (1888), are collected in *Life's Little Ironies*.
23. Letter to Edmund Gosse, 20 November 1895. (*The Life of Thomas Hardy*,
    pp. 272–3.)

Casterbridge, and it is this which I wish to consider at greater length.

The plot of *The Mayor of Casterbridge*, it hardly needs emphasizing, is dependent on the theme of respectability. Although Henchard commits his original sin with drunken abandonment, he soon repents, and even after his many years of success which have brought him to the position of Mayor of Casterbridge, he is sensitive to the damage which public knowledge of his past would do to his reputation. When meeting the returned Susan, he chooses the Amphitheatre as 'safest from observation', for 'As Mayor of the town, with a reputation to keep up, he could not invite her to come to his house...' (Chapter 11). It is a guilty secret, however, and the choice of the Amphitheatre – following the Hardy practice which causes psychological states to be expressed in terms of environment – is dictated by more than convenience. 'Melancholy, impressive, lonely . . .' the Amphitheatre had associations which 'had about them something sinister', including the bloodshed of Roman games, hangings, and, what might well be the subject of a chilling Wessex ballad, the half-strangling and then burning of a woman who had murdered her husband.[24]

These sinister undertones, as well as the impulsiveness of Henchard's character, may also account for his telling the secret to Farfrae and then being recurrently suspicious that Farfrae intends to blackmail him. Certainly when the furmity-woman makes her dramatic disclosure of Henchard's past Hardy's handling of the scene generates a sense that far more than a piece of long-forgotten youthful folly has been revealed. The furmity-woman represents all that is lacking in respectability. In the opening scene it is her contraband rum, surreptitiously added to the furmity, which precipitates Henchard's crime, and eighteen years later, when Susan finds her way back to Weydon Priors, Elizabeth-Jane tries to stop her mother speaking to the furmity-woman with the words: 'Don't speak to her – it isn't respectable!' (Chapter 3). When the furmity-woman herself claims to have done 'business with the richest stomachs in the land' (Chapter 3), she merely deepens the reader's sense of the great gulf between her and polite society; though there is a sense in

24. The grotesque humour makes it still more ballad-like: 'Tradition reports that at a certain stage of the burning her heart burst and leapt out of her body, to the terror of them all, and that not one of those ten thousand people ever cared particularly for hot roast after that' (Chapter 11).

which she is justified, for the greed she satisfies is a sinister leveller.
As she puts it: 'I knew the clergy's taste, the dandy gent's taste;
I knew the town's taste, the country's taste. I even knowed the taste
of the coarse shameless females' (Chapter 3). But out of this disreputable mouth-piece comes a dramatically heightened, and thereby
all the more effective, denunciation of respectability.

Hardy's treatment of the scene at the Casterbridge Petty Sessions
when the furmity-woman is to be tried by Henchard mingles broad
comedy and tragic melodrama. Constable Stubberd is a nineteenth-
century Dogberry: ' "Hearing a illegal noise I went down the street
at twenty-five minutes past eleven P.M. on the night of the fifth
instinct, Hannah Dominy" ' (Chapter 28). He is particularly shocked
by her offence of 'disorderly female and nuisance' because it was
committed 'By the church, sir, of all the horrible places in the
world!'. This reflects a conventional notion of sacrilege, but in practice 'church' in *The Mayor of Casterbridge* has social rather than
religious implications. The town has its upper and lower church at
which sermons of appropriate length are preached to congregations
of respectively higher and lower social standing, and the social range
is completed by a passing comment on the most disreputable part
of the town: 'The inn called Peter's Finger was the church of Mixen
Lane' (Chapter 36). This ambiguous meaning of 'church', coupled
with the furmity-woman's double-edged attitude towards respectability, prepares the way for Henchard's exposure in a passage
which is reminiscent of *King Lear*. His own impatience with Stubberd's linguistic coyness (' "Come – we don't want to hear any more
of them cust dees and bees! Say the words out like a man, and don't
be so modest, Stubberd . . ." ' Chapter 28), leads to a contrastingly
plain and direct relation by the furmity-woman of Henchard's wife-
selling. This is pronounced irrelevant by the second magistrate, but
it is, as the furmity-woman claims, highly relevant since it questions
Henchard's moral right to judge her: ' "That bears on the case. It
proves that he's no better than I, and has no right to sit there in
judgement upon me" ' (Chapter 28). It is the same perception of social
hypocrisy that leads Lear to say:

Thou rascal beadle, hold thy bloody hand!
Why dost thou lash that whore? Strip thine own back;
Thou hotly lusts to use her in that kind
For which thou whipst her. The usurer hangs the cozener.

Through tatter'd clothes small vices do appear;
Robes and furr'd gowns hide all. Plate sin with gold,
And the strong lance of justice hurtless breaks;
Arm it in rags, a pigmy's straw does pierce it.
                                    (*Lear*, IV. vi. 162–9)

Henchard is guilty, but it enhances his stature that he immediately accepts the basic relevance of the furmity-woman's disclosure: ' "'Tis as true as the light," he said slowly. "And upon my soul it does prove that I'm no better than she" ' (Chapter 28).

The dramatic heightening given to this exposure of Henchard is justified both in thematic and in structural terms. Indeed, the two are closely interlocked. It is a climax and a turning-point in Henchard's career:

> Small as the police-court incident had been in itself, it formed the edge or turn in the incline of Henchard's fortunes. On that day – almost at that minute – he passed the ridge of prosperity and honour, and began to descend rapidly on the other side. It was strange how soon he sank in esteem. Socially he had received a startling fillip downwards; and, having already lost commercial buoyancy from rash transactions, the velocity of his descent in both aspects became accelerated every hour (Chapter 31).

From here on, as Hardy says, Henchard's fortunes decline. Something is broken in Henchard – his image of himself as a successful public man, a man of consequence – and his desire to be respected gives way to private and personal concerns. His abortive greeting of the Royal Personage is perhaps a feeble attempt to recover some of his lost prestige, but it springs mainly from personal resentment towards Farfrae; and its sequel, the fight in the barn, is entirely personal. He cannot carry out his intention to kill Farfrae because his sense (a false sense, of course) of public wrongs is overwhelmed by private feeling. The change in him is emphasized by the way he sits afterwards on the sacks in the loft: '. . . in a crouching attitude, unusual for a man, and for such a man. Its womanliness sat tragically on the figure of so stern a piece of virility' (Chapter 38). His deception of Elizabeth-Jane with regard to her true father, Newson, is again on the personal level. It is a pathetic attempt to keep hold of at

least one person's close, intimate affection – a selfish act, and yet
devoid of self-importance.

The later Henchard, though he is somewhat sulkily despondent,
suffers less from wounded vanity than from his sense that the furmity-
woman's denunciation is just. Loss of respectability leads to loss of
self-respect and a suicidal state of mind which is deflected from its
purpose only by Henchard's seeing an image of himself floating in
Ten Hatches Hole. The precise way in which this works on Henchard's consciousness is not explained by Hardy – it is rarely his
practice to describe the inner workings of the mind – but the implication must surely be that to see his purpose symbolically realized
in this way ('. . . he perceived with a sense of horror that it was *himself*. Not a man somewhat resembling him, but . . . his actual double'
Chapter 41) pulls him up, and makes him feel the enormity of doing
away with even as worthless-seeming a life as his own. Self-disgust
and the will to endure are set in a peculiarly tragic tension which
finds its most telling expression in the words Henchard utters as he
shoulders his basket to leave Casterbridge: 'I – Cain – go alone as I
deserve – an outcast and a vagabond. But my punishment is *not*
greater than I can bear' (Chapter 43). Yet the poor value of self
comes out again after his repulse by Elizabeth-Jane on her wedding
day. He cannot make an effective self-defence because 'he did not
sufficiently value himself to lessen his sufferings by strenuous appeal
or elaborate argument' (Chapter 44). And, finally, his will ('That
Elizabeth-Jane Farfrae be not told of my death', etc., Chapter 45)
expresses a wish for complete self-annihilation. It is true that this
final gesture also shows an enduring strength and dignity which
makes him more compelling as a tragic figure; but what Henchard
shows at his end is not, for example, the sense of a revived public
image which comes to Othello as he dies re-enacting on himself the
death he had formerly inflicted on 'a malignant and turban'd Turk',
but rather the naked humanity of King Lear.

All this is in striking contrast to the fall of Lucetta, the other main
victim in *The Mayor of Casterbridge* of society's cult of respectability.
Her story is closely bound up with Henchard's, since it is their
liaison in Jersey which provides the guilty secret in her past equivalent to Henchard's wife-selling. The published version of the novel
leaves the exact nature of this liaison vague, but such vagueness is
due only to the bowdlerizing forced upon Hardy by nineteenth-
century publishing conditions and exemplified in other novels such

as *The Return of the Native, Tess of the d'Urbervilles* and *Jude the Obscure*.[25] According to a note in the New Wessex edition, 'In the manuscript, relations between Lucetta and Henchard in Jersey were explicitly sexual...'[26] Nothing less could really account for Lucetta's terrified sense of being compromised; and the skimmity-ride which exposes her, though it might make a sardonic point about the scandal-mongering and vindictive nature of provincial Casterbridge, would not be nearly so effective if based on merely unconventional appearances rather than deeds.

According to Ian Gregor, *The Mayor of Casterbridge* is 'an intensely public novel in its drive' and 'one of the very few major novels – or, for that matter, very few novels – where sexual relationships are not, in one way or another, the dominant element'.[27] The truth of this statement very much depends on the amount of emphasis given to the qualifying 'dominant'. As Gregor says, *The Mayor* is a novel which includes little or nothing of the Lawrentian struggle for self-fulfilment through personal relationships; and there is nothing at all of the Lawrentian sense of exploring 'unknown modes of being' through the sexual experience. But sexual relationships in their public aspect are certainly of great importance. The emphasis which both Hardy's plot and commentary throw on to this public aspect was, in fact, seen by Lawrence as a weakness in all Hardy's major novels. Of Eustacia, Tess and Sue Bridehead, along with Tolstoy's Anna Karenina, he asks, '... what was there in their position that was necessarily tragic? Necessarily painful it was, but they were not at war with God, only with Society'.[28] Without going into all the complex issues which this criticism raises, one thing that can be said is that Lawrence underestimates the influence of convention. Each of these women, like Ibsen's Hedda Gabler, is a mixture of the

25. See *Hardy, The Tragic Novels*, pp. 13–14, and, for fuller detail, John Paterson, *The Making of 'The Return of the Native'* (University of California, 1960); Mary Ellen Chase, *Thomas Hardy, from Serial to Novel* (University of Minnesota, 1922); and R. L. Purdy, *Thomas Hardy, A Bibliographical Study* (London, 1954).
26. *The Mayor of Casterbridge*, New Wessex (hardback) edition (London, 1975), p. 351.
27. Op. cit., Introduction, p. 17.
28. D. H. Lawrence, *Study of Thomas Hardy*. In *Phoenix* (London, 1936, reprint of 1961), p. 420.

conventional and *un*conventional, or in the case of Sue Bridehead, of the conventional and the *would-be un*conventional.

Nothing like the same depth of analysis is to be found in the presentation of Lucetta and her entanglement with the conventional, but its power over her is strong and Hardy does not make the mistake of underestimating it simply because she is a shallow person. The importance she attaches to dress, for example, is a mark of her triviality, but it is also an indication of the significant role that it plays in her life:

> 'But settling upon new clothes is so trying,' said Lucetta. 'You are that person' (pointing to one of the arrangements), 'or you are *that* totally different person' (pointing to the other), 'for the whole of the coming spring: and one of the two, you don't know which, may turn out to be very objectionable' (Chapter 24).

How she appears to others conditions what she is. Or perhaps that is going too far, since her situation in Casterbridge is made 'painful', as Lawrence puts it, by the new feeling which she has for Farfrae coming into conflict with the craving for respectability which had brought her there in the first place. Not for the first time she experiences conflict between her improper private feelings and the external demands of propriety-conscious society. She had been through something like this in Jersey and tries pathetically to justify herself to Henchard: 'Knowing that my only crime was the indulging in a foolish girl's passion for you with too little regard for correctness, and that I was what *I* call innocent all the time they called me guilty, you ought not to be so cutting' (Chapter 25). Her improper feelings carried her away then, in Jersey, and threaten to do so now, in Casterbridge, but she is really terrified of the social opinion which for the moment she tries to defy. When Henchard says, 'But it is not by what is, in this life, but by what appears, that you are judged' (Chapter 25), he voices Lucetta's own true conviction.

The story of Lucetta's Jersey affair with Henchard; her 'artfulness' in getting Elizabeth-Jane to live with her in order to bring about a meeting with Henchard, only to find that the meeting is then an embarrassment to her; the elaborate business of the love-letters, which again carries a sting in the tail, since the letters, via Jopp, are a cause of the skimmity ride; the preparation of the skimmity ride going on as a kind of shadow to the preparations for the welcome to the Royal Personage, in which Lucetta's former lover, Henchard, and present husband, Farfrae, are each to figure so prominently – all this is elaborate and rather melodramatic plotting, but not mere catering to the tastes of contemporary magazine readers. It effectively highlights the tensions which torment poor Lucetta's limited consciousness. When the skimmity ride occurs, Hardy's narrative method throws all the emphasis on appearance in a way that is peculiarly appropriate to the appearance-conscious Lucetta. She hears one maid describing it to another with that same preoccupation with feature and dress that is so characteristic of Lucetta herself: 'The man has got on a blue coat and kerseymere leggings; he has black whiskers, and a reddish face. 'Tis a stuffed figure, with a false-face... What's the woman like?... 'tis dressed just as *she* was dressed when she sat in the front seat at the time the play-actors came to the Town Hall!... Her neck is uncovered, and her hair in bands, and her back-comb in place; she's got on a puce silk, and white stockings, and coloured shoes' (Chapter 39). When Lucetta herself has a direct view of the skimmity-ride Hardy again emphasizes the identification of self with appearance. 'She's me,' exclaims Lucetta, 'she's me – even to the parasol – my green parasol!' She then loses consciousness, and the curiously objective-subjective image disappears immediately, vanishing into air: 'Almost at the instant of her fall the rude music of the skimmington ceased. The roars of sarcastic laughter went off in ripples, and the trampling died out like the rustle of a spent wind' (Chapter 39).

Because the fainting of Lucetta is also virtually her death there is no sequel to her exposure equivalent to the sequel to Henchard's. This is partly a matter of the form of the novel, which coheres around Henchard and demands that Lucetta's affairs be subordinated to his. After the skimmity ride her part in his career is played out, and death is a better exit for her than any other. But it is also an appropriate exit, because she lacks the strength of character that enables Henchard to endure his punishment and the emotional resonance which sustains him in his personal life, even when his confidence in his public role has gone. Respectability is important for both, but more nearly the whole of life for Lucetta than it is for Henchard.

The evidence so far examined points towards *The Mayor of Casterbridge* as a vigorous exposure of the hollowness of so-called respectability; but, powerful as this element is, it is not what the novel is really about. The motivation of those who contrive the

skimmity-ride, traditional part of Wessex life though it may be, is
seen by Hardy much as Duke Senior in *As You Like It* sees Jaques'
wish to be a privileged satirist who will 'cleanse the foul body of
th' infected world'. 'What, for a counter, would I do but good?'
asks Jaques, and the Duke replies:

> Most mischievous foul sin, in chiding sin:
> For thou thyself hast been a libertine,
> As sensual as the brutish sting itself;
> And all th' imbossed sores and headed evils,
> That thou with licence of free foot hast caught,
> Wouldst thou disgorge into the general world.
>
> (II. vii. 64–9)

These are singularly appropriate words to apply to satire emanating
from Mixen Lane, for that part of Casterbridge is a place where
'Vice ran freely in and out certain of the doors'; in one of its blocks
of cottages 'there might have been erected an altar to disease in
years gone by'; and it exists as a 'mildewed leaf in the sturdy and
flourishing Casterbridge plant' (Chapter 36). The vindictiveness of
Jopp ('One that stands high in this town. I'd like to shame her.')
and the hypocrisy of Nance Mockridge (''Tis a humbling thing for
us, as respectable women, that one of the same sex could do it.')
point to the attack on Lucetta's morals as springing from motives
as infected as the place in which it is bred. Mixen Lane is, in fact,
symbolic of the corrupt aspect of respectable Casterbridge, and the
satire bred of such corruption is shown as being itself tainted.

Just as the attack on respectability is denied wholehearted approval, so the conventional judgements associated with respectability
do not necessarily evoke the author's mockery. Near the beginning
of the novel, as I have already shown, Elizabeth-Jane does not want
her mother to speak to the furmity-woman ('It isn't respectable'),
and when she learns that dancing in Farfrae's tent should be beneath
the dignity of the Mayor's stepdaughter 'her ears, cheeks, and chin
glowed like live coals at the dawning of the idea that her tastes were
not good enough for her position, and would bring her into dis-
grace' (Chapter 17). Such comments are not meant, however, to
diminish sympathy for Elizabeth-Jane. Even when Hardy seems to
condemn her compulsion towards respectability as excessive, the
criticism is in fact checked. When, for example, Lucetta tries to con-

fess to Elizabeth-Jane that she has broken her promise to Henchard and married Farfrae, Hardy comments:

> Any suspicion of impropriety was to Elizabeth-Jane like a red rag to a bull. Her craving for correctness of procedure was, indeed, almost vicious. Owing to her early troubles with regard to her mother a semblance of irregularity had terrors for her which those whose names are safeguarded from suspicion know nothing of. 'You ought to marry Mr Henchard or nobody – certainly not another man! ' she went on with a quivering lip in whose movement two passions shared (Chapter 30).

'Almost vicious' is a strong phrase, yet characteristically holds back from actual condemnation, and it is followed by a reference to Elizabeth-Jane's earlier background which explains the excess as a consequence of insecurity ('Owing to her early troubles . . .'). Finally, the emphatic words of judgement that come from the girl herself ('You ought to marry Mr Henchard or nobody') are qualified by 'certainly not another man' – a phrase which, since it refers indirectly to Farfrae and Elizabeth-Jane's suppressed feeling for him, is seen to be ambiguously motivated. Both the over-emphasis of insecurity and a touch of jealousy lie behind the seemingly rigorous judgement, and in causing us to sense this Hardy also wins sympathy for Elizabeth-Jane.

This is perhaps a dogged, even pedestrian, effort to understand and condone, which may make some readers impatient with Hardy, but seems to me entirely characteristic. The fact that attitudes appear to shift from sentence to sentence is a natural consequence of his readiness to acknowledge the various facets that experience may wear. Not, however, that I want to present Hardy as a studiously impartial writer. What I have already said about Henchard and the furmity-woman shows that he has instinctive reactions which provide the particular thrust and driving energy of his work. Education and experience, however, induce other attitudes which may counter these and, without necessarily leading to a new synthesis, serve to alert the reader's imagination to the complexities and contradictions which focus on the theme of respectability.

The relationship between the individual and the rural community (or 'rustic chorus', as it is often called) further illustrates this. In *Under the Greenwood Tree* Tranter Dewy and the quire embody sympathies which are instinctive to the country-bred Hardy whose father was a fiddler at church, and who played the fiddle himself. Fancy Day, as school-teacher and organist, and as refined individual, is a threat to that community. In the end she marries Dick rather than Parson Maybold, and yet as organist displaces the quire. The conclusion is thus part-victory, part defeat for traditional ways – a studied uncertainty which is reflected in the mixed mood of the novel. In *Far From the Madding Crowd* Gabriel Oak is an individual distinctly above the level of Jan Coggan, Mark Clark, 'Henery' Fray and the other frequenters of Warren's malthouse, and he rounds on them if they dare to criticize Bathsheba; but he can also merge into the democratic, undifferentiating atmosphere of the malthouse, he ignores the dirt on the 'God-forgive-me' and the grittiness of the bacon which has been dropped on the road, and, as the old maltster puts it, 'Ah, he's his grandfer's own grandson! – his grandfer were just such a nice unparticular man!' (Chapter 8). This is perhaps the ideal relationship as Hardy sees it, continued in the marvellous individual craftsmanship of Giles in *The Woodlanders* and his almost mythic identification with community and nature as 'Autumn's very brother' (Chapter 28). But Gabriel Oak, and more particularly Giles Winterborne, lack qualities which Hardy also consciously values and which are possessed in the last resort by even the pernicious Fitzpiers. As David Lodge reminds us, 'Fitzpiers survives because he is fitter, not better, than Giles – fitter to survive in a "modern" age'.[29]

In the tragic novels, of which *The Mayor* is one, this rural community is seen as coarser-grained, still commanding the instinctive sympathies, but itself more critically viewed than previously. In the interesting scene where Donald Farfrae sings his Scottish song to the drinkers at the *Three Mariners* individual and community are alike sympathized with and distanced.

> 'What did ye come away from yer own country for, young maister, if ye be so wownded about it?' inquired Christopher Coney, from the background, with the tone of a man who preferred the original subject. 'Faith, it wasn't worth your while on our account, for, as Maister Billy Wills says, we be bruckle folk here – the best o' us hardly honest sometimes, what with

29. *The Woodlanders*, New Wessex (hardback) edition (London, 1975), Introduction, p. 24.

hard winters, and so many mouths to fill, and God-a'mighty sending his little taties so terrible small to fill 'em with. We don't think about flowers and fair faces, not we – except in the shape o' cauliflowers and pigs' chaps' (Chapter 8).

Hardy certainly does not idealize Farfrae (the latter is heard at his wedding to Elizabeth-Jane 'giving strong expression to a song of his dear native country that he loved so well as never to have revisited it', Chapter 44), and Christopher Coney's speech is therefore effectively deflating. It says something that comes out of the community's experience. But at the same time the drinkers in the *Three Mariners* sense it as churlish and ill-timed. Solomon Longways on their behalf smooths over the slight awkwardness by getting Farfrae to sing some more songs, and as he does so the community warms to him, 'including', adds Hardy, 'even old Coney'. Nevertheless Hardy, the narrator, maintains his stance between the two, and it is from this position that he comments:

Notwithstanding an occasional odd gravity which awoke their sense of the ludicrous for the moment, they began to view him through a golden haze which the tone of his mind seemed to raise around him. Casterbridge had sentiment – Casterbridge had romance; but this stranger's sentiment was of differing quality. Or rather, perhaps, the difference was mainly superficial; he was to them like the poet of a new school who takes his contemporaries by storm; who is not really new, but is the first to articulate what all his listeners have felt, though but dumbly till then (Chapter 8).

In moving from Coney's sarcasm to this comment on Farfrae as the voice of Casterbridge sentiment and romance, 'the poet of a new school', Hardy does not move from a false to a truer view; nor even quite from one attitude sensed as false to another sensed as equally so. Each has some validity; each is in some respects defective; and the shifting tones of Hardy's prose are what make us feel this. Farfrae's 'odd gravity' awakes the drinkers' 'sense of the ludicrous', but only 'for the moment', and the rather formal 'Notwithstanding' has already created an expectation that it will be offset by something more in Farfrae's favour. This comes with the 'golden haze' which Farfrae's 'tone of mind' raises around him, indicative of a refinement which appeals to the drinkers precisely because it is on a higher, more respectable, level than 'cauliflowers and pigs' chaps'. 'Golden haze' is already a touch ironic, however, and this is a note which grows much stronger in the expansive rhetoric of 'Casterbridge had senti-ment – Casterbridge had romance; but this stranger's sentiment was of differing quality'. This might be taken as simply dramatizing the increasingly sentimental response of the drinkers, but the next, more reflective, sentence is essentially authorial comment, eradicat-ing the difference (it was 'mainly superficial') and generalizing the relationship between Farfrae and the community in terms of a newly-fashioned poet and his ravished audience in a way that can be taken either as a genuine compliment to a Romantic – Words-worthian or Burnsian – figure who voices the feelings of the people, or as a deflating comment on the spuriousness of a poet who is flashy rather than original and on the essential inertness of his audience who can only respond to a flatteringly novel version of their own banal ideas.

One doesn't have to choose between these interpretations. Hardy himself offers the last sentence only tentatively and with typically academic caution: 'Or rather, perhaps . . .' It is part of the tone of *his* mind that he should prefer to offer alternatives in this way rather than to take sides. Raymond Williams has written of Hardy's 'real identity' as being that of 'both the educated observer and the pas-sionate participant'.[30] The 'passionate participant' is that aspect which sympathizes with the not particularly respectable Christopher Coney, and also with the gradually warming response of the drinkers to Farfrae's song; but the final ambiguous sentence is the expression of the respectable, but alienated 'educated observer'. The point, however, is that they are part of the same identity, one that is – if it is not too much of a contradiction in terms to say so – a divided identity. The greatness of Hardy is that he knows this, and accepts it' and creates his art out of this acceptance. As he puts it in the poem 'Welcome Home':

> Back to my native place
> Bent upon returning,
> Bosom all day burning
> To be where my race

30. Raymond Williams, *The English Novel from Dickens to Lawrence* (London, 1970), and *The Country and the City* (London, 1973). Extract reprinted *Hardy, The Tragic Novels*, p. 100.

Well were known, 'twas keen with me
There to dwell in amity.

    Folk had sought their beds,
    But I hailed: to view me
    Under the moon, out to me
    Several pushed their heads,
And to each I told my name,
Plans, and that therefrom I came.

    'Did you? . . . Ah, 'tis true,'
    Said they, 'back a long time,
    Here had spent his young time,
    Some such man as you . . .
Good-night.' The casement closed again,
And I was left in the frosty lane.

SOME THOUGHTS ON THE REVISION OF THE *O.E.D.*[1]

Robert W. Burchfield

Sir William Craigie's important paper read to the Philological Society on 4 April 1919[2] contained the following observation:

> The Society's Dictionary[3] has easily outstripped anything else of the kind in existence, and contains such a general survey of the English language down to the present day as may never be entirely superseded; but its own plan on the one hand, and the immensity of the material on the other, prevent it from being absolutely final. Dealing as it does with all periods of English, from the seventh century to the twentieth, it has been impossible for it (beyond certain limits) to devote special attention to any one of these. Yet each definite period of the language has its own characteristics, which can only be appreciated when it is studied by itself, and which are necessarily obscured when it merely comes in as one link in the long chain of the language as a whole. To deal adequately with each period it is necessary to take it by itself and compile for it a special dictionary, as full and complete as may be.

This is the paper in which Craigie advocated the preparation of what are now conventionally called period and regional dictionaries. The dictionaries that he specified as calling for this special exhaustive treatment have not all appeared. Conversely some that he did not

1. This is a revised form (January, 1976) of part of a Special University Lecture entitled 'The *O.E.D.* in 1974' that I gave at the University of London on 14 March 1974. It has not previously been published. Professor Mackie contributed to the 1933 Supplement of the *O.E.D.* (his contribution was acknowledged in the Preface by the Editors) and to the Revised Supplement and it therefore seems particularly appropriate to offer this paper on *O.E.D.* matters for inclusion in a volume of essays prepared in his honour.
2. 'New Dictionary Schemes Presented to the Philological Society, 4th April 1919', *Transactions of the Philological Society, 1925–1930* (1931), pp. 6–11.
3. The *O.E.D.* is called 'the Society's Dictionary' in the *Transactions of the Philological Society* because it was 'founded mainly on the materials collected by the Philological Society'.

mention have been prepared. I shall begin by giving a brief account of both kinds.

a) *A Supplement,* in which
  (i) it will be necessary to correct any important errors in the Dictionary which have been discovered by the Dictionary Staff and others.
  (ii) Wherever the new material makes any real change in the history of a word, or a particular sense of a word, a place must be found for it in the Supplement, and its importance indicated.
  Result: the 1933 one-volume Supplement, now being replaced by a four-volume Supplement in the 1970s.

b) A revised edition of Bosworth and Toller's *Anglo-Saxon Dictionary.*
  Result: A plan for a new *Dictionary of Old English* to be edited by Mr Angus Cameron and Mr C. J. E. Ball, announced after an international conference held at the University of Toronto in March 1969.[4] Some preparatory work has been done, and the first parts are expected to appear about 1980.

c) 'A complete dictionary of Middle English (1175–1500) would be a work of marvellous richness and interest . . . Such a work can never be undertaken on practical grounds, but in the interests of English scholarship I hope that by some means or other it may yet be carried out' (p.7). Sir William went to America in the 1920s and the work was undertaken there.
  Result: *circa* 1930–52 preparatory work
    1952–1975 *A – manere* of the *Middle English Dictionary,* published in fascicle form, and edited by H. Kurath, S. M. Kuhn, and J. Reidy.

d) The Tudor and Stuart Period (from 1500–1675). 'The English of these two centuries can only be dealt with in an adequate

---

4. See for example, A. Cameron *et al., Computers and Old English Concordances* (Toronto, 1970); C. J. E. Ball and A. F. Cameron, 'Some Specimen Entries for the Dictionary of Old English', in *Lexicography and Dialect Geography,* ed. H. Scholler and J. Reidy (Wiesbaden: *Zeitschrift für Dialektologie und Linguistik,* Beihefte N.F., no. 9, 1973), pp. 46–64. Bosworth and Toller's dictionary has itself been supplemented: the late Professor A. Campbell's Supplement to it was published in 1972.

manner when it has been made the subject of special study and
has its own dictionary – a dictionary which would be one of the
greatest proofs of the wealth and dignity of the English tongue'
(p.8).
Result: Some false starts, but no dictionary yet. There is, however, an interesting by-product. In 1975, 38 000 citations from
the Tudor collections at Ann Arbor in Michigan were made
available in microfiche form in a project entitled *Michigan Early
Modern English Materials*. A handbook,[5] containing a biblio-
graphy of all the sources cited in this first collection, was published at the same time.

e) 'The period from 1675 to 1800 is less remarkable' and Sir William
Craigie was not certain how far it would be worth while to treat
it separately from the modern period, 'which sets in definitely
with the nineteenth century' (p.8).
Result: No dictionary.

f) The older Scottish period, extending from the fourteenth to the
seventeenth century. In an addendum in 1925, Craigie also men-
tioned the need for a Scottish dictionary for the modern period
(from about 1700).
Result: *The Dictionary of the Older Scottish Tongue*, edited by
W. A. Craigie and A. J. Aitken. 1931–1975. A – O published.
The Scottish National Dictionary, edited by William Grant and
David D. Murison. 1931–1976, 10 volumes.

g) In the addendum of 1925, Craigie said that 'for the modern
period of English, a perfectly new element has come into consideration', namely the need for a dictionary of American English
on historical principles.
Result: *The Dictionary of American English*, ed. W. A. Craigie
and J. R. Hulbert (1938–44). *The Dictionary of Americanisms*,
ed. M. M. Mathews (1951).

Two other regional dictionaries on historical principles have been
published, both of them in 1967, namely *A Dictionary of Canadian-
isms* and *A Dictionary of Jamaican English*, and similar dictionaries

5. Richard W. Bailey *et al.*, *Michigan Early Modern English Materials* (Xerox
University Microfilms and The University of Michigan Press, Ann Arbor,
Michigan, 1975).

are planned for Australian English,[6] Newfoundland English,[7] and South African English.[8]

This bare chronicle reveals in outline what has happened since the *O.E.D.* was completed in 1928, and it is instructive to examine the pattern a little more closely. In particular, it is of interest to go into the question of relationship between the progress and policy of these specialized dictionaries and the eventual revision of the *O.E.D.* itself.

From time to time it is said that the moment has arrived for a full-scale revision of the *O.E.D.* to be attempted. Thus, for example:

> *O.E.D.* is now obsolete in so many respects that, without complete revision, it must soon become, like Dr Johnson's *Dictionary*, an object of veneration rather than a tool for modern use . . . The *O.E.D.* is still – just – a working tool that is deservedly a world-famous glory of English culture. Soon, now, it will be a magnificent fossil.
>
> Marghanita Laski, *Times Literary Supplement*
> 13 Oct. 1972, p. 1226.

This is one view, and I believe that it may be widely held. A fortnight later (*T.L.S.*, 27 Oct., p. 1287), the Editor of the *Dictionary of the Older Scottish Tongue* pointed out that one difficulty about this suggestion was the usual one: 'where are we to find the wherewithal to carry it out?'

> What I do not know is how to persuade the governments of the English-speaking nations to spend (perhaps between them?) in this way a sum which could otherwise, I suppose, maintain a few military aircraft, or a small naval vessel, or one of the scientific research centres.

The 'wherewithal' is certainly a problem. Like Mr Aitken, I do not know whether a British government, of whatever complexion, would

6. See especially *Occasional Papers* 1–16 of the Australian Language Research Centre, Sydney, 1964–71, and J. R. Bernard, 'The Need for a Dictionary of Australian English', *Southerly* (1962) XXII: 2: 92–100.

7. G. M. Story *et al.*, 'Collecting for *The Dictionary of Newfoundland English*', in *Annals of the New York Academy of Sciences* (1973) Vol. CCXL. 104–108.

8. *Towards a Dictionary of South African English on Historical Principles*, Fifty Draft Entries. Institute for the Study of English in Africa, Rhodes University, Grahamstown, South Africa, 1971.

be willing to invest the price of 'a small naval vessel' in the defence
of the language instead of the defence of our shores. Some other
discouraging factors may be mentioned.

a) The size and the incompleteness of the period and regional
   dictionaries. First, the size. The *O.E.D.* itself contains just under
   15 500 pages. The period and regional dictionaries already
   published contain more than 21 000 pages, and I estimate that
   when these are completed the total number of pages will be
   something like 45 000.[9] This huge figure needs to be qualified
   by the fact that each page of the *O.E.D.* contains more material
   than a page of any of the other dictionaries, but it remains true
   that the period and regional dictionaries, when completed, will
   together contain more material than is included in the *O.E.D.*
   itself.

   No prudent editor would set about revising the *O.E.D.* before
   his main sources stood in a complete and exploitable form on the
   shelves. It will be many a long day before this state of affairs
   exists. Two of the major potential sources, the *M.E.D.* and the
   D.O.S.T., at their present rate of progress, are unlikely to be
   completed before the 1990s;[10] and no date can even be posited
   for the completion of a dictionary of Early Modern English, or
   for the commencement of an exhaustive dictionary of the period
   1675 to 1800.

b) These are practical, non-lexical, considerations, but perhaps
   even more important are problems arising from the varied
   policies adopted in the major source dictionaries. I shall give an
   indication of the problem by describing what happens when one
   tries to absorb into the *O.E.D.* two different kinds of material.
   For this purpose I revised the *O.E.D.* entry for the adjective
   actional, and I compared the *O.E.D.* entry for the noun *action*
   with that in one of the source dictionaries, namely the *M.E.D.*

   The *O.E.D.* entry (omitting the formal sections):

   actional, *a.* Of or pertaining to action or actions.
   1731 In BAILEY. **1870** J. GROTE *Exam. Util. Philos.* xviii. 307
   The actional principle of conservatism.

9. See the Appendix.
10. But see note 17 below.

is easily convertible to the following:[11]

> **actional,** *a.* †1. Of, pertaining to, or of the nature of a legal action. *Obs.*
>
> *c* **1450** *Godstow Reg.* 225 Gefrey brocher of blechesdon gaf... iij. d of yerly rent in þe town of blechesdon . . . with all hys Ryht & accionall maner, within the towne. **1662** *Rec. Colony of Rhode Island* (1856) I.497 It shall be alowed on the actionall case aforesayd. **1664** *Ibid.* (1857) II.31 That two Courts of Triall in the yeare be held . . . for the triall of any actionall matter. **2.** More generally, of or pertaining to action or actions; *spec.* in *Gram.*, expressing an action (opp. *statal*).
>
> *a* **1834** COLERIDGE *Omniana* in *Lit. Remains* (1836) I. 377 His outward senses, the subjugation of which to faith, that is, the passive to the actional and self-created belief, is the great object of all religion! *a* **1866** J. GROTE *Treat. Moral Ideals* (1876) 188 Actional or direct thought is objective and unconscious. *a* **1866** — *Exam. Utilitarian Philos.* (1870) xviii. 307 The actional principle of conservatism. **1935** G. O. CURME *Gram. Eng. Lang.* II. 218 The common actional form is employed also as a statal passive . . . 'The door *was shut* (state) at six, but I don't know when it *was shut* (act).' **1958** PRIEBSCH & COLLINSON *German Lang.* (ed. 4) I.iii.106 A dative singular in *-anne* (with doubling caused by *j* on the analogy of neuter actional *ja*-stems like *gikōsi* 'chatter'). **1971** *Black World* Oct. 5/1 *Negritude* is not only a concept, it is also actional. **1973** QUIRK & GREENBAUM *Univ. Gram. Eng.* 359 A sentence such as *They were married* is ambiguous between an actional interpretation (*They were married in church yesterday*) and a statal interpretation (*They were married when I last heard about them*).

The dictionaries drawn on for the revised entry were *M.E.D.*, *D.A.E.*, and Volume I of *A Supplement to the O.E.D.* The first *a* 1866 example was given in *N. & Q.* 1966, p. 55. The *a* 1834, 1971, and 1973 examples were obtained from unpublished material in the *O.E.D.* quotation files.

In this very simple type it is worth noting:

a) There are undoubted improvements: a ghost-date (1731) in the *O.E.D.* has disappeared: and the word *actional* is recorded more

---

11. *O.E.D.*'s '1731 In BAILEY' turned out to be a false reference.

than 400 years before the earliest genuine example in the Dictionary.

b) The number of senses is doubled, and the two examples are replaced by ten, thus already posing the problem of scale in any revision of the Dictionary.

c) Most importantly, the revision of such an entry is feasible.

Whereas *actional* is revisable by an additive process, it is not at all a simple matter to reconcile the *O.E.D.* and *M.E.D.* entries for the word *action*. This becomes clear when skeleton details of the corresponding entries are set down in tabular form. The *O.E.D.* senses listed are restricted to those which are first recorded in the Middle English period.

O.E.D.	*M.E.D.*
1. The process or condition of acting or doing.	**1.** (a) Something done, an act, a deed. (c 1390) Chaucer *CT. Pars.* I.95.
(a) Of persons. (Distinguished from *passion*, from *thought* or *contemplation*, from *speaking* or *writing*.) **1393** LANGLAND *P.Pl.C.* II.94.	
(b) Of things. (Distinguished from *inaction, repose*.) c **1386** CHAUCER *Persone's T.* (Ellesmere) 82.	(b) The operation or effect (of heat or fire); the activity or function (of a bodily organ) (a1398) *Trev. Barth.* 212 a/a.
2. The exertion of force by one body upon another: influence. c **1360** CHAUCER *A.B.C.* 20.	**2.** *Law.* (a) The right to take legal steps for the redress of a wrong, right to bring suit in a court of law; cause or grounds for a lawsuit; also *fig.* ?a1400 (a1338) Mannyng *Chron. Pt.2* p. 196.
7. The taking of legal steps to establish a claim or obtain judicial remedy; legal process; the right to raise such process. **1330** R. BRUNNE *Chron.* 196.	(b) A formal demand of one's right from another in a court of law, a lawsuit. ? a 1425 *Mandev.* (Eg) 141/3. c1450 (c1370) Chaucer *ABC* 20.
8. A legal process or suit. **1483** CAXTON *Gold. Leg.* 431/3.	

Some points are worth noting:

a) The non-correspondence of the senses: senses la and lb in the *O.E.D.* do not correspond to senses la and b in the *M.E.D.* The only ME. example in *O.E.D.*'s sense 2, a non-legal use, is given in the *M.E.D.* under *M.E.D.*'s sense 2b, a legal use, and the same example is dated *c.* 1360 in the *O.E.D.* and *c.* 1450 (*c.* 1370) in the *M.E.D.* The *O.E.D.* has four ME. senses (including la, b); the *M.E.D.* has 2 (la, b, 2a, b).

b) The discrepancy between the dates given for the same work would require a reconsideration *de novo* of the conventional dates assigned to every Middle English work cited in the *O.E.D.*

c) The *O.E.D.* cites for the most part from Victorian editions of medieval English Works. These would need to be converted throughout, in terms of pagination, etc., to standard modern editions.

d) The *O.E.D.* has 8 ME. illustrative examples, the *M.E.D.* has 57. It is possible that further examination would show that the incompatibility of corresponding entries in the *O.E.D.* and the *M.E.D.*, and in the *O.E.D.* and other period and regional dictionaries, is not as apparent as seems to be the case from the word *action*, but I doubt it.

Some of the main considerations, therefore, seem to be as follows:

1. The period and regional dictionaries provide material on an ample scale beyond what could conveniently be presented in a single amalgamated dictionary. The large number of main entries in the North American historical dictionaries for words like *buffalo*[12] and *Indian*[13] could only be accommodated in a 'parent' dictionary by drastic pruning and curtailment. Similar considerations apply in the case of the other period and regional dictionaries.

2. Doubtless the problem of absorption could to some extent be

---

12. In the *D.A.E.* alone there are 80 main entries (*buffalo beat, buffalo beef, buffalo beetle, buffalo berry, buffalo-berrying, buffalo boat, buffalo bug, buffalo bull*, etc.) and many other undefined combinations and subordinate senses.

13. The *D.A.E.* lists 117 main entries (*Indian affairs, Indian agency, Indian agent, Indian arrow, Indian barn, Indian basket, Indian beads, Indian bean*, etc.) apart from those for *Indian* n., adj., and v.

alleviated by the provision of traffic directions within a revised *O.E.D.*, that is some system of signals meaning essentially 'For further information on this word or sense see (as appropriate) *M.E.D.*, *D.O.S.T.*, *S.N.D.*, etc.'

3. It is also possible that far from an expansion of the *O.E.D.* from 12 volumes to say 30 volumes (which in present-day money terms would sell at about £500) the pattern of the future might be a reduced *O.E.D.*, the contraction to be achieved by regarding it as a dictionary of the Literary English of the British Isles, with its specialized regional (i.e. specifically North American, Australasian, etc.) vocabulary removed, and excluding scientific and technical vocabulary except that necessary for the understanding and elucidation of literary works. Such a development would bring the *O.E.D.* more into accord with the major European dictionaries on historical principles, which have traditionally omitted overseas forms of the home language (for example Canadian French and Afrikaans), and have rigorously excluded scientific and technical vocabulary.

4. In such a reduced dictionary it might be possible to introduce new features into the *O.E.D.* For example, some of the historically based dictionaries produced in recent years, or in preparation, draw on oral sources as well as on written ones and the *O.E.D.* could follow suit. I quote from Professor G. M. Story's paper on Newfoundland English:

> From such [oral] sources spotty printed evidence has been substantially supported and clarified (or exploded), and – most important – whole new fields of the lexicon have been brought to light.[14]

Similarly, the planned new Dictionary of Old English will provide, it is hoped, information about frequency of occurrence of individual items of vocabulary, and about synonyms and antonyms, and will present typical collocations more systematically than has been attempted in any of the published historical dictionaries. Similar features might usefully be introduced into the *O.E.D.* itself. For example, one aspect of frequency of occurrence that goes largely unspecified in the *O.E.D.* at present may be illustrated by the treatment of such words as *Establishment, hopefully, Iron Curtain,*

14. *Annals of the New York Academy of Sciences* (1973) CCXL, p. 106.

juggernaut (lorries), and *know-how*. In each case the new word or sense came into wide use in a particular year or years. Then each went into a kind of intensive-care unit with virtually the whole community searching for earlier examples. Inevitably some were found. The diachronic method tends to suffer from the excessive zeal of its supporters in such circumstances and the resulting entries, lengthened to absorb the results of massive research, often prove to be disproportionately long, apart from the fact that they give a misleading impression of the word's currency.

In such a revised *O.E.D.* it would also be desirable to bring out more clearly than hitherto the downward movement of expressions from acceptability to unacceptability (e.g. *disinterested* acceptable in the sense 'not interested, uninterested' between 1612 (John Donne) and 1770 (Junius letters), unacceptable in the twentieth century), and the reverse. I gave a brief indication of this problem in a paper in *Encounter*,[15] but much more detailed study is called for.

15. Feb. 1974, pp. 54–7.

APPENDIX

Scale of the Period and Regional Dictionaries

Dictionary	*No. of pages*		*Date of Completion*
	Already published	When com-pleted, *circa*	(* = estimated date of completion
O.E.D.	15 488		1928
D.A.E.	2 528		1944
D.A.	1 911		1951
Dict. Canad.	879		1967
Dict. Jamaican E.	489		1967
S.N.D.	4 734		1976
²Suppl. to O.E.D. (A-G, 1972, H-N, 1976)	2 613	5 000	*1982
D.O.S.T. (A-O, 1975)	3 471	5 850[16]	*1995
M.E.D. (A-manere, 1975)	6 067	11 300	*1996[17]
Dict. E. Mod. E.	–	10 000	?
Dict. Newfoundland E.	–	900	?
Dict. S. Afr. E.	–	900	?
D. Austral. E.	–	900	?

Note: M.E.D. *A. – manere* has about 394 000 illustrative examples (based on an average of 65 examples a page). The completed dictionary will probably therefore contain between 700 000 and 800 000 examples, compared with some 1 800 000 examples in the *O.E.D.*

16. 'I am chary of committing myself when I don't have to about the extent of the completed work, but the figure you extrapolated is close to one I arrived at some years ago, which assumes a lot of self-discipline from the editors as to space allowed. So the answer is, yes, it seems reasonable. I now fear, though, we will go somewhat beyond it rather than fall within it, even exercising adamant self-control.' Private letter from A. J. Aitken, 7 February, 1974.

17. Possibly much earlier: plans were announced in 1975 for the supplementation of staff and facilities made possible by a large financial grant. It is hoped that the dictionary will now be completed in the early 1980s.